Contents

www.contentextra.com/customerservice

The accompanying website includes the following additional units for this qualification:

A5: Promote additional services or products to customers

A8: Make customer service personal

A11: Deal with incoming telephone calls from customers

A12: Make telephone calls to customers

A13: Deal with customers in writing or electronically

C3: Resolve customer service problems

Plus additional coverage of the Technical Certificate units

How to use this book

This book has been written to help you achieve your NVQ (or SVQ, if you are based in Scotland) Level 2 qualification. It covers the mandatory units and a range of optional units from the 2010 standards, giving you a broad choice of content to match your needs.

Throughout this book, you will find the following learning features.

Key terms

Essential terminology and phrases are explained in clear and accessible language. Where these appear in the book, the first instance of the word is shown in bold so you know there is a definition nearby.

Portfolio Task

These are tasks that cover grading criteria from the NVQ standards. You can use these tasks to generate evidence for your portfolio. Some portfolio tasks will be supported by downloadable editable forms, which are available from www.contentextra.com/customerservice

Functional Skills

You may be taking Functional Skills alongside your NVQ – if so, these are opportunities for you to apply your English, mathematics or ICT skills in a business enivronment.

✓ Checklist

These features help you to identify important information, or steps in a task that need to be completed.

Working Life

See how the units applies to the real world of work, and receive top tips for making the most of your time in the workplace.

Check your knowledge

At the end of each unit, use this feature to check how well you know the topic and identify and areas you need to recap. The answers for these questions can be found at www.contentextra.com/customerservice

About the website

www.contentextra.com/customerservice

Username: CSLevel2

Password: Customer

The website accompanying this book will support you in a number of ways as you complete your NVQ.

Extra free support

For the units covered in this book, you will find the following additional support materials:

- Downloadable forms and templates for Portfolio Tasks

- Answers to 'Check your knowledge' questions

- Links to useful websites for further reading

Additional free units

The website contains additional units, not covered in the book, providing you with a broader choice of units to better suit your needs. Each unit is available as a downloadable PDF for your personal use, and also includes answers, template forms and links to useful websites.

The additional units on the website are:

A5: Promote additional services or products to customers

A8: Make customer service personal

A11: Deal with incoming telephone calls from customers

A12: Make telephone calls to customers

A13: Deal with customers in writing or electronically

C3: Resolve customer service problems

Plus additional coverage of the Technical Certificate units

Bonus support for Apprentices

If you are taking the NVQ as part of an Apprenticeship, you will also be taking a Technical Certificate. This qualification assesses the knowledge and understanding that underpins the NVQ.

The website includes concise unit-by-unit summaries of the key knowledge and understanding you need to complete your Technical Certificate — perfect for revising for on-screen assessment.

CUSTOMER SERVICE
Level 2   NVQ/SVQ

Username:
Password:

Login

Home page
FAQ

Welcome to Customer Service

This website provides additional support to complements the Heinemann NVQ/SVQ Level 2 Customer Service Candidate Handbook.

Here you will find:

Additional content for book units

Including web links, answers to questions and sample forms to use when completing Portfolio Tasks.

Additional optional units

Full coverage of additional popular units from the NVQ/SVQ.

Technical Certificate units

Doing an Apprenticeship? Use the dedicated Technical Certificate units to revise for your on-screen assessment or develop your knowledge and understanding to help you produce a portfolio.

Getting started

Log into the website using the user name and log-in details in the book (on page XXX), and select the content you want to see from the left-hand menu.

About | Privacy Policy | Terms and Conditions | Contact Us | © Copyright 2011 Pearson Education Ltd

Unit F1

Communicate using customer service language

What you will learn:

- To identify customers and their characteristics and expectations
- To identify their organisation's services and products

Introduction

Delivering great customer service is rather like building a jigsaw; all the pieces need to fit together before the total picture can be seen. Understanding how the part you play – your one piece in the jigsaw – impacts upon your organisation, your colleagues and, most importantly, your customers will help you to see the whole picture and be good at customer service.

In this unit we look at who your customers are, their expectations and how you can work with colleagues to deliver great service. To do this you need to be able to communicate using language and concepts which are easy to understand.

You need to know all about the **services** or **products** your organisation offers (see the key terms on page 21). You must be able to understand and explain what your organisation offers. It's more than that though: you need to understand *why* customer service is important to your organisation in order to fully play your part and bring your knowledge and skills into action.

When you are clear about what your organisation is willing and able to provide, you will be on your way to being able to use the right language with customers and colleagues.

So, providing good customer service starts with knowing and understanding all about how you can help your organisation deliver great customer service. Remember, you must:

- identify customers and their characteristics and expectations
- identify their organisation's services and products.

Doing an Apprenticeship

If you are taking your NVQ as part of an Apprenticeship, you will find that the knowledge and understanding for this unit links to your Technical Certificate. Go to www.contentextra.com/ customerservice to find summaries of the Technical Certificate units.

Customers can have very different characteristics and expectations.

Identify customers and their characteristics and expectations

What you need to know and learn

- Which types of customer your organisation does business with
- Who's who and who does what to provide customer service
- How customer satisfaction is affected by customer expectations
- Why good customer service is important to any organisation

Many people will think customer service is all about making customers happy by giving them what they want when they want it. However, we all know life isn't quite that simple in the fast-moving world of customer service. Products change, services change, your customers' expectations change. You need to react to these changes and must often anticipate how to deal with your customers.

To do this, you will need the help or assistance of people you work with – your colleagues. The people your organisation does business with (suppliers) also play an important part. So, teamwork is very important.

You will need to know all about the products or services you are expected to use as well as about the rules and regulations which state what you can and cannot do. We look further at this in **Unit F2 Follow the rules to deliver customer service**.

Perhaps most importantly, you will need brilliant communication skills. You need to know how your behaviour and the behaviour of customers can make the difference between a great customer service experience and an ordinary or poor one.

Learning from situations and experiences will also help you develop. Almost every day something will happen that can be used to help with your personal development.

YOU are very important! You have the opportunity to have a real and lasting impact on other people, to have personal job satisfaction and to help your organisation be successful.

Customers appreciate a friendly service.

Unit F1 Communicate using customer service language

We will start your journey to achieving your qualification by asking you to explore what is meant by 'customer service'. They are, after all, words which you hear and read all the time. But what do they actually mean? When you are a customer what do you think customer service is all about? What does customer service mean to you in your daily work?

An undertaker might say:

> 'The job is dealing with customer needs – 70% is about supporting the people, 30% is about dealing with the arrangements. If I fail to show I care about the relatives, I might as well not bother to do a quality job with the administration.'

A market stall holder might say:

> 'My customers know they will find a happy, smiling face whatever the weather. That is what they expect, and that is what they get.'

A call centre agent might say:

> 'I give good service to customers by answering calls promptly and dealing with what they want without the need for them to call back. They get an efficient service, they can trust me to carry out their instructions. I keep my promises.'

Which types of customer your organisation does business with

Here is a definition from the Institute of Customer Service (the professional body which deals with developing customer service people and systems):

> 'Customer service is the sum total of what an organisation does to meet customer expectations and produce customer satisfaction. It usually involves service teamwork and service partnerships.'

A customer service practitioner might simply see it as 'helping people'.

Who are your customers?

Just as you have many different friends and colleagues, so too there will be a variety of customers for you to deal with. Good customer service depends on fully understanding the needs of your customers so that you can provide a good product or service.

A customer is someone who receives customer service from you. They may be an **external customer** or an **internal customer**. It's usually easier to think of customers as living breathing people. However, sometimes your customers will be other organisations or departments.

Both internal and external customers require the same great level of service from you. Your internal customers are working with you to provide an overall level of service which supports the needs of customers wherever they are. If the chain breaks down, service suffers.

Key terms

External customer – a customer who works in another organisation

Internal customer – a customer who comes from another part of your organisation

So, everyone where you work is responsible for service somewhere along the line.

Portfolio Task   Links to f1a, f1i, f1j

Portfolio Task

1   Find out who some of your internal customers are. On a separate piece of paper, complete this sentence: My internal customers are…

2   Now think about your external customers and complete this sentence: My external customers are…

3   Thinking about customer types — who are your organisation's customers? Complete this sentence: My organisation's customers are…

4   Make a list here of any other customer types you deal with. Indicate whether they are internal or external customers.

Keep the lists for your portfolio.

Functional skills

English: Writing
If you use accurate punctuation and spelling and correct grammar when completing the sentences and making your list, you may be able to count it as evidence towards Level 1 Functional English: Writing.

Customer types

To understand what products or services to offer, your organisation has to understand what types of customer it wishes to attract and keep loyal.

Customers may be described according to areas like age, gender and special needs. Don't forget, your organisation will also look at how to win the business of potential customers too.

Take a look at Figure 1. Are there any other customer types you deal with?

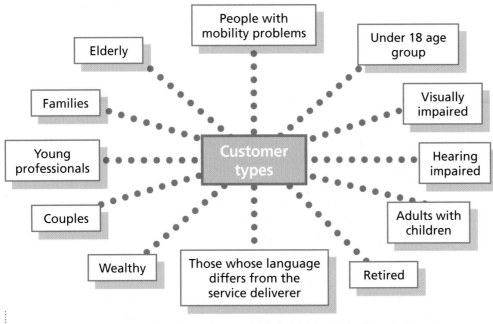

Figure 1: Categorising customers into groups can be helpful when identifying their needs.

Unit F1 Communicate using customer service language

Customers fall into a wide range of different groups.

Perhaps the obvious place to think about dealing with all of these different customer types is a supermarket. How does a supermarket manage to meet the needs of all these different people? One way would be to ensure its checkout staff are trained to recognise the needs of different customer types. For example, a mum with a baby may need help with packing. So too may a person with mobility problems. An elderly person may well want to chat as his or her shopping is dealt with. Often men want to get out quickly! However, only by asking questions to accurately tell what a customer wants will you be able to manage expectations effectively.

However, asking questions may not always be appropriate, as in this supermarket example. In this case, giving an 'invisible check' will help you in managing expectations.

Portfolio Task   Links to f1.1.1, f1.1.2, f1h

Discuss with a colleague what specifically your organisation does to meet the needs of these customer types:

- elderly
- disabled
- under-18s
- non-English speaking
- adults with children.

Discuss only those which are appropriate to your working environment. Make notes of key points from your discussion.

Using these notes, write a report which details the part you personally play in meeting these customers' needs.

Discuss this report with your assessor.

Who's who and who does what to provide customer service

Any organisation should have a clear structure to help it meet the needs of its customers. This structure is a bit like a family tree; people and departments or different parts of the business have connections to one another.

In smaller organisations one person may have to take on many of the roles looked after by specialised departments in larger organisations.

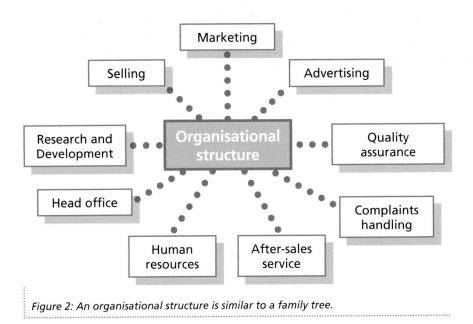

Figure 2: An organisational structure is similar to a family tree.

Teamwork and good customer service

It's highly unlikely that your organisation's products or services can be delivered by one single person. Several people — team members — will be involved when dealing with a single customer.

Unless you work entirely on your own, everybody performs as part of a team. Sometimes people belong to more than one team.

Here are some activities customer service people are involved in. Remember, these can be either face-to-face or using technology.

- greeting customers
- answering questions
- giving information
- solving problems
- handling complaints
- building relationships (with customers and colleagues/suppliers).

You will need skills to ensure you carry out your responsibilities well. These include:

- communication skills – written, oral, non-verbal
- call-handling skills – for the telephone
- listening skills
- questioning skills
- information-gathering skills
- IT skills
- teamworking skills
- personal development skills.

You will learn more about these skills as you work towards achieving your qualification.

Teamwork fits nicely into the concept of thinking of customer service as a jigsaw with the pieces all fitting together at the same time. To make this happen, team members need to work co-operatively with one another. It helps if you all know each other's roles and responsibilities.

To understand where you fit, think about the key customer service requirements of your job. Just what is it you are expected to do?

Portfolio Task

Links to f1f

Looking at teamwork and its impact on customer service, write a report which aims to show you understand the importance of teamwork in delivering good customer service. Base your report on a typical week at work. Use these questions to help you get started.

- Who works with you in your team? What role do they play?
- What is your role within the team?
- What happens if somebody is off sick or away on holiday?
- Who do you miss the most if he or she is not there? Why is this?

- Who helps you the most? Why is this?

Keep your report for your portfolio.

Functional skills

English: Writing

You may be able to use your report as evidence towards Level 1 Functional English: Writing. Make sure your report is structured appropriately to make it logical for the reader to understand and check it through for punctuation, spelling and grammar.

Who to go to for information or help when dealing with customer service issues

It really is all about teamwork: knowing who to go to for help or information when you deal with customer service issues and who might come to you for help too.

People you work closely with (your colleagues) may be the right people to ask. Or you might need to go to someone in another department, building, office or organisation. It very much depends on what it is you need.

It's not just about people. There are all sorts of things you can do to access information providing you know where to find it.

Here are some places you could look:

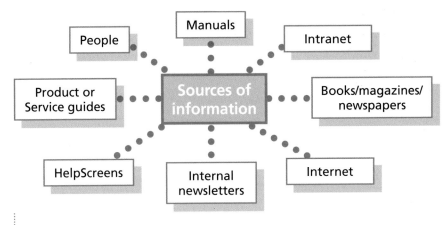

Figure 3: Some of the places you can look for information.

Information your colleagues may need from you so that they can give good service to customers

Thinking about your customer service responsibilities — there will be times when you can help a colleague to give great customer service. You will know the answers when he or she does not.

You may well know much more than you think you know. It's great when you can help out a colleague by providing information. That way, customers' needs and expectations continue to be met or exceeded and the reputation of your organisation is sustained.

Remember, it is important to keep yourself up to date, especially with product or service information — more about this later.

> Versions of the tables used in this task, ready for you to complete, are available to download from www.contentextra.com/customerservice

Portfolio Task

Links to f1f, f1h, f1l

1 Make a list of colleagues, suppliers or other individuals who you regularly work with to deliver customer service. Use the table below.

How people I work with help me deliver customer service.

Name and job role	How they help me provide good customer service

2 Now write down what happened when another person say, a colleague, came to you for information.

- What did he or she ask *you*?
- Were you easily able to give the information?

- Why did you know the answers to the questions?
- How did you feel when you were able to help a colleague?
- Would you do anything differently next time?

Use the table below to describe what happened.

How I provided good customer service.

I was asked to do this	How I helped provide good customer service

Keep your report for your portfolio.

> If we all pull together, we can win!

Figure 4: Everyone pulling together as a team leads to success.

If you had not helped out and all those people who have helped you had also not bothered, service would have suffered. Being part of a team of people can be hugely rewarding because you know each and every one of you can pull together to make life easier for the customer and for yourselves.

Teamwork is at the heart of everything you do.

✔ Checklist – Being an active team player

- Understand your role in the team.
- Listen to other team members.
- Have a positive attitude.
- Work co-operatively to produce solutions.
- Respect other people's needs.
- Share ideas and information.
- Support colleagues.
- Keep your promises.

Portfolio Task   Links to f1h

1   a.   Find out what your key customer service responsibilities are. Talk with a colleague if necessary. Write a list.

    b.   Use the list to discuss with your assessor how you provide good customer service to differing customer types.

2   Now think about the team you play a part in. Use these questions as a basis of discussion with your assessor about teamwork.

    a.   What are your team's main objectives?

    b.   What is your role within this team?

    c.   What responsibilities as a team member do you have to your team leader (if any), your organisation, and your colleagues in the team?

Teamwork and internal customers

You should treat your internal customers in the same way as you treat external customers. You might like to think in terms of a jigsaw puzzle – you wouldn't treat pieces of a jigsaw differently just because some were of a different size and shape. They all have a value in making the whole come together.

If you communicate effectively with other team members you will soon develop a reputation for being a good person to work with and a solid team member.

Teamwork and external customers

Remember that external customers are not just those people who come to you to access your organisation's products or services. Suppliers and other partner organisations are also your external customers.

How customer satisfaction is affected by customer expectations

What makes your organisation different from its competitors? **You do!** Service failings frequently revolve around employees and their attitudes and behaviour, for example, staff who are helpful, are willing to take responsibility and have the right level of knowledge to help customers will be on their way to providing the right level of customer service.

You, your colleagues and the systems and processes that support customer service in your organisation are what make or break the customer service experience. **You** have an enormous part to play in ensuring that customers are dealt with properly and to everyone's satisfaction.

Each customer will have their own ideas as to what to expect from organisations. These **customer expectations** are based on a number of factors including:

- advertising and marketing
- word of mouth from friends or family
- past experiences with the organisation, product or service
- reputation of the organisation and its staff.

You will probably have some expectations about what will happen when you do business with various people and organisations. These will be **your** expectations; other people might think differently.

Key term

Customer expectations – what people think should happen and how they think they should be treated when asking for, or receiving, customer service.

Looking at the scenarios in Table 1, select three which are appropriate to you. On a separate piece of paper, write down what your expectations are from the organisation and people you deal with.

Table 1: Typical activities involving customer service.

Scenario	My expectations are...
Shopping over the Internet	
Phoning a call centre	
Having a meal out	
Ordering a takeaway	
Shopping at a supermarket	
Using public transport	
Seeing your GP or dentist	

What kind of thoughts and emotions did you feel when completing this activity? Were you able to recall instantly both good and poor experiences? What level of **customer satisfaction** did you experience? For the good memories, your expectations were probably met and therefore you were satisfied. With the poor ones, you may have ended up disappointed, perhaps even angry, because your expectations were not met.

Organisations which are known for the quality of their service generate positive expectations. When dealing with organisations with a good reputation, customers expect things will be done right first time and that they will get value for money. They expect the organisation to be easy to do business with.

Part of this positive perception may be built on an organisation's advertising. For example, is it portraying a young, fresh image or a traditional image? Does it promise to do things through its advertising and do customers trust these promises?

Key term

Customer satisfaction – the feeling a customer gets when he or she is happy with the product and service provided.

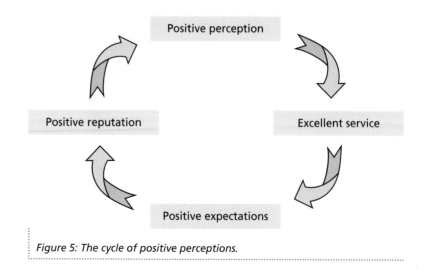

Figure 5: The cycle of positive perceptions.

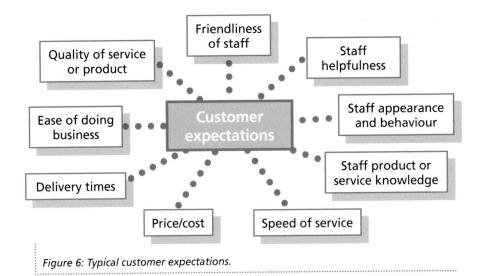

Figure 6: Typical customer expectations.

Notice how many customer expectations are associated with the people working in customer service. You and your team are at the heart of everything a customer expects from an organisation, so remember to:

- play an active part in your team
- act appropriately so that customers and team members trust you
- do what you say you will do
- treat your customer like an individual
- go the extra mile for your customer
- provide the personal touch
- resolve any problem well
- give your customer a good experience from start to finish.

You can make the difference

People make the difference. You can show by your behaviour and your actions that things can change for the better. If every customer service practitioner had this attitude, the pace of change would accelerate and your customers would soon sit up and notice the difference. Imagine how powerful you could be if you and your team members all do this.

One way you can deliver great service on a consistent basis is to ensure you are **reliable.**

Being reliable means:

- being trustworthy
- keeping promises
- being accurate
- doing things on time
- being efficient
- being professional
- being dependable.

Portfolio Task

Links to f1.2.3, f1c, f1d

1 Discuss with colleagues the part you play in delivering reliable customer service. Make sure you ask for specific examples of your behaviours and actions.

2 Based on this, write a short report which explains how being reliable helps to ensure customer expectations are met so that customer satisfaction is achieved.

A version of the table used in this task, ready for you to complete, is available to download from www.contentextra.com/customerservice

The effect of customer expectations being met, exceeded or not met

You have seen that customers typically have expectations about the same areas regardless of the product or service involved. When the reality differs from the customer's expectations — either because the expectations have not been met or because they have been exceeded — there will be an impact on the customer.

Portfolio Task

Links to f1.1.2, f1c, f1d

1 Imagine you are the customer in each of these situations. Describe the effect the scenarios might have on you. We have given you one example to start you off.

2 For each scenario, discuss with colleagues how they might feel.

3 Where you have said your expectations were not met, discuss with your colleagues how customer satisfaction has not been achieved and its likely impact on the organisation.

Impact of different scenarios on me

Situation	Expectations not met or exceeded?	Impact
Your car is unexpectedly cleaned during a routine service	Exceeded	Will use company again and will tell my friends
A tune fails to download from the Internet		
You find a slug in your lettuce		
Repairs to your car are more costly than the quote		
The call centre deals with your query quickly		
The sales person tells you where you can get help when unable to help you personally		
Your train arrives on time		
The supermarket has no queue		
Your written complaint is dealt with by return of post		
Your takeaway meal arrives 30 minutes late		

What makes your customers happy?

You will have had many opportunities to recognise when a customer is happy or not, so we will now look at customer satisfaction with your organisation.

Customers might tell you (verbally or in writing) about things which really impressed them. You may have gone the extra mile with a customer and positively surprised them by what you did. Or, you yourself might observe something happening which indicates whether all is well or not.

Portfolio Task
Links to f1.1.1, f1c, f1h, f1k

Think about a time when a customer told you he or she was not happy. Why was this? On a separate piece of paper, write down your answers to these questions.

1 Describe the customer's expectations.

2 Why did the customer feel dissatisfied?

3 Which was the most significant cause for concern:
  a. the product or service itself?
  b. the behaviour of the service deliverer involved?

4 What did the organisation do (or not do) to cause this dissatisfaction?

5 What could you or your organisation do differently to ensure customer expectations were met next time?

Thinking about typical customer expectations, you may have heard comments like these:

Quality of service or product

'Why does this always break?' 'I love your new workshop.' 'Your opening hours are much more convenient.' 'I hate that answerphone!'

Friendliness of staff

'It's always a pleasure coming here.' 'Thank goodness for a smiling face!.' 'You always remember me.' 'Miserable lot! Why don't they find another job!?'

Staff helpfulness

'Thank you. You're really kind.' 'It's good to find someone who really knows what they are doing.' 'Why are you rushing me?' 'What's the matter? Don't you want to help?'

Staff appearance and behaviour

'Your uniform is really smart and it helps me to find where you are.' 'All of you work so well together as a team.' 'Wow! That's a really professional attitude. Thank you!' 'I really appreciate you trying.' 'They can't be bothered to help. I'm going elsewhere in future.'

Figure 7: Poor service can leave customers frustrated and upset.

Unit F1 Communicate using customer service language

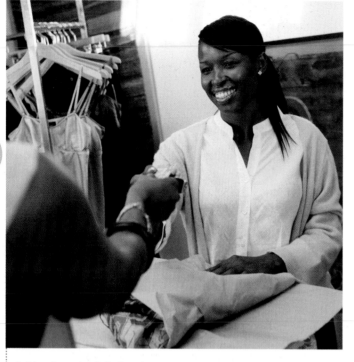

A friendly attitude helps give customers a positive impression.

Staff product or service knowledge

'I'm really confident you know what you are talking about.' 'I'm really upset, you can never find what I want.'

Speed of service

'I'm really happy; I never have to queue here.' 'Why do you never answer the phone? It's so frustrating!'

Price/cost

'Many thanks. I didn't expect you to give me a discount.' 'I'm getting really frustrated your prices are so high.'

Delivery times

'That's amazing! I didn't expect it so quickly.' 'As usual, I'm waiting weeks when it should be days. It's so annoying!.'

Ease of doing business

'The lack of form-filling makes it a real pleasure to come here.' 'I'm very annoyed; your website is hard to navigate.'

Remember, impressing people is going to take more than doing your job well. You need to do that little bit extra!

Portfolio Task   Links to f1.1.2, f1.2.3, f1c, f1h, f1k

To prepare for a discussion with colleagues, make lists about things which impress or annoy your customers.

1   What specifically does your organisation do to impress customers?

2   What does your organisation do which appears to annoy customers? To help with this, think about things you have heard or seen repeatedly. Think about complaints you have dealt with.

3   Now think about your own actions and behaviours. What do you do which consistently pleases and impresses your customers?

4   Finally, what about the things you have done which have annoyed your customers?

Now discuss your findings with colleagues.

Why good customer service is important to any organisation

Key term

Reputation – the general opinion customers have about an organisation.

If expectations are met, a customer will be satisfied. If they are exceeded, the customer may end up both surprised and delighted with the service he or she has received. Quite simply, if you and your organisation do not provide good service, somebody else will. Business will be lost, your competitors will gain, your business **reputation** suffers and ultimately, your organisation (or parts of it) may cease to exist.

So it is really important to make sure your customers' expectations are met or exceeded. One small blip in service and reputation will be damaged. If expectations are not met, disappointment, anger and frustration might set in.

That all sounds pretty bad so you should by now see what a very important job you have. You can actively contribute to giving good customer service and ensuring your customers remain loyal.

Working for an organisation that has a positive reputation is immensely satisfying as well as challenging. Customers have high expectations of you and your organisation and you should feel proud to be part of that and proud that customers come back to you with their business time and time again.

An organisation's reputation is directly linked to meeting customer expectations and achieving customer satisfaction. To achieve and sustain a good reputation, service delivery must be consistently good. In other words, a customer needs to see you and your organisation are reliable.

Building a strong reputation leads to customer loyalty.

Having a strong reputation will mean that your organisation has the building blocks to:

- attract customers to use its products or services – acting as a 'reputation magnet'
- put things right if they go wrong
- create a positive impression
- change its reputation over time.

Unfortunately, some organisations will have a reputation that is so poor that customers expect virtually nothing from them by way of good service. This can mean that, even when there are signs of improvement, these go unnoticed because customers' minds are always fixed on the fact that certain organisations are simply a pain to deal with.

✔ Checklist – Building and sustaining your organisation's reputation

- Do what you say you will do.
- Treat your customer like an individual.
- Go the extra mile for your customer.
- Provide the personal touch.
- Resolve any problems well.
- Give your customer a good experience from start to finish.

Figure 8: Make sure you maintain a positive reputation.

The difference between having a strong reputation and a poor reputation is often down to the difference between excellent and poor customer service.

Looking at the checklist above, organisations with strong reputations are a pleasure to do business with. They make things easy for the customer. Promises are kept, employees go the extra mile on behalf of customers and provide a 'personal touch'. If things do go wrong, problems are solved well.

So, it follows that reputations are easily damaged by poor customer service. If promises are not kept, if service is impersonal and employees simply do not make the effort to help, then a reputation will suffer. There are likely to be more complaints leading to more problems which will probably in turn not be resolved very well.

Your organisation's reputation is something you need to live up to. If it is strong, your customer's expectations will be high.

For example, if your organisation has a reputation for doing things quickly and on time, the reputation will suffer if things go slowly and promises are not kept.

Similarly, organisations with poor reputations suffer from customers thinking there will be hassle. In this case, it will be important for employees to help build the reputation so that customer expectations rise.

How your organisation's procedures support good customer service

Your organisation will have systems and procedures for supporting the delivery of a consistent and reliable service to customers. These include feedback systems, complaints procedures and service standards. By following these, you will be helping to build and sustain a positive reputation.

You will be expected to follow your **organisation's or company's procedures**. Some of these will relate to external customers and some will be internal procedures designed, for example, to help staff deal with each other, such as HR (Human Resource) procedures.

Some typical organisation or company procedures include:

● procedures for obtaining and dealing with customer feedback

● staff training procedures

● health & safety procedures

● security procedures

● HR procedures (for example, sickness procedures)

Key term

Organisation/company procedure – the detailed guidelines or rules that an organisation uses to deliver customer service.

Unit F1 Communicate using customer service language

- complaints procedures
- service standards.

For example, a cosmetics mail order firm will have procedures for exchanges or refunds and delivery times; both customers and employees know what to expect. If customer expectations are not met, there will be a complaints procedure to follow.

By following the steps laid down in the complaints procedure, a customer service practitioner will help to contribute to consistent and reliable customer service.

This is because the procedure will help employees to understand how to deal with the complaint.

It might tell you to:

1 Log the date and time the complaint was made.

2 Seek feedback as to why the item is being returned.

3 Record the reasons.

4 Offer an alternative product.

5 Log how the complaint was resolved.

Notice this procedure asks for feedback on why a complaint was made. In this way, procedures can help organisations understand if service standards are being met. By collecting this information, customer satisfaction can be sustained.

> A version of the table used in this task, ready for you to complete, is available to download from www.contentextra.com/customerservice

Portfolio Task

Links to f1.1.3, f1c, f1d, f1e

1 Find out about your organisation's procedures. We have given you some to get you started. Add any other procedures which have an impact on customer satisfaction. Write a report against each one which details how you use them to achieve customer satisfaction.

2 Now discuss with your assessor how you use these procedures to deliver good customer service.

Functional skills

English: Speaking, listening and communication and Writing
Your discussion with your assessor might be able to count as evidence towards Level 1 Functional English: Speaking, listening and communication. Present the information from your research using appropriate language. The report you write to prepare for the discussion may be used as evidence for Level 1 Functional English: Writing. Check it for spelling, grammar and punctuation and print out a copy.

Effect of my organisation's procedures on customer satisfaction.

Company procedure	Key points leading to customer satisfaction
Health & safety	
Complaints	
Customer feedback	
Teamworking	

> ☑ **Checklist – Organisational procedures help to:**
>
> - let customers know what to expect in specific situations
> - advise employees on how to deal with customer complaints or queries
> - resolve problems in a consistent way
> - monitor service standards
> - improve service delivery.

Service standards

Some organisations will lay down service standards against certain criteria. These standards are simply things an organisation expects of its employees when dealing with customers. This could cover anything from how to answer the telephone and what to say, to the timescales involved when replying to a letter.

Service standards vary between organisations. For example, it may be appropriate in some organisations to dress casually, for example, in a call centre. In others, a uniform may be necessary, for example, in an airline.

Table 2 shows what some service standards might include.

Table 2: Examples of service standards

Area for action	Service standard
Face-to-face initial greeting	• Smile at customers as they approach • Say 'good morning' or 'good afternoon' • Make eye contact within 3 seconds • Use customer name at least twice
Telephone answering	• Answer the phone within 3 rings
Returning phone calls	• Return all calls within 24 hours
Take responsibility	• Give customers your name, phone number and extension

A version of the table used in this task, ready for you to complete, is available to download from www.contentextra.com/customerservice

Portfolio Task

Links to f1.1.3, f1c, f1d, f1e

1 Find out about your organisation's service standards, for example, for workplace behaviour and appearance.

2 Make a list here of any other service standards which have an impact on customer satisfaction. Include the key points from each standard which you believe help you to achieve customer satisfaction.

3 Now discuss with your assessor how you use these service standards to deliver good customer service.

Effect of my organisation's service standards on customer satisfaction.

Service standard	Key points leading to customer satisfaction

Checking expectations are met

The existence of service standards and other company procedures does not mean organisations can sit back and stay as they are. They need to check service delivery continues to meet customer needs. This is necessary because people's opinions and preferences will change over time.

Portfolio Task   Links to f1.1.2, f1c, f1d

Discuss with a colleague how **you** meet or exceed your customers' expectations.

To prepare for this, complete these sentences on a separate piece of paper.

1 What do customers generally expect from your own organisation? Write down five key expectations.

2 I make sure I follow company procedures by...

3 I check I have done what the customer wants by...

4 I sometimes go the extra mile by...

5 I am reliable because I...

6 How does doing all this help you to meet or exceed customer expectations? Think about specific times you have done this and write down some examples.

Show the answers to these questions to your assessor.

Identify your organisation's services and products

What you need to know and learn

- What services or products your organisation provides
- How you can help to deliver your organisation's service offer
- How the way you behave affects your customer's service experience.

Key terms

Product – a physical good providing benefits to customers, for example, food, clothes, furniture, mortgages, savings accounts.

Service – an activity carried out providing benefits to customers, for example, rail and bus services, health services, providing information and advice.

We have looked at who your customers are, teamwork and using company procedures to help with meeting customer expectations. We will now help you to understand how you can deliver great customer service by understanding all about your organisation's **services** and **products**.

What services or products your organisation provides

Organisations tend to offer a mixture of products and services. **Customer satisfaction** results from the overall effect of what you offer (see the key term on page 12).

A shoe shop will rely heavily on the boots and shoes it sells, that is, on its products. But a good shoe shop will know that the service it provides during the sale is also important. Some retailers will also be involved with before- and after-sales care, for example, a furniture showroom, car dealership or computer store.

Organisations which provide **only** services rely totally on the quality of the customer service offered by employees. These include rail and bus services, the local authority recycling service and your GP or dentist.

You need to become an expert in knowing all about the products or services that are appropriate to your job role. You will then feel confident in explaining them to your customers and your customers will have confidence in you.

Get to know your products or services inside out.

Finding information about services or products

There are probably lots of places or people you can go to in your organisation to find out about services and products. Figure 9 gives you some examples.

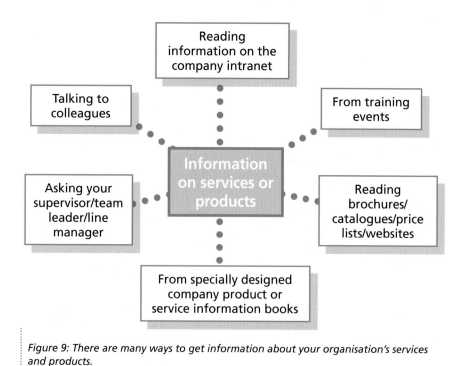

Figure 9: There are many ways to get information about your organisation's services and products.

Product leaflets are one source of information.

You are not expected to know about **all** the products or services your organisation offers. The first thing to do is to find out which ones you **must** know all about and which would simply be **nice** for you to know about.

If you do this, you will be able to direct customers to other people in your organisation who can help your customers with things which are outside your responsibility. Knowing who to go to is all part of giving good customer service and helps your organisation's reputation.

Figure 10: Do you know which key services or products you need to know all about?

Unit F1 Communicate using customer service language

Portfolio Task

Links to f1.2.1, F1.2.3, f1b, f1n

1 a. Find out which are the key products or services you are expected to know about.

   b. Make a list.

2 Now think about all the sources of information you use to find out about these products or services.

   Match each source of information to the products or services you have identified. Add this to your list.

3 a. Now find out about some of the other services or products dealt with by other people in your organisation. Make a list.

   b. Use this to discuss with a colleague why it is important to know what other people can do for customers.

   c. Reflect on what you have discussed and write a personal statement which summarises your discussion.

   d. Show your list and this statement to your assessor who may also want to observe you communicating service or product information to customers.

Functional skills

English: Reading

When doing your research, you will need to read and understand a variety of texts and be able to use this information to write lists, enter into discussions and write a personal statement. You may be able to use this preparatory reading work as evidence towards Level 1 Functional English: Reading.

Keeping your product or service knowledge up-to-date

Organisations are always looking to improve their products or services which means changes are frequently made. You need to make sure you are always up to date so the information you give to customers is accurate. Customers must be able to trust what you tell them. We look further at this in **Unit B2 Deliver reliable customer service**.

Telling your customers about services or products

People buy services or products for different reasons; we all have our individual preferences. It is important you identify what your customer needs by asking questions and listening carefully to what you are told. You can then match the best product or service to your customer's needs.

To do this, you will need to know the **features** and **benefits** of your products or services. This will help you to answer simple questions and to give great customer service.

Features describe characteristics, for example, size, colour, shape, speed, accessibility. A benefit describes what the feature will do for a customer. The best explanation you can give to a customer is to talk about both. For example:

> 'Our skirts have elasticated waistbands so it doesn't matter how much you eat at Christmas!'

> 'This chair has a built-in lumbar support to help prevent backache.'

> 'We always phone you before arranging delivery to make sure the time is convenient.'

> 'This broadband connection is ultra-fast so you will save time.'

Key terms

Feature – describes what a product or service does.

Benefit – describes how the product or service can help a customer.

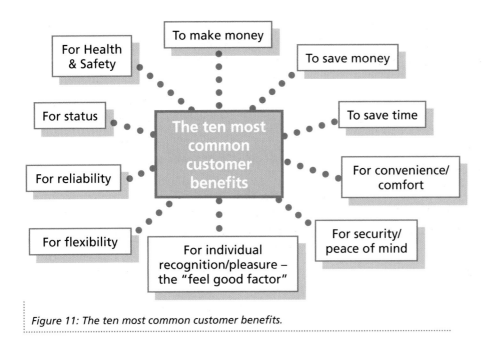

Figure 11: The ten most common customer benefits.

When listening to what your customer wants always keep the ten key customer benefits in mind.

When you outline a product or service to a customer make sure you do not over-complicate things. For example think about whether any of the following over-complicate things:

- Is it right to tell customers every single thing there is to know?
- Do you tell customers just enough to make them buy or want to use the product or service?
- What about telling them about products or services they did not ask about?

It's all too easy to make life more difficult for your customer than it need be.

Portfolio Task

Links to f1.2.1, f1b, f1m

Imagine you are the customer service professional in each of these situations. With a colleague, practise talking about features and benefits by completing these sentences. Then write down the best sentences which show you understand how to talk about features and benefits.

Travel agent to a disabled person
The holiday complex has lifts to all floors making it...

Shop assistant to a mother
This sun tan lotion has a high SPF making it suitable for...

Gym instructor to a client
I have just updated my qualifications in sports nutrition which means that...

Car salesperson to a potential car buyer
This car reaches 0–60 in 4.4 seconds; you will be able to...

Tree surgeon to a customer
I am fully insured so you will be ...

Now look back at the list of services or products you deal with. For each one, write down how you would best describe them to a customer in terms of both their features and benefits.

Make sure you are observed outlining products or services to customers.

What customers want is to leave you feeling their needs have been met. It is even better if you have managed to exceed their expectations.

It is all about identifying each customer's individual needs and then matching your products or services closely to them.

With up-to-date product or service information, you will have enough knowledge to be able to answer questions from customers.

To do this well you will need to decide what to say or write:

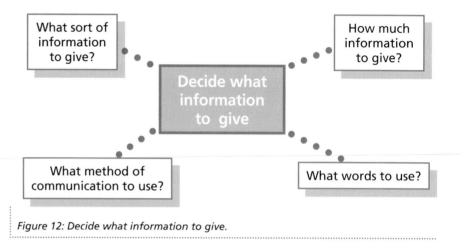

Figure 12: Decide what information to give.

You can only do this if you truly understand what the customer wants and needs. It's all about great communication – you and your customer must understand each other!

Always communicate in a clear, polite and confident way. You can do this by:

- listening
- asking questions
- checking understanding
- providing information
- using language appropriate to the individual customer
- using appropriate body language.

We look at communicating with customers in more detail in Unit A4 Give customers a positive impression of yourself and your organisation.

Key term

Service offer – the extent and limits of the customer service that an organisation is offering.

How you can help to deliver your organisation's service offer

Think about a **service offer** as a set of promises your organisation makes to its customers. If you look at it in this way, you will instantly see that if a promise is broken, customer satisfaction will suffer. Expectations will not be met. Potentially, the organisation's reputation will be damaged.

Clearly, you will need to know all about your organisation's service offer to help you deliver great customer service. It will help you to decide:

- what and how much information you need about services and products

- what your organisation is prepared to do for its customers

- what it is not prepared to do.

Promises made in service offers might include things like:

- friendly service

- money back if goods returned

- next day delivery if ordered by 12 noon

- call-back in 24 hours

- dedicated helpline

- fully qualified staff

- evening opening.

These promises create customer expectations. For example, if a company promises to send goods by next day delivery then customers will expect to receive their order in that time. If a coffee bar promises never to ask customers to leave their comfortable sofas, then customers will expect to be able to enjoy a leisurely coffee even if they buy just one steamy latte.

Perhaps the most difficult service offer promises to live up to are the ones which involve staff behaviour. Many organisations say they have friendly, professional staff who are always on hand to be of help. Can organisations consistently live up to this promise? By working towards your qualification, you are doing your best to help them do so.

If you look through any magazine or newspaper you will see plenty of promises made to customers in advertising, for example:

- *No deposit, 4 years free credit with nothing to pay for the first year.*

- *Book with 100% confidence, fully bonded, fully protected.*

- *Because our recorders are available with either Freeview+ HD or freesat+ HD built in, you can bring your High Definition television to life no matter where you live in the UK***
  ** Offering up to 95% coverage of the UK

- *Reupholster 2 items and we will reupholster a 3rd item FREE on selected designs!*

- *If you can find the same product at a lower price, in stock locally, within 7 days of purchase — we promise to beat that competitor's written quotation.*

Imagine what would happen if staff working at these organisations did not know about the service offer, that is, the promises made to customers.

Portfolio Task

Links to f1.2.3

In relation to the services or products you deal with, find out now what your organisation's service offer is.

- How is it communicated to customers?
- How do you keep up to date with any changes to the service offer?
- What part do you play in living up to the promises made in the service offer?

Discuss this with your colleagues. Make an audio for your portfolio.

Managing expectations through service offers

There is no point promising things will happen if there is no chance of people or systems being able to deliver what has been promised. So, an organisation can use service offers to set customer expectations at a level it knows it can achieve or exceed.

Service offers help staff because you need to live up to the promises made in them. This means behaving in such a way so as to ensure the service offer is fully met.

A service offer is often made by considering what competitors do. An organisation can then try to beat this but it would only be sensible to do so if it knows it can fully meet the promises made. For example, if a new coffee shop opens in the High Street, it may well look to do something a little different from others nearby. This could be by adding a new service such as Wi-Fi access or it may be around price. Perhaps a loyalty scheme would help show its potential customers it promises to do more than the competition.

Service offers and saying 'no'

To be able to explain your organisation's service offer you will also need to know the procedures and regulations which support them. This might include what you are not able to do for customers because, for example, health and safety regulations do not permit it.

Customers who feel organisations and staff have not lived up to their expectations will probably be frustrated and even angry. Sometimes this is because they have misunderstood what a service offer is all about or have not read the small print. For example, if you refer back to the promise made by one company, it said HD televisions could be brought to life no matter where somebody was in the UK. However, in the small print it states that coverage is up to 95% of the UK.

In this example, a customer service practitioner would be wrong to say 'Read the small print' but should simply point out exactly what the promise meant.

Saying no is not about refusing to help. It's more a case of helping a customer to understand that on this occasion you are unable to help but can offer a suitable alternative. It's all about offering options or alternatives rather than a straightforward 'no'.

Your organisation's service offer will help you to decide what you can and cannot do for customers. Also, knowing who to go to for help if you are unable to provide information would also support your explanations to customers.

Knowing the limits of your authority is vital. It would be wrong to promise you will do something if you do not have the authority to act. Make sure you know about your organisation's complaints procedure as this will often help you to know how the service offer and promises work in practice.

Portfolio Task   Links to f1.2.2, f1.2.3, f1b, f1e, f1g, f1m, f1n

In relation to the services or products you deal with, consider how your own job is affected by your organisation's service offer.

1   Make a list of the key features of the service offer which you need to be able to explain to customers.

2   Now think about the procedures and regulations which affect the areas you have identified. How do you keep yourself up to date with any changes? Make a list.

3   Ensure your lists include details of the information you need to deliver effective customer service and where it can be found.

4   Discuss this with colleagues and make a recording for your portfolio.

How the way you behave affects your customer's service experience

Your attitude will drive forward just how good you are at customer service. Get it wrong and customers will soon react. Be confident with your organisation's service offer. Be an ambassador for your organisation. Speak from the heart. Believe in the products or services you deal with. Being up to date with product or service information will give you the confidence to know you are giving accurate explanations and living up to the customer service promise. Customers want to do business with organisations and people who believe in the products or services they deliver.

Sounds so easy? Sounds difficult? It's up to you to make this happen. You are already showing the right attitude by taking this qualification. It will arm you with knowledge you need to be a customer service professional. It's now all about putting this knowledge into practice alongside developing your customer service skills.

Delivering the service offer starts with using the right words and actions. You will learn more about this in the units dealing with communication. To get you started think about choosing the right words and actions to support your organisation's service offer.

The impact of your appearance

When you are a customer, one of the key factors in creating an image in your mind will be the appearance of the people you do business with. Many organisations now have dress codes which lay down rules regarding what employees are expected to wear to work. This is all about portraying the right image to customers and creating the 'picture' the organisation wishes to portray.

It helps create a sense of identity. Customers will instantly be able to recognise members of staff. In turn, many staff feel a sense of pride or belonging. A dress code can also help to foster teamwork.

However, many employees resent being told what to wear. Perhaps they feel it is like going back to school. If you fall into this category, try to make the most of following your organisation's dress code. Understand how it can help you to deliver great customer service. In turn, you will do your job well and achieve recognition for that. Be positive and supportive despite any personal reservations you may have.

Portfolio Task

Links to f1.2.3, f1g, f1h, f1p

Think about the type of organisation you work for. Discuss these questions with colleagues. Make an audio recording for your portfolio.

1 What does the organisation stand for?

2 What image does it create through its advertising, its premises and its services or products?

3 What is the dress code, if any?

4 How does it help you to deliver your organisation's service offer?

5 Are there any aspects of the dress code which you do not like?

6 What do you need to do to ensure you comply with the dress code?

The impact of your behaviour

Taking care of your appearance is not the only thing you need to do. Consider the impact of your behaviour too. Successful delivery of the service offer requires you to be confident in your actions and behaviour. It's not only about **what** you say, it's also about **how** you say it. There may be times where you do not fully agree with what your organisation is doing. Perhaps you think some of the promises are unrealistic or perhaps you feel it is almost impossible for every customer to receive great service. However, in all situations you must do your best to help customers understand the service offer by being enthusiastic about the services or products regardless of any personal reservations you might have.

Show your customer respect. Show interest by actively listening – if you are on the telephone, make encouraging noises. If face-to-face, nod your head. and use eye contact to show you are interested and paying attention. Make sure your working environment is creating the right image.

If your organisation's procedures recommend you use the customer's name, do so.

Most importantly, keep the promises you personally make to customers as well as following those made in the service offer.

Choose your words carefully

Be positive with your choice of words. Nobody wants to hear what cannot be done so say what you can do and offer options and alternatives if you are unable to help.

Avoid using jargon as this will confuse your customers. Be clear when describing services or products to avoid misunderstandings. Check your customers have understood you.

Speak with a smile in your voice. Yes, even on the telephone, customers truly will know if you are smiling and it will also help instil confidence in them that you know what you are doing.

Remember – It's not only about **what** you say, it's also about **how** you say it.

> A version of the table used in this task, ready for you to complete, is available to download from www.contentextra.com/customerservice

Portfolio Task

Links to f1.2.3, f1p

1. On a separate piece of paper or using the table on the website, complete the table below by thinking about the impact you have on customers and listing this in the left-hand column.

2. Now ask a colleague to observe you dealing with customers. Ask colleagues to make notes on what they see and hear you doing. Record this in the right-hand column.

3. Use these notes to discuss how the way you behave affects your customer's service experience. Include in your discussion how you help to deliver the service offer.

   Make an audio of the discussion for your portfolio.

My impact on customers

The impact on customers of ...	My colleagues say:
my working environment is....	
my appearance is....	
my behaviour is…	
the words I use is…	
my service or product knowledge is...	

Remember– if you get your attitude and behaviour right, your customers are more likely to trust you.

What to do if problems occur

Of course, there will be times when things do not go to plan. Sometimes this will be largely outside your control. For example, strike action, travel disruptions, equipment failure or extreme weather conditions.

There are, though, plenty of things that can go wrong which are within your control or which you can help to resolve.

Spotting there is a problem is the first thing to do. This may sound like commonsense but you have probably wondered why the same things seem to go wrong with certain companies you use. Is nobody listening? Do they have their heads buried in the sand? Or, do they simply not care? If this is the case, nothing will change for the better, reputation will suffer and customers will go elsewhere.

By spotting the problem, you can help to make things better for customers, your organisation and yourself.

Becoming aware of problems

You may become aware of problems in a variety of ways. Some might be brought to your attention by customers and you will see or hear things going wrong yourself. Your colleagues too might share what they have noticed. This is called feedback. It can happen verbally, that is, customers talking to you, or in writing – perhaps in a letter of complaint.

It is important for customers to trust you.

You might spot a problem simply by noticing a customer's behaviour. Does he or she look angry or frustrated? It is important to interpret behaviour accurately. Refer to **Unit A10 Deal with customers face to face** for more information.

Some organisations also have processes to help with seeking feedback. These include customer comment cards, suggestion boxes, surveys and questionnaires.

Having spotted the problem, you need to know who to go to for help. The work you have already done earlier in this unit will help with knowing who does what to solve customers' problems.

Portfolio Task

Links to f1.2.3, f1o

Make a list of the types of problems which occur frequently in your organisation.

Think about:

- problems brought to your attention by customers

- problems with systems and procedures

- problems with colleagues and/or suppliers

- problems which are outside the control of you or your organisation.

Make a list of who to go to for help against each problem you identify.

What part do you play in helping to resolve these problems? Discuss this with colleagues.

Working Life

I'm Adam and I work on a helpline in a call centre dealing with queries from customers who have bought from a range of electrical goods. I am well aware of my company's service offer which is:

- free helpline open 24 hours a day 7 days a week

- friendly staff

- problems solved quickly and efficiently or your money back.

I am always taking calls from people about vacuum cleaners. Customers know my company has a strong reputation for both its products and its after sales service.

This morning I took a call from a customer who was concerned about the amount of air blowing out from the cleaner. I get this type of call every day! I asked her if the suction was still good and she said it was. I then told her that she had bought one of the most powerful cleaners on the market which meant that the powerful suction mechanism which took in air (and therefore dirt) had to come out somewhere and that was why she had a gale blowing out of the front of her machine. 'But it frightens my dog,'. she said. 'Also, it's blowing dust about off my furniture.'

I told her not to worry and that what was happening was perfectly normal. I then asked her if there was anything else I could help her with and there wasn't. However, I am not convinced she appreciated my explanation as, when she said goodbye, she sounded a bit flat.

Ask the expert

Q Why wasn't customer satisfaction achieved?

A Although Adam knew all about the service offer he had perhaps grown tired of hearing the same question over and over again. He did not ask questions about how the machine had been put together and so failed to check it was being used properly. Always ask questions to check understanding.

Q Did Adam do enough?

A He could have done more when realising the customer didn't sound satisfied. Remember, the customer experience is all about what a customer feels and remembers about their dealings with you. Sometimes, it is not enough to offer an explanation. More is needed to reassure customers and to rebuild confidence.

Top tips

Adam knew his organisation's service offer and was mindful to be friendly and to try to sort the issue out promptly. He was polite and tried to offer an explanation. He also asked if there was anything else he could help with.

Check your knowledge

1 Both external and internal customers should be given:

a. standard customer service

b. service which is discounted

c. the best possible service

d. exactly the same service.

2 External customers are people who:

a. do not access products or services or communicate with your organisation

b. do not pay for products or services until your organisation sends an invoice

c. access products or services from a competitor industry or organisation

d. access products or services but do not work for your organisation.

3 A good way of beginning to understand what customers expect is to:

a. always deliver the same level of service

b. ask senior colleagues for advice.

c. see it from the customer's point of view

d. always give a refund when requested.

4 The customer experience is all about:

a. ensuring customers have the most up-to-date technology to use when ordering goods

b. what a customer feels and remembers about the customer service he or she receives

c. the cleanliness of premises and the professional behaviour of staff towards customers

d. providing staff uniforms and name badges to create a professional image for customers.

5 How can a customer service practitioner help build an organisation's reputation?

a. By attending training courses and reading books.

b. By helping colleagues to exceed their sales targets.

c. By keeping promises and offering a consistent quality service.

d. By participating in team meetings about sales targets.

6 Where might customer service practitioners find out about their organisation's services or products?

a. From brochures, manuals, colleagues and the Internet/intranet.

b. From competitors and similar organisations operating nearby.

c. From health & safety manuals and maintenance procedures.

d. From government directives and European regulations.

7 Why are company procedures important to good customer service?

a. They are a cost-effective way of selling a service.

b. They ensure budgets are never exceeded.

c. They ensure competitors know about staff changes.

d. They help to deliver a consistent quality service.

8 You cannot plan to delight customers until you know something about their:

a. motivation

b. decisions

c. movements

d. expectations.

9 Customers often decide between competing services or products by comparing:

a. colour schemes

b. staff uniforms

c. service offers

d. company brochures.

10 Customer satisfaction is all about:

a. the feeling a customer gets when he or she is happy with the service provided

b. making sure the customer is happy with the price paid for a service

c. making customers aware of additional products or services

d. inviting customers to events to get to know staff and the management team.

Unit F1 Communicate using customer service language

Unit F2
Follow the rules to deliver customer service

What you will learn:

- To follow your organisation's customer service practices and procedures
- To follow legislation and external regulation that relate to customer service

Introduction

Rules exist to help you do your job well. They make sense because they can help both customers and service deliverers understand what can and cannot be done.

Some rules will be set by your organisation and are the result of general responsibilities set by legislation and so apply to many situations and workplaces, for example, laws relating to data protection and health and safety. Other rules apply only to specific industries, for example, distance selling regulations and so are followed by your organisation because of the business you are in. If your organisation has a firm strategy for delivering customer service it may choose to set its own rules to run alongside those rules which exist because of legislation.

Showing you are able to work within the rules will help you with your career because it shows you are a responsible person capable of understanding and using both external and internal sets of rules in order to deliver great service. There are advantages for both customers and any employer of you doing so.

This unit requires you to show you know and understand all the rules that apply to customer service delivered by your organisation and how they apply to your job. You need to show that you:

- Follow your organisation's customer service practices and procedures

- Follow legislation and external regulation that relate to customer service.

Note

As you work through this unit, not all the procedures, rules and legislation may be applicable to you, your job role and/or your working environment. Make sure you take advice from an appropriate person if you are unsure which are the rules you should be familiar with.

Follow your organisation's customer service practices and procedures

What you need to know or learn

- How to use organisational practices and procedures which relate to your job
- How to work in a way which protects the security and health and safety of your customers and their property

How to use organisational practices and procedures which relate to your job

Procedures exist to help you and your customers know what to expect. They assist everyone by stating what happens, when it happens and how it will happen. Timescales might also be included, for example, a complaints procedure would set out what a customer might expect to happen after they've made a formal complaint, and how long this should take.

A customer service procedure might be:

- about behaviour, for example, a dress code or how to deal with abusive customers
- administrative, for example, a complaints procedure or how to handle customer feedback
- technological, for example, about operating a piece of machinery.

Organisations may have many systems and procedures in place such as those shown in Figure 1.

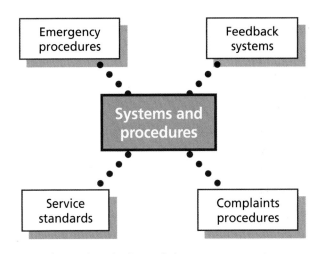

Figure 1: Systems and procedures in the workplace.

Feedback systems

A feedback system is a process that enables your organisation to listen to what the customer has to say. This is important if it is to improve the service it gives. It may be an informal process in which you pass on comments made to you by customers to an appropriate person. Alternatively, it could be a formal process of writing to customers with questions about the service they receive.

Successful organisations understand that both verbal and written comments should be taken very seriously. After all, if a customer has taken the time to write a letter or email, he or she must be either very angry or very happy. Comments made informally, almost in passing, are just as important. For example, in the airline industry if several passengers mention their in-flight meals were too salty, the cabin crew member could pass the feedback on to his or her manager who will then contact the food and beverages department, who take the issue up with the suppliers. If cabin crew ignore this informal type of feedback nothing will change, the meals will continue to be cooked in the same way and this could result in significant customer dissatisfaction.

Feedback is very useful to your organisation. Without it, things will stay the same or be changed as a result of what your organisation wants to impose regardless of what the customer actually wants or needs. Feedback ensures a cycle of continuous improvement can occur.

Portfolio Task   Links to f2.1.1, f2a

1   Find out about feedback procedures you need to follow by asking an appropriate person.

   a. What is your role in using these procedures?

   b. Describe these to your assessor.

2   If applicable to your role, obtain witness testimonies which show how you have used your organisation's feedback procedures.

Complaints procedures

Your organisation may have a process in place for dealing with customer complaints, for example, when to say 'sorry', when to give refunds, what information to record and how to reach a satisfactory conclusion. Depending on your own organisation's practices, you may have full authority to give a refund or a sum of money as a gesture of goodwill. Alternatively, you may have to refer to someone else for permission to do so.

Many organisations actively encourage people to contact them with complaints and comments. This is because a complaint is a form of feedback; it tells an organisation about specific addresses which need attention. Once the organisation knows something has gone wrong, it can take steps to put things right and protect its relationship with the customer.

A complaint could be about a member of staff, a faulty product, poor communication, literally anything which has caused the customer to feel dissatisfied.

Many organisations go as far as describing in detail what a customer needs to do in order to make a complaint. This shows a willingness to help and to use the information to try to improve customer service in the future. For example, an organisation may describe the procedure in its literature or on a 'How to complain' page on their website.

Typically this will include answers to frequently asked questions such as:

- How does the complaints process work?
- Who will reply and when?
- What if I have not had a reply?
- If I don't like the reply what happens next?
- Can I complain to an outside body?

Clearly, you need to know how any complaints procedures operate because if a complaint is handled badly, a difficult situation will quickly escalate into something much worse. Make sure you know how to record details of any complaint made so that it can be followed up appropriately.

Figure 2 illustrates a typical example of what a customer complaint form might look like. It has been completed by a customer service practitioner who has just dealt with a phone call from a customer who is unhappy about a change to her refuse collection.

If there is no complaints procedure where you work, answering these questions will help you to understand what role you need to take. You may need to seek guidance from an appropriate person to help you with the answers.

1 Are you personally authorised to deal with a complaint?

2 If not, who do you need to refer to?

3 What records do you need to make about the complaint?

4 What authority do you have, if any, to compensate the customer where appropriate?

5 What types of compensation can a customer claim?

6 What information is available to a customer to help him or her make a complaint?

Customer Complaint/Comment

Date	Customer name/details	Dealt with by
28 September 2010	Greta O'Shea Manor House, Sea Lane	Paul Tomlinson

Description of Complaint/Comment

New bin men not taking recycling bin away on today's round. Complaints about Council Tax being too high and customer feels her efforts to recycle are wasted.

Action Taken (include here what you have promised the customer)

Mrs O'Shea very angry. Calmed her down. Listened and explained Council policy re what cannot be placed in recycling bin. Asked her if she has seen recycling information leaflet. She had been missed off leaflet drop. Promised to send one to her together with details of new compost bin offers as she clearly wanted to do her bit to recycle.

Customer kept informed of progress (include dates & details of action taken)

N/A

Feedback given to colleagues (if necessary)

Copy of complaint forwarded to bin-round team leader & leaflet dispatched.

Figure 2: Providing customer complaint or comment forms helps organisations improve customer service.

Portfolio Task

Links to f2.1.1, f2.1.2, f2a, f2b

1 Find out about your organisation's complaints procedures.

Write down your answers to these questions.

a. What promises are made concerning what will happen if a customer has a complaint?

b. What is the customer required to do (if anything) when making a complaint?

c. What are your responsibilities to your customers?

d. What are the limits of your authority when dealing with a complaint?

e. What are your responsibilities to your organisation?

f. What guarantees (if any) does your organisation make to its customers for the products or services you deal with? How do these promises affect the possibility of complaints being made?

2 Show your answers to your assessor and obtain witness testimonies which describe some of the times you have used your organisation's complaints procedures.

Service standards

Some organisations have service standards. These are rules which tell its staff how to behave or what to do in certain situations. You could think of service standards as things an organisation expects of its employees when dealing with customers. This could involve anything from how to answer the telephone and what to say, to timescales involved when replying to a letter. Table 1 shows what some service standards might include:

Table 1: Examples of service standards

Area for action	Service standard
Face-to-face initial greeting	• Smile at customers as they approach • Say 'good morning' or 'good afternoon' • Make eye contact within 3 seconds • Use customer name at least twice
Telephone answering	• Answer the phone within 60 seconds
Returning phone calls	• Return all calls within 24 hours
Take responsibility	• Give customers your name, phone number and extension

Portfolio Task

Links to f2.1.1, f2.1.2, f2.1.3, f2a, f2b, f2c

1 Find out if your organisation has service standards.

Make a list of those which are applicable to your role.

2 Describe to your assessor the role you play in making sure these standards are met. Include in your discussion how they limit what you are able to do for customers.

3 Obtain witness testimonies which show you work within your organisation's service standards.

Ethical standards

Some organisations may have their own ethical standards which affect what you can and cannot do for customers.

These ethical standards may be written and influenced by professional sector standards. They have a big impact on helping you understand what you can and cannot do for customers especially when resolving customer problems e.g. when giving refunds an organisation might do more than it is legally bound to do.

For example, the Co-operative Bank has a series of ethical statements based on extensive consultation with customers. These statements reflect ethical concerns about how their customers' money should and should not be invested and whom the bank chooses as its partners and suppliers. It covers areas such as:

- human rights
- international development
- social enterprise
- ecological impact
- animal welfare.

The ethical standards of an organisation influence its policies, procedures and the behaviour of its staff towards customers. This is particularly true of organisations which recognise their customers will want them to act in a responsible manner and they devise ethical policies to reflect this.

For example, the John Lewis Partnership (Waitrose, John Lewis, Greenbee) aims to:

'deal honestly with its customers and secure loyalty and trust by providing outstanding choice value and service.'

This organisation takes things one step further in that its relationship to its staff (known as Partners) is one where it states it 'puts the happiness of its Partners at the centre of everything it does'. For business relationships, the John Lewis Partnership aims to act with 'integrity and courtesy and to honour scrupulously every business agreement'. It also aims to contribute to the well-being of the communities in which it operates. The John Lewis Partnership consistently wins or is recognised in a variety of national customer satisfaction surveys.

Portfolio Task
Links to f2a f2b

1 Find out about your organisation's ethical policies.

 a. How does what you have found affect what you can and cannot do for customers?

 b. How does the ethical policy affect the products or services your organisation offers?

2 Discuss your findings with your assessor.

Codes of conduct and codes of practice

Your organisation's ethical policies may be included within codes of conduct or codes of practice. Think of them as a set of rules which state how people should behave with one another. For example, public bodies such as local authorities, schools and universities, and police, fire and rescue services have codes of conduct which govern the behaviour of members. Similarly, members of a trade, profession or occupation (for example, social care workers, physiotherapists and solicitors) will have codes of practice to follow. They are sets of guidelines or regulations and are not usually legally binding.

These codes cover areas such as:

- unlawfully discriminating against someone
- failing to treat people with respect
- failing to report another member's misconduct
- damaging the reputation of their office or authority.

There may be other more informal but equally important codes which your organisation has, such as a dress code. This will tell employees what is expected of them in terms of what they wear to work, including items of jewellery or how to wear a uniform. Often there are health and safety reasons behind a dress code such as in the food or health industries. A dress code also helps to promote the right image with customers. Following it helps you to show you are a customer service professional.

Portfolio Task

Links to f2a, f2b

1 If applicable to your role, find out about your organisation's code of conduct and/or practice.
 - How does the code affect what you can and cannot do for customers?
2 Discuss your findings with your assessor.

Functional skills

English: Speaking, listening and communication
If you clearly discuss your findings with your assessor using appropriate language, you may be able to count this as evidence towards Level 1 Functional English: Speaking, listening and communication.

Working within the limits of your authority

When working with your organisation's procedures there will be times when you are required to refer to somebody in authority. This could be a manager, a supervisor, an experienced colleague, a team leader or a recognised specialist or expert or your line manager.

The situations in which you are required to do this will depend on both your organisation's procedures and your job role. Here are some examples when it might be necessary:

- giving refunds
- giving discounts
- dealing with complaints.
- dealing with returns or exchanging items
- dealing with health and safety issues

Portfolio Task   Links to f2a, f2c

1   Thinking about your role and your organisation's customer service practices and procedures, identify the limits of what you are allowed to do. Include in your investigations who you should refer to and why.

2   Make a list and use this to explain to your assessor the limits of your authority.

Emergency procedures

From time to time, you might be involved in something which puts your customers at risk so it's important you know what to do in the event of an emergency. Do you know what to do if a routine fire drill happens while customers are with you? What contingency plans are in place to deal with industrial action which might affect your job, for example, tube strikes?

What about health and safety issues if your customer has an accident whilst with you? Something as simple as someone spilling a cup of hot tea can escalate into a full-blown emergency if you do not know what emergency procedures are in place to help you.

Your organisation will have its own procedures to help manage customer expectations during emergency situations. One of the most common is dealing with a fire drill.

A typical fire drill procedure might include these points:

1   the locations (assembly points) in your workplace which are considered safe areas

2   any specific locations which should not be used

3   advice about not using lifts

4   how to help people with impaired mobility – such as wheelchair users or a disability not immediately obvious, for example, heart problems, poor sight or hearing

5   what to do in the event of a fire

6   location of fire safety equipment.

Portfolio Task   Links to f2a, f2b, f2c

1   Find out about your organisation's emergency procedures:

   a.   Who are your company's first aiders?

   b.   Who is the fire warden?

   c.   How do you raise the alarm in the event of a fire?

   d.   Where are the fire drill assembly points?

2   What other procedures does your organisation have that affect your job? List them and describe your role in each?

Discuss your findings with your assessor.

How to work in a way which protects the security and health and safety of your customers and their property

Different workplaces have different things that can harm people, called hazards. A risk is the chance, high or low, that the hazard will actually cause somebody harm.

There are lots of risks or hazards faced by customers and/or their property. For example, your customer might be at risk from a less than honest person who spots a handbag left open, a car door left unlocked or a coat left behind. You can help by keeping your eyes and ears open to what is going on around you so that you can gently point out to customers that the handbag needs zipping up, the car is vulnerable or their coat needs collecting. That way you will be doing your job in a way which protects the security of customers and their property. Try putting yourself in the customer's shoes and thinking about what you would personally do to ensure you kept yourself and your own property safe.

Acts of terrorism

We live in times when the threat of a terrorist attack is a possibility so, another emergency procedure you should be aware of, is what to do in the event of an act of terrorism. It is important you have the confidence to cope with such a situation to keep both yourself and your customers safe.

What action should you take if you see something unusual like a suspect package left at your workplace? Some organisations use the guidance 'Think HOTT':

Hidden — is the package hidden or simply something left behind, that is, lost property?

Obviously suspicious — are there any wires or batteries showing?

Typical — is it typical for the environment it is in, for example, a shopping bag left in a library?

Threat — has there already been a specific threat to the location or to the organisation?

What would you do?

- If you received a telephoned bomb threat, what do you need to do?

- What is your role in any evacuation procedures?

- You might simply see a person behaving suspiciously. What counts as suspicious behaviour in the eyes of your organisation? Do you need to report it?

Some organisations have special codes which their staff are aware of and which indicate the level of threat the organisation believes they are under at any moment in time. Each code would have special procedures attached to it for staff to follow.

Portfolio Task — Links to f2.1.4, f2.2.1, f2c, f2d

1 Do some research to find out if your organisation has emergency measures in place to deal with security threats.

a. In particular, find out your role in:

- dealing with unattended packages
- reporting suspicious behaviour
- helping with evacuation procedures.

b. In which situations do you need to refer to somebody in authority?

c. Discuss these with your assessor.

2 Obtain witness testimonies which show how you have specifically acted to protect the security of customers and their property.

The health and safety risks and hazards customers might face

As you look around your own working environment what can you spot which might be a potential hazard to yourself, your customers and your colleagues?

Some examples of hazards are:

- chemical substances
- dust and fumes
- excessive noise
- moving vehicles
- moving parts in machinery
- electricity
- extremes of heat/cold
- animals
- uneven floors
- exposed wiring/cabling over the floor/ground.

Slips, trips and falls are the major cause of accidents in the workplace.

Portfolio Task — Links to f2.2.1, f2f

To be risk aware, you need to identify the hazards in your workplace and find out what measures are in place to combat them.

1 Make a list. For each hazard answer the following questions.

a. How badly could a person be hurt?

b. How likely is this to happen?

2 Find a possible hazard in your workplace and describe it.

a. What precautions/controls are there to combat it?

b. If there was an accident, how serious could the injury be?

c. How likely (or unlikely) is such an accident to happen?

d. Are there any extra precautions you need to take to make sure you and your customers are safe?

3 Using your responses to these questions, describe to your assessor your health and safety responsibilities and how these enable you to work in a way that is safe for your customers and your colleagues.

Figure 3: Always ensure you are in control of your own and your customer's health and safety.

☑ **Checklist – Working safely to protect yourself, your customers and your colleagues**

- Report things (for example, equipment or machinery) that seem dangerous, damaged or faulty.

- Only use tools, machinery or substances after you have been trained and given permission to do so.

- Don't leave things lying around – keep work areas tidy and clear.

- Clean up spills straight away.

- Always close drawers.

- Keep fire doors unlocked and free from obstruction.

- Know about first aid arrangements.

The Health and Safety at Work Act 1974 is a piece of legislation which covers the responsibilities employers have to employees and also to customers who are on their premises. We deal with this on pages 48 – 51.

It is also important to work in a way which protects the security of information about customers. After all, we all have the right to expect information we give to organisations about ourselves to be treated with respect and kept confidential. This is dealt with by the Data Protection Act 1998 and is covered in detail on pages 53 – 57.

Follow legislation and external regulation that relate to customer service

What you need to know or learn

- How to work within Health and Safety legislation
- How to work within Data Protection legislation
- How to work within Consumer Protection legislation
- How to work within Equal Opportunities legislation

Legislation refers to laws which are made to prevent something happening. Regulation refers to rules which set out to control what happens. Parliament passes laws. Regulators use these laws to work out what needs to happen in order for laws to be kept.

There are three legal systems in the UK:

- English law which also covers Wales
- Scottish law
- Northern Irish law.

There is little difference between English and Northern Irish law but Scotland is different – the courts have different names and follow different procedures. English laws do not apply to Scotland and vice versa (though some may be similar).

You need a sound understanding of how the relevant laws and regulations guide what you can and cannot do in your job. The laws that will affect you are those relating to health and safety, data protection, equal opportunities (including disability discrimination) and consumer protection.

Note
There are often changes made to legislation and regulations so it is important you keep yourself up to date. The website www.legislation.gov.uk, which is run by The National Archives, is a useful reference source.

Key term

Health and Safety at Work Act 1974 – covers the general duties employers have towards employees and members of the public, and employees have to themselves and to each other.

How to work within Health and Safety legislation

The basis of British health and safety law is the **Health and Safety at Work Act 1974**.

An employer needs to take steps as far as is reasonably practicable to put in place measures to control health and safety risks. Really, this is just commonsense and good management should mean that an employer identifies potential risks and takes steps to reduce them. Figure 4 shows some of the responsibilities an employer has under health and safety legislation.

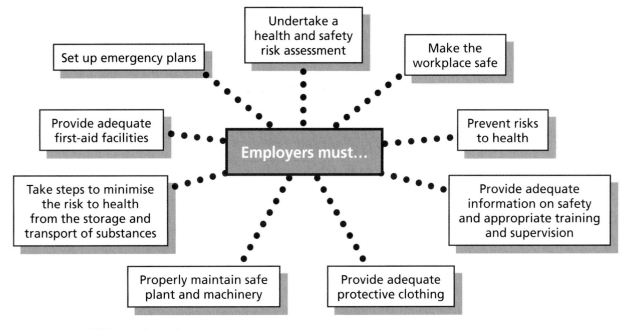

Figure 4: Responsibilities employers have to employees.

Making the workplace safe and healthy

So what exactly does it mean to make the workplace safe and healthy?
Measures that your employer should take include:

- making sure there is proper ventilation with clean and fresh air

- keeping temperatures at a comfortable level – a minimum of 13 degrees C where the work involves physical activity or 16 degrees C for 'sedentary' workplaces, for example offices, but there is no maximum limit

- lighting premises so that people can work and move about safely

- keeping the workplace and equipment clean and in good working order

- providing workstations to suit employees and the work

- making floors, walkways, stairs, roadways etc. safe to use

- storing things so they are unlikely to fall and cause injuries

- providing suitable washing facilities and clean drinking water

- if necessary, providing somewhere for employees to get changed and to store their own clothes

- setting aside areas for rest breaks and to eat meals, including suitable facilities for pregnant women and nursing mothers

- letting employees take appropriate rest breaks and their correct holiday entitlement

- making sure that employees who work alone or off-site can do so safely and healthily.

Portfolio Task

Links to f2.2.1, f2.2.4, f2.2.5, f2f, f2i

If you are completing Unit B2 Deliver reliable customer service:

1 Review how the portfolio tasks associated with the section mentioned above, can be used to provide evidence for this unit.

2 Complete question 4 below.

If you have *not* selected Unit B2 Deliver reliable customer service as one of your optional units:

1 Complete Questions 1–3 below (these are the relevant portfolio tasks from **Unit B2**.

2 Also complete Question 4.

1

a. Make a list of the types of equipment you deal with.

b. Create a diary note to remind you to check the equipment is in good and safe working order.

Keep these for your portfolio.

2

a. In the context of your working environment, complete these sentences on a separate piece of paper and keep the responses for your portfolio.

My work area can be kept tidy by...

The things I need to do to make my work area safe for my customers to use are...

For my colleagues to be safe, I should make sure...

The impact and benefit of being well organised in my working environment is...

b. Create your own daily checklist based on Table 1 in **Unit B2 Deliver reliable customer service**, use it and keep it for your portfolio.

3

1 Write a personal statement for your portfolio which details what you have done recently to ensure the area in which you work is tidy, safe and organised efficiently. Use the questions below to help you.

a. Take a look at your working area.

- Is it neat and clean?
- Have you put away everything that you are not using at the moment?
- Are there electrical cables running all over the floor that you or your customers might trip over?
- Are there tears in the carpet someone might get their foot caught in?
- Have you put chairs or other pieces of equipment in places which make it difficult for customers to get access?
- What does your organisation expect you to do to ensure your working area is tidy, safe and organised efficiently?
- What can you do to improve the safety of your workplace?
- What impression do customers get from it?
- What about colleagues? Have they made any comments?

b. Find out what your organisation's guidelines are for keeping your work area tidy, safe and organised. Show in your report how you make sure you follow these guidelines.

c. Ask an appropriate person to give you a witness testimony about how you keep your workspace tidy, safe and organised effectively.

d. Make sure your assessor observes you dealing with customers in your workspace.

4

Using the results of these tasks describe to your assessor your health and safety responsibilities as they relate to your customer service work.

How to work within Data Protection legislation

If you are in a role where you ask for, receive and have access to lots of personal information about your customers (for example, account details, addresses, shareholdings, doctors' notes on patients etc.) it is important you absolutely understand that you *cannot* disclose this information to anyone who might want to see it.

The Data Protection Act 1998 (DPA)

Most organisations and government store information about customers, manually, in electronic format or both. The types of information stored include:

- names
- addresses
- contact details
- medical information
- buying preferences
- employment history
- credit history
- convictions.

People want to know information about them is being kept private and that it will be used appropriately. Your customers will have concerns about their information being misused or falling into the wrong hands. They might have concerns about:

- who could access the information
- how accurate it is
- it being copied
- it being stored without their permission.

The **Data Protection Act 1998 (DPA)** is legislation passed by Parliament to govern the use of personal data in the UK.

Data is information without content, for example, a list of people's names with numbers against them is data. When it becomes clear the numbers represent something, for example, a credit rating or standing in a league table, the data becomes information.

The Act does not stop organisations storing information about people. It just ensures they follow rules. It covers information stored in manual formats (for example, ring binders or filing cabinets) or in computer format (for example, computers or DVDs) about living people.

For example, if someone accessed your medical records without your permission it would be unauthorised access. The DPA sets up rules to prevent this happening and the rules are enforced by the **Information Commissioner**.

Key term

Information Commissioner – the person responsible for enforcing the DPA.

Personal data

There are two types of personal data:

- **Personal data** is about living people and could be:
  - o their name
  - o their address
  - o their medical details or banking details.

- **Sensitive personal data** is also about living people, but it includes one or more details of a **data subject**'s:
  - o racial or ethnic origin
  - o political opinions
  - o religion
  - o membership of a trade union
  - o health
  - o sexual life
  - o criminal activity.

There are more safeguards about sensitive data than personal data. Usually, a person must be asked specifically if sensitive data can be kept.

The Data Protection Act 1998 established eight enforceable principles of good practice, which you need to know about when dealing with personal customer service information (see Figure 6).

The Act covers the processing of information relating to individuals including, obtaining, holding, using or disclosing information.

Key term

Data subject – anyone who has data stored about them which is outside their direct control.

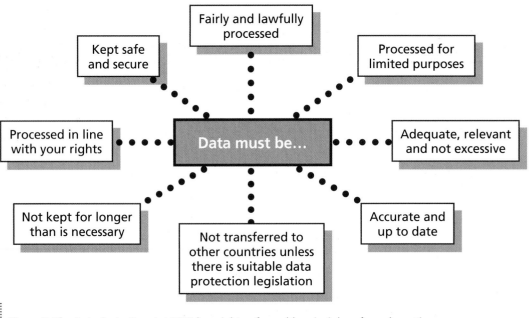

Figure 6: The Data Protection Act 1998 has eight enforceable principles of good practice.

Putting the principles into practice

The main issues which relate to most customer service roles are to remember:

- Data should only be used for the reasons given to the Information Commissioner and not disclosed to unauthorised people.

- Data cannot be sold or given away without authority to do so.

- You must hold only enough detail to allow you to do the job for which the data is intended. Make sure the information you request from a customer is needed for a genuine reason, so asking for frivolous and unnecessary information is wrong.

- You must keep data away from people who are not authorised to access it. Leaving information out on a desk or not password-protected may mean it could be misused. Data should be stored in a way that prevents unauthorised access, accidental loss or destruction.

- Data should not be kept for longer than is necessary. The Act does not state how long this should be. There may be other laws which state how long data must be kept in certain industry sectors. For example, the financial services sector may have to keep some information for up to six years in accordance with the financial services regulations.

As a general rule, sensitive information (such as details on race or ethnic origin, health or medical conditions and sexual orientation) may not be collected and processed unless your customer has given his or her consent. It is your organisation's responsibility to obtain this consent.

Your customer's rights

The Data Protection Act 1998 gives people rights concerning the data kept about them. They are:

- **Right of Subject Access** – anyone can request to see the personal data held about him or her. The **data controller** can charge for this (the charge is usually around £10).

- **Right of correction** – the data controller is obliged to correct any mistakes in data held once these have been pointed out.

- **Right to prevent distress** – there is a right to prevent the use of information if it would be likely to cause the person distress.

- **Right to prevent direct marketing** – people can stop their data being used in attempts to sell them things (for example, by junk mail or cold calling).

- **Right to prevent automatic decisions** – people can specify that they do not want a data user to make 'automated' decisions about them (for example, computerised credit scoring of a loan application).

- **Right of complaint** to the Information Commissioner – people can ask for the use of their personal data to be reviewed by the Information Commissioner who can enforce a ruling using the Act; the Commissioner may inspect a controller's computers to help in the investigation.

- **Right to compensation** – people can use the law to get compensation for damage caused ('damages') if personal data about them is inaccurate, lost, or disclosed.

> **Key term**
>
> **Data controller** – the nominated person in a company who applies to the data commissioner for permission to store and use personal data.

Exemptions

There are some circumstances where personal data is not covered by the DPA and the people storing data do not need to keep to the rules. There can be *complete exemptions* or *partial exemptions*:

- *Complete exemptions* cover:
  - o any personal data that is held for a *national security* reason
  - o personal data held at home for *domestic purposes*; for example, a list of your friends' names, birthdays and addresses does not have to keep to the rules.

- *Partial exemptions* cover some personal data. The main examples of this are:
  - o HM Revenue & Customs do not have to disclose information being processed in connection with the assessment or collection of tax or duty if it would harm any investigations. The police do not have to disclose information being processed to detect or prevent crime.
  - o A data subject has no right to see information stored about him or her if it is to do with his or her health. This allows doctors to keep information from patients if they think it is in their best interests.
  - o A school pupil has no right of access to personal files, or to exam results before publication.
  - o A data controller can keep data for any length of time if it is being used for statistical, historical or research purposes.
  - o Some research by journalists and academics is exempt if it is in the public interest or does not identify individuals.
  - o Employment references written by a previous employer are exempt.

Why it is important to protect the security of information about customers

To allow themselves access to many goods and services, customers need to give personal information to all sorts of organisations, for example:

- credit card numbers when shopping online
- health details to get insurance cover
- household details ranging from which newspapers are read, what brand of dog food they buy or which television channels they watch in order to get supermarket loyalty points.

Customers have the right to expect that the people they give their personal information to, treat it with respect. As you have seen, The Data Protection Act provides the framework to make sure personal information is properly protected. This is known as keeping information *confidential*.

The loyalty and goodwill built up between service providers and customers will be destroyed if there is a breach of confidentiality. Trust will be broken and therefore the relationship between the customer and the service provider will be badly (and sometimes terminally) affected.

Although there are clearly benefits to providing personal information, for example, the service provider can make sure the customer gets an appropriate product or service, this information needs to be handled correctly in order to avoid problems.

For example, if personal information is recorded inaccurately, it could lead to an individual being unfairly refused a product or service. A job application might be rejected, an application for housing benefit or a loan request could be refused.

Many people use the Internet to buy goods or services. Organisations using the web to sell products or services have to show they have taken appropriate legal and technical steps to keep their customers' personal information safe from unlawful access. It is, of course, in their own interests to do so; customers will not make purchases using the Internet if the website they wish to use is not secure.

Sensitive company information

On a day-to-day basis there may be some information passed between colleagues or between different departments that should not be seen by everyone. This is not to say there are 'secrets' deliberately held within organisations. It is more about having respect for the privacy of individuals. If the information is commercially sensitive then a simple rule states that, the fewer people who know about it, then the less likely it is for sensitive information to fall into the wrong hands. For example, an organisation developing a new product would not want its competitors to know the details until it is ready for the product to be formally launched.

This means you should consider how the way in which you pass information on to others is going to impact upon your ability to maintain confidentiality.

The Information Commissioner's Office (ICO) is responsible for looking after customers' rights and making sure that personal information is not misused. You can find out more about its work by visiting their website www.ico.gov.uk.

Access to official information – for public authorities

The Freedom of Information Act and Environmental Information Regulations give people the right to request official information (often known as the 'right to know') held by public authorities in England, Northern Ireland and Wales. Both came into force in January 2005.

Public authorities include:
- government departments
- NHS bodies
- state schools, colleges and universities
- the police.

Once a request has been made, the appropriate body has 20 days in which to respond unless it is not in the public interest to disclose information (for example, national security would be in danger). Customers can ask for reports about air quality, pollution, flooding problems or minutes of meetings held at their local school. They have a 'right to know'.

Scotland has its own Environmental Information (Scotland) Regulations 2004 and the Freedom of Information (Scotland) Act 2002. These are regulated by the Scottish Information Commissioners Office.

Portfolio Task

Links to f2.1.4, f2.2.4, f2.2.5, f2e, f2h

1 Find out if your organisation has its own code of conduct for dealing with information in order to comply with the Data Protection Act 1998 and to maintain confidentiality.

2 Make a list of your key responsibilities (as they relate to your customer service role) under:

   a. any internal rules or codes of conduct

   b. the Data Protection Act.

3 Write a personal statement which shows how you follow any internal rules and/or the principles of the

Data Protection Act in order to protect the security of information about customers. In your report, include:

   a. what you need to do to ensure you work within your organisation's rules and the DPA.

   b. why it is important to respect customer and organisation confidentiality.

Keep this for your portfolio.

4 Obtain witness testimonies about specific times you have protected the security of information about customers.

How to work within Consumer Protection legislation

Note

This section will only apply if you work in a role which involves your customers using a product or service.

The government introduced legislation to help to protect **consumers** against unfair selling practices. The key legislation which may affect the way in which you and your organisation operates is:

- Sale of Goods Act 1979 (as amended)
- Supply of Goods and Services Act 1982
- Unsolicited Goods and Services Act 1971
- Trade Descriptions Act 1968
- Consumer Protection Act 1987
- Consumer Credit Act 1974
- Consumer Protection (Distance Selling) Regulations 2000.

We'll now outline how each Act is designed to protect the consumer. As you work through these, keep in mind how the legislation affects what you must do and not do in your job.

Sale of Goods Act 1979 (as amended)

This law is very important if you are involved with selling goods. (There is a separate law covering services which we deal with shortly). All goods bought or hired from shops, street markets, car boot sales, mail order or door-to-door sellers are covered by this Act. It also covers goods bought in sales, for example, the winter sales that start around Christmas.

Key term

Consumer – an individual who receives or seeks to receive goods or services from a supplier.

This Act also applies to goods and services purchased via the Internet, providing the trader is based in the UK.

In the 1990s, two further Acts extended the basic 1979 Act: the Sale and Supply of Goods Act 1994 and the Sale of Goods (Amendment) Act 1995. That is why the bracketed words 'as amended' are included in the title of the Act.

The Sale of Goods Acts lay down several conditions that all goods sold by a trader must meet. The goods must be:

- of merchantable, that is, satisfactory, quality

- as described

- fit for purpose.

It is important to understand how fair trading laws protect customers.

Satisfactory quality – goods must have nothing wrong with them (unless any defect was pointed out at the time of sale) and should last a reasonable time. This means the Act does not give a customer any rights if a fault was obvious or pointed out, when the customer bought the product. The Acts cover the appearance and finish of the goods, their safety and their durability.

As described – refers to any advertisement or verbal description made by the trader. If yoghurt is described as '100% fat free' then it must be.

Fit for purpose – covers not only the obvious use or purpose of an item, but also anything you say the item will do when you are trying to sell the product. If you tell a customer that the jacket you are selling is 'waterproof even under extreme conditions' then it must not leak water in a shower!

The customers' rights under the Sale of Goods Act 1979

If a product bought by a customer does not meet any of the conditions set out in the Sale of Goods Act 1979, they are entitled to a full refund. They cannot be expected to accept a repair, a replacement or a credit note if they don't want to.

Remember – The Act also covers second-hand items and goods purchased in sales.

Customers are only entitled to their money back from the trader they originally bought the item from, not from the manufacturer. Technically, it is up to the trader to collect the faulty item, although customers usually find it easier to return the faulty good themselves.

If customers wish to accept a repair, and many people do, they would be wise to put in writing that they 'reserve the right to "reject" the item if the repair is not satisfactory'. All this is pretty straightforward and easy to remember, although if there is a dispute, the customer, not the trader, has to prove their case.

Unit F2 Follow the rules to deliver customer service

Portfolio Task

Links to f2i, f2j

1 Looking at all the various pieces of consumer protection legislation, work out which acts apply to your job role. Make a list.

2 Now write down a summary in list format of the main things you
   a. must do
   b. must not do
   in your job under consumer protection legislation.

3 Use the results of the other portfolio tasks in this section to help you.

Functional skills

English: Reading and Writing

To be able to prepare your lists you will need to read and understand a variety of texts. You may be able to use this as evidence towards Level 1 Functional English: Reading. The summary list you produce may be counted as evidence towards Level 1 Functional English: Writing. Check it for grammar, punctuation and spelling.

How to work within Equal Opportunities legislation

It's important to treat people fairly and equally regardless of who they are, where they live or how much you like or dislike them. In other words, while you should treat people as individuals, what makes one person different from another does not mean he or she should have any advantage or disadvantage over anybody else in relation to customer service delivery.

All your customers should be treated fairly regardless of their age, gender, race, sexual orientation, disability, gender reassignment, religion or belief.

The Equality Act 2010

The Equality Act 2010 came into force on 1 October 2010 and replaces the Disability Discrimination Act 1995 (known as DDA). It is one of the most important pieces of legislation you are likely to need to know about regarding disability discrimination and equal rights. People who access your goods, facilities or services are protected from discrimination because of certain 'protected characteristics'. These are:

- age
- disability
- gender reassignment
- marriage and civil partnership
- pregnancy and maternity
- race – this includes ethnic or national origins, colour and nationality
- religion or belief
- sex
- sexual orientation

Notes – some definitions

- *Gender reassignment* is the process of transitioning from one gender to another.
- *Marriage* is defined as a union between a man and a woman. Same sex couples can have their relationships legally recognised as civil partnerships.

- Civil partners must be treated the same as married couples on a wide range of legal issues.

- *Maternity* refers to the period of 26 weeks after the birth, which reflects the period of a woman's ordinary maternity leave entitlement in the employment context.

- *Race* refers to a group of people defined by their race, colour and nationality (including citizenship), ethnic or national origins.

Disability defined

Disability has a broad meaning. It is defined as a physical or mental *impairment* that has a *substantial* and long-term adverse effect on the ability to carry out normal day-to-day activities:

- *Substantial* means more than minor or trivial.

- *Impairment* covers long-term medical conditions such as asthma or diabetes and fluctuating or progressive conditions such as rheumatoid arthritis and motor neurone disease. A mental impairment would include learning difficulties such as dyslexia and learning disabilities such as Down's syndrome and autism.

Some people are automatically protected as disabled people by the Act, including those with cancer, multiple sclerosis and HIV/AIDS.

Helping disabled people

Disabled people must not be treated less favourably than others because they are disabled. Businesses have an obligation to make reasonable adjustments to help disabled people access their goods, facilities and services. Some organisations build ramps to ensure wheelcair users can access their premises or provide information in braille for visually impaired customers.

What is a 'reasonable' adjustment? This will depend on a number of circumstances, including cost. The Equality Act 2010 requires that service providers must think ahead and take steps to put right things that may stop disabled people using their goods, facilties or services. Your organisation should not wait until a disabled person experiences difficulties using a service, as this may make it too late to make the necessary adjustment. This could mean making:

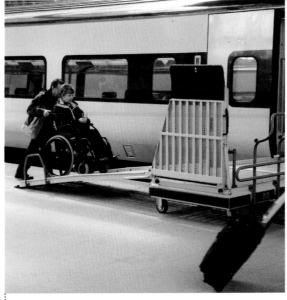

- 'reasonable' changes to the way things are done – for example, changing practices, policies or procedures where disabled people would be at a 'substantial disadvantage', such as amending a 'no dogs' policy.

- 'reasonable' changes to premises – for example, changing the structure of a building to improve access, such as fitting handrails alongside steps

- providing auxiliary aids and services – for example, providing information in large print or an induction loop for customers with hearing aids.

Figure 8: Businesses must make reasonable adjustments to help disabled people access their goods, facilities and services.

Under the Equality Act 2010, protection is extended to anyone who has, or has had, a disability. The Act also protects people from being discriminated against by association. For example, if a mother is refused a service because she is caring for her visually impaired child, this would be unlawful discrimination.

A disabled person does not have to prove their impairment affects a particular capacity (for example sight, hearing or mobility) in order to qualify for protection.

Remember

The main problem disabled people face on a day-to-day basis is often the attitude of other people towards them. Make sure you treat all people with respect.

Customer service practitioners and employers must have the right attitude: give people with disabilities the same level of service as you would give to non-disabled customers. Disabled people make a huge contribution to the economy. Treating them fairly makes sense.

You should now refer to the section on *Establishing and maintaining rapport with people with disabilities* in **Unit A10 Deal with customers face to face**, on pages 128 – 129. This will give you some pointers for helping your disabled customers.

You can find out more information about the Equality Act 2010 at www.equalities.gov.uk and www.direct.gov.uk.

The Equalities and Human Rights Commission (EHRC) is the statutory body responsible for protecting, enforcing and promoting equality. We recommend you visit their website at www.equalityhumanrights.com for guidance and information, including equality matters within different industry sectors. Please also use these websites to keep yourself up to date with changes to equal opportunities legislation.

Portfolio Task

Links to f2.2.2, f2.2.4, f2.2.5, f2g, f2i, f2j

1 Access the Government Equalities Office's *Equalities Act 2010: What do I Need to Know? Disability Quick Start Guide* for businesses who sell goods and services. You can find it at www.equalities.gov.uk

2 Use it to make a list of what you must do and must not do when helping people with disabilities.

3 Thinking about your own organisation, what arrangements are in place to accommodate disabled people? Make a list.

4 What is the impact, if any, on your customer service role? Explain your responsibilities to your assessor.

Functional skills

English: Speaking, listening and communication and Reading

If you access the Internet to do your research and use the information you read to prepare for your discussion, you may be able to use this as evidence towards Level 1 Functional English: Reading. If you clearly, and by using appropriate language, explain your findings to your assessor, you may be able to count this as evidence towards Level 1 Functional English: Speaking, listening and communication.

Discrimination – it's all about your attitude

It doesn't make sense to treat your customers unfairly because of their sex or marital status or because a woman is pregnant. That would be sex discrimination. For example, it would be unlawful for a bank to ask a woman to provide security for a loan and not ask a man in similar circumstances to do so. If a nightclub wishes to attract more women into the club, it would be unlawful to run a promotion offering women free entry or reduced price drinks unless they offered the same to men.

It doesn't make sense to treat your customers unfairly because of their race. If this happens it would be racial discrimination. This occurs when an individual is treated less favourably than someone else in a similar situation because of his or her race, skin colour, nationality or ethnic or racial origin.

It doesn't make sense to treat your customers unfairly because of their age. That would be age discrimination. Many elderly people feel invisible to service providers. Do not let this happen to your customers.

Stop and think! It can sometimes get confusing to try to remember what the law says you can and cannot do.

How about just using your commonsense and thinking about delivering customer service in a fair way to everyone regardless of who or what they are?

Remember – discrimination means the act of treating people unfairly for some reason. This could be because of:

- their age
- a disability that they have
- their marital or civil partnership status
- a woman's pregnancy and subsequent maternity period
- their race
- their religion or belief
- their sex
- their sexual orientation
- their gender reassignment.

Portfolio Task   Links to f2.2.2, f2.2.4, f2.2.5, f2g, f2i, f2j

You have done a portfolio task relating to the protected characteristic of disability. Now think about the other protected characteristics.

1   Make a list of what you must do and must not do to ensure you do not discriminate against your customers.

2   Think about the types of customers you deal with and the impact of legislation. How does this link into your customer service role? Explain your responsibilities to your assessor with regard to treating your customers equally.

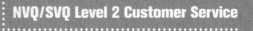

Working Life

Hello, my name is Dai and I work in a large hotel as part of the Conference and Events team. One weekend we had a booking for both a wedding and a group of people from a charity holding a fun day out for children with learning disabilities. This is a regular booking and we enjoy helping out this worthwhile charity.

The wedding party organisers had become aware of the children's event and were concerned this would disturb or even upset the wedding guests. So as not to upset them, my manager moved the charity booking to a different room which was situated at the far end of the hotel. He did not tell the charity.

As a consequence, when the carers from the charity arrived, I had to deal with some very upset, angry and disappointed people. They told me the room was inferior to the one they had booked, too far away from the toilets and that having the same familiar room was important for the children's well-being. I was then told they felt they had been discriminated against and they asked to speak to my manager. I went to fetch him but couldn't really understand what the problem was as the room was of a similar size.

Ask the expert

Q Would it have made a difference had the charity booking been for people who did not have a disability?

A Not in terms of the need to treat everybody fairly and with respect. However, the rooms were changed purely on the assumption by the wedding organisers, that children with learning disabilities might disrupt their wedding. This is a form of prejudice and, therefore, the charity had experienced disability discrimination.

Q What should the manager have done?

A He did have a balancing act to perform. He is not responsible for the views of the wedding party. However, he is responsible for not allowing these views to influence his behaviours and actions so as to discriminate against other customers.

Hopefully, a discussion with both parties might have resolved things. A great deal of tact would have needed to be shown. By discussing it, the carers may themselves have preferred to be kept away from a wedding party. However, any change to their booking should have been agreed and be of a similar or higher standard. If the charity receives an inferior service, they are being discriminated against.

Q What about Dai? What can he do to ensure this does not happen again?

A Being on the front-line, Dai was the first person to be at the receiving end of the charity's frustrations. He would have needed to use all his skills to calm the customers down. For example, listening, showing empathy and quickly arranging for the manager to talk with the carers.

As he seems to be unaware of the legislation which aims to protect disabled people from discrimination he needs to bring himself up to date and recognise his legal responsibilities. Of course, this also applies to Dai's manager.

Top tips

Regardless of the fact that the booking was for people with a disability, basic best practice had not been followed by not telling the charity about the proposed change. Always use your commonsense and show respect to everybody. The charity had not been treated fairly.

Unit F2 Follow the rules to deliver customer service

Check your knowledge

1 Which statement contains examples of unlawful reasons to discriminate against people?

  a. Because of the time of day they require help.

  b. Because of the number of staff at work.

  c. Because of disability, age, religion or belief.

  d. Because of budgets, cost, time or safety.

2 Under the Data Protection Act 1998, personal information must be:

  a. obtained in writing from customers and businesses

  b. stored on an easily accessible computer system

  c. provided in writing to anybody who requests it

  d. stored in a way that prevents unauthorised access.

3 Under the Equalities Act 2010, it is unlawful to:

  a. provide extra assistance, support and guidance

  b. install environmentally approved equipment

  c. refuse to provide a service without justification

  d. communicate in a very assertive manner.

4 Equal opportunities legislation aims to protect people from:

  a. discrimination and harassment

  b. fraudulent traders and companies

  c. personal information being misused

  d. unwanted mailshots and phone calls.

5 When following equal opportunities legislation you should always aim to ensure people are:

  a. offered credit facilities regardless of their financial situation

  b. given the most up-to-date product or service information

  c. treated fairly by recognising and respecting their differences

  d. dealt with in accordance with a company's service standards.

6 What do you need to know in order to prevent health and safety hazards occurring?

  a. How to travel to work economically.

  b. How to communicate assertively.

  c. How to keep information confidential.

  d. How to reduce risks in the workplace.

7 Which of the following include procedures set by organisations to protect the interests of customers?

  a. Consumer legislation and data instructions.

  b. Complaints procedures and feedback systems.

  c. Advertising and marketing promotions.

  d. Health & safety legislation and help desks.

8 Health and safety legislation aims to protect:

  a. customers from fraudulent traders or organisations

  b. management from staff who are under-performing

  c. customers and staff from hazards in the workplace

  d. organisations from damaging their good reputation.

9 Under consumer protection legislation:

  a. traders must not falsely describe something on sale

  b. advertisements must be colourful and innovative

  c. newspaper and TV campaigns must be run monthly

  d. posters and leaflets must be updated regularly.

10 Why is it important to respect customer confidentiality with regards to personal information?

  a. Because competitors might try to obtain information about our customers to win business.

  b. Because not all colleagues can be trusted to handle private information in an appropriate way.

  c. Because organisations need to keep records of customer types to develop their products and services.

  d. Because by law customers have the right to have their personal information treated with respect.

11 My responsibilities under health and safety laws include:

  a. co-operating with requests to do overtime or extend my hours

  b. taking the initiative to ensure colleagues can operate equipment

  c. taking reasonable care for my health and safety and that of others

  d. becoming fully qualified in first aid and displaying the certificate.

12 Under the Supply of Goods and Service Act 1982, people who supply goods or services:

a. must work overtime during busy periods to avoid customer complaints.

b. should achieve a qualification in order to ensure customer satisfaction.

c. can report customers who behave badly to the equalities ombudsman.

d. must act with reasonable care and skill when dealing with customers.

13 Health and safety legislation aims to ensure employers:

a. make the workplace safe and without risk to health.

b. give compassionate leave to staff who are under stress.

c. repair plant and machinery on at least a weekly basis.

d. carry out daily risk assessments before customers arrive.

14 Why is it important to follow your organisation's service standards?

a. Because they notify suppliers of changes to personnel and stock ordering procedures.

b. Because legislation requires all organisations to have customer charters.

c. Because they tell me what my organisation expects of me when dealing with customers.

d. Because they tell customers how to request a discount and obtain value for money.

15 Under the Equalities Act 2010 it is important to:

a. speak loudly to hearing impaired customers when offering help.

b. make reasonable adjustments to premises to help accessibility.

c. offer special discounts to visually impaired people who complain.

d. speak to a carer or companion before speaking to the customer.

Unit A3

Communicate effectively with customers

Introduction

Think back to a situation when you were a customer, where you were delighted with the service you received. Think too about those times when you were less than happy. It may well be that, in both cases, the feelings you experienced were down to the way in which the customer service practitioner dealt with you rather than anything to do with the product or service involved. So, being a skilled communicator is not only about listening well and using the right words but also about being sure you understand how customers feel.

You will need to have effective communication skills to ensure you have understood what your customers want and that they understand you. This is the case whether you deal with customers face to face, on the phone or electronically.

Aspects of this unit are also covered in **Unit A4 Give customers a positive impression of yourself and your organisation** and **Unit A10 Deal with customers face to face**. You may choose to refer to these in this book to supplement your learning.

This unit will help you in all aspects of your career because effective communication is at the heart of everything you do with customers whether they be external to your organisation or internal. This is why it is important that you consistently:

- communicate effectively with customers.

Positive body language can help effective communication.

Communicate effectively with customers

What you need to know and learn:

- How to listen actively
- Why body language is an important factor in effective communication
- How to deal with customers' questions and comments
- How to manage customers' reactions when you are unable to help

How to listen actively

Do you think most people involved in a conversation generally do intend to listen to each other? Or, are they just taking turns to speak? Do you listen carefully without interrupting or voicing an opinion? There are so many opportunities for misunderstandings to occur and this frequently happens when people fail to listen for the true meaning behind the words used.

How can you expect customers to listen to you, if you do not fully understand what they are saying because you have not listened properly?

Dealing with customers in a respectful, helpful and professional way is simply showing you are polite. You can achieve this by using **active listening**, *really* listening when *they* are talking. You will get things right first time which will stop misunderstandings happening and potential complaints being made. Everybody wins!

This will involve you using your eyes as well as your ears. You will need to:

- listen for content as well as underlying emotions
- respond to feelings — sometimes the true meaning is in the emotion not the words used
- tune in to your customers' body language — what are the non-verbal cues telling you?

> ### Key term
>
> **Active listening** – paying careful attention to understand more than the words being spoken.

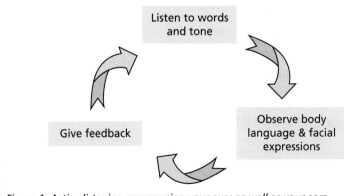

Figure 1: Active listening means using your eyes as well as your ears.

Figure 2: Facial expressions can tell you what customers are really thinking.

Give your customer your full attention — make sure you give enough eye contact to develop rapport. Make encouraging 'noises', for example 'OK' — especially on the telephone — to indicate you are listening. Customers will take this as an acknowledgement you have heard them.

Manage your reactions — you are listening so try not to interrupt! The person speaking the most should be your customer.

Look for signs of the true meaning behind the words. Does the facial expression match the words being used? Does the tone of voice tell you anything about what the customer is really feeling?

Give feedback by confirming you have understood by nodding or using phrases like 'I see', 'I understand', 'oh yes' and 'OK'.

If you do not understand, ask questions to find out more information.

You can still be an active listener on the telephone — it's not only what your customers say, it's how they say it. Listen carefully for changes in tone of voice and how each word is stressed. Tone is how things are said, for example, too loud, too soft, impatiently, too quickly, with sensitivity, with respect. We expand on the importance of tone of voice later in this unit on pages 82 – 83.

Portfolio Task   Links to a3.1.1, a3.1.2, a3.1.9, a3a, a3b

Ask your colleagues if you can observe them. Make a list of the skills they use to show they are listening actively to customers. Ensure your list shows how they have managed to listen and not just hear.

Discuss this list with your assessor. Describe how you use these skills yourself. You will also need to be observed by your assessor or provide a witness testimony.

The difference between hearing and listening

We hear sounds all day long. It could be music, birdsong or the spoken word. There may be a great deal of other noise going on too. When hearing words, it's fairly easy to stop at just that: *hearing* a list of words all joined together. They mean something but need careful attention if you are to understand the feelings and emotions behind them. When you can do that, you are truly *listening*.

Listening is emotional. Hearing is passionless. Listening means digging deep into the true meaning. Hearing is stopping at the surface.

To discover the true meaning, you need to be an active listener.

Unit A3 Communicate effectively with customers

Why body language is an important factor in effective communication

Being able to read body language is an important factor in understanding the difference between hearing and listening. Of course, it is not just about you reading your customers' body language, they too will be interpreting messages you give out through your own body language.

We look now at the impact of body language on effective communication because it will help you to discover the true meaning behind the words being spoken. It will also help you to calm down any difficult situations as behaviour breeds behaviour.

The signals given out through our body language can be positive or negative. It is important to combine words used with body language in order to get the best understanding. This means you should not take one in isolation from the other. For example, it is often said, if you are talking with a person who has their arms tightly crossed, he or she must be angry or confused or simply unhappy with the situation. In fact, he or she may just be comfortable in that position or even cold.

Figure 3: Consider both the words and the body language together.

Positive and negative body language

You should always strive to use positive body language in order to show your customers you are willing to help and are respectful of their wishes. This will also give them a positive impression of your organisation.

Examples of positive and negative body language are shown in Table 1.

Table 1: Positive and negative body language.

Positive body language	Negative body language
Smiling with mouth and eyes	Pursed lips
Leaning forward (but not too much)	Invading personal space
Giving eye contact	No eye contact/ looking around
Relaxed facial expression	Frowning
Head nodding occasionally	Staring
Head leaning to one side	Yawning
Steady breathing	Rapid breathing
Gesturing with hands whilst speaking	Pointing hands or fingers
Raised eyebrows whilst smiling	Tapping fingers

Gestures

Gestures are important when used with words because they act to emphasise speech. Gestures include movements of the head and moving hands to emphasise what you are saying. If you understand the gestures you tend to use and can recognise them in other people, you can use them successfully to achieve customer satisfaction.

Positive or supportive gestures will help create **empathy**.

For example, your customer will definitely want to know you are listening. You can show this without interrupting, by having your head leaning to one side and nodding occasionally. Make sure your eyes also really show you are listening. Do not grin from ear to ear but the occasional smile will help with **rapport**. This will mean you and your customer have empathy. You will both understand each other's feelings.

Please refer to **Unit A10 Deal with customers face to face** to help you with the next task.

Key terms

Empathy – understanding and sharing the feelings of others.

Rapport – a sense of being comfortable with someone whether or not you know him or her well.

Customers can read your body language.

Unit A3 Communicate effectively with customers

Portfolio Task

Links to a3.1.7, a3.1.9, a3c, a3d

Some examples of positive and negative body language are listed in the table below. Work out which are examples of positive and which are examples of negative body language and write this against each one. Use a separate piece of paper or download a copy of the table from the website.

Now imagine you behave like this with a customer. For each one, write down what a customer might think about you. Include the emotions a customer might feel.

Discuss your completed list with your assessor. Make sure you are also observed dealing with customers by your assessor and/or somebody who can write a witness testimony describing how you use appropriate body language when dealing with customers.

Functional skills

English: Writing

If you write down your interpretation of each statement, you may be able to use this towards evidence for Level 1 Functional English: Writing. Make sure you check for grammar, punctuation and spelling and include an appropriate level of detail against each statement.

The impression I give with different types of body language.

If I do this....	My customer might think I am
smile with my mouth and eyes	
lean forward until I get quite close	
lean forward occasionally	
give eye contact	
frown	
yawn a great deal	
raise my eyebrows whilst smiling	
nod my head occasionally	
lean my head to one side	
gesture with my hands when I speak	
stand very close to my customer	
look around the workplace	
point my hands or fingers directly at the customer	
tap my fingers on something	
stare at the customer	
talk without giving eye contact	

Clearly, at the same time a customer is reading *your* body language, you too will be interpreting theirs. The rules are the same. The most important rule is to always remember that words count too.

A version of the table used in this task, ready for you to complete, is available to download from www.contentextra.com/customerservice

Portfolio Task

Links to a3.1.7, a3.1.8, a3.1.9, a3c, a3d

Keep a diary over a one-month period of how you have been able to use your skills to interpret your customers' body language. Make sure you include things that have surprised you. For example, you may have thought a customer was angry when this did not turn out to be the case. Complete these headings. We have given an example to get you started.

Show your diary to your assessor and make sure you are observed dealing with customers.

Functional skills

English: Writing

Your completed diary could be counted as evidence towards Level 1 Functional English: Writing. Consider the format you use and check for grammar, punctuation and spelling.

How I've interpreted customers' body language

What I heard	What I saw	What I did and thought	What happened next
'I've been told you've increased the price?'	Customer was red in the face, kept looking at his watch and tapping the counter.	Used intranet to get information on new prices. It took a while. He looked angry and frustrated so I kept him informed of what I was doing and also gave good eye contact.	He told me he had just had some bad news and had to get home quickly. I had thought he was annoyed with the price increase but this was not the case.

A version of the table used in this task, ready for you to complete, is available to download from www.contentextra.com/customerservice

How to deal with customers' questions and comments

We've looked at how using listening skills and interpreting body language can help you to be an effective communicator. We will now concentrate on doing this in the context of dealing with customers' questions and comments.

Whether your work involves you being face to face with customers or on the telephone or communicating by electronic means, you will always need to be respectful, helpful and professional. You can achieve this by being polite and confident and by making it very clear what you can and cannot do for your customer. Do this and you are on your way to being a customer service professional.

> **Appearance** (you & your surroundings) + **Appropriate behaviour** + **Product or service knowledge** = **Professional behaviour**

Figure 4: Professional behaviour means creating the right impression across lots of factors.

We will now look at the impact of each of these factors on your ability to answer questions and comments.

Your appearance

Your appearance and that of your surroundings (if applicable) need to convey the right professional impression. You can achieve this by following your organisation's dress code and keeping your working environment clean and tidy. You will find it easier to find information you need to help customers if you are well organised so, keep your workspace free of clutter.

Even if you are not dealing with a customer face to face, your colleagues can see you. You need to create the right impression with them too. You need to convey respect and trust through your appearance and your surroundings.

If you do this you are making the right start. You will already be giving a positive signal and conveying trust and reassurance.

Your behaviour

Effective handling of questions and comments relies heavily on your behaviour towards your customers. Equally you will be affected by your customers' behaviour towards you. You should always behave in a manner that shows you care.

If you are faced with hearing the same thing many times during the day, it would be very easy to get bored. If this happens, your behaviour might indicate you are not interested in your customer. Your voice might sound flat or you may get easily distracted and your listening skills will suffer. If your customer is with you, they will be able to see you gazing blankly into space.

Answer any queries at the appropriate time. If you have to research information or seek help from others, do so. Never guess the answer! If the answer is taking longer to find than anticipated, keep your customer informed of progress.

If a customer has spent time queuing (either on the telephone or face to face) acknowledge this before you answer the query. This shows you care and you will be treating your customer with respect.

Behaviour refers to everything you do and say. People will draw conclusions about you and your organisation based on your behaviour towards them.

Product or service knowledge

Make sure you know where to access information about all the products or services you deal with. Keep this information up to date. This will help to ensure your responses to queries and requests are accurate.

Know the limits of your authority. Do not make promises which cannot be kept. Know who to ask for help if you are unable to deal with your customer's request.

> ### ✓ Checklist – Dealing with questions and comments in a positive and professional way
>
> - Follow your organisation's guidelines for appearance and behaviour.
>
> - Acknowledge any query or request as soon as possible.
>
> - Be friendly and welcoming in the language you use.
>
> - Be respectful – treat your customer with courtesy.
>
> - Give accurate information.
>
> - Say what you can do rather than what you cannot do.
>
> - Know about your organisation's products and/or services.
>
> - Know where to seek assistance if you are unable to help.

Portfolio Task   Links to a3.1.6, a3.1.9, a3e, a3f

Make a list of questions you are frequently asked. For each one, write down how you ensure you deal with them in a professional way.

Now consider two or three questions you have been asked recently which you were unable to respond to. Make a list. Write down how you dealt with them including how you believe you had to adapt your behaviour to deal with them. Discuss these examples with your assessor.

You will also need to ensure you are observed dealing with questions and comments from customers.

How to use questions to check your understanding

To avoid misunderstandings and making assumptions, you will sometimes need to check you have understood what your customer is telling you.

Try using checking phrases such as:

'I didn't quite hear what you said. Did you mean…?'

You can use this type of question when you simply cannot hear what has been said. For example, 'Did you say you wanted to book a table for 11 July?'

'To be sure I have understood correctly, let me repeat back what you need… Is that right?'

Sometimes, you may feel confused by what the customer has said. Repeating back key words you think you have heard could help to clarify things. For example, 'Did you say you wanted a table for six on 11 July at 7 p.m. and you need one with easy access to help your wife who has walking difficulties?'

When repeating back try to use key words the customer has used. In this example, it would be wrong to say 'you want a table which your wife can get to because she is a wheelchair user' if the customer has specifically mentioned 'walking difficulties'. Making assumptions could cause offence.

'Let me briefly summarise what you've said.... Have I got that right?'

This is simply a case of extending the repeating back by adding in what you and your customer have agreed. It enables you to confirm understanding, agreements made and actions to be taken. For example, 'I've booked a table for six on 11 July at 7 p.m. As this is a wedding anniversary, champagne will be available on arrival and there will be red roses on the table which will be situated away from a wall so that your wife has easy access. We look forward to seeing you on 11 July.'

By listening actively, asking the right questions, repeating information back and summarising, you will ensure you have fully understood your customer.

Checking understanding ensures customer satisfaction.

Portfolio Task   Links to a3.1.1, a3.1.2, a3.1.3, a3.1.4, a3.1.5, a3.1.7, a3.1.8, a3.1.9, a3b, a3c, a3d, a3e, a3f, a3g, a3h, a3i, a3k

Ask an appropriate person to write a report on how you deal with customers' questions and comments. Request specific feedback on the questions you use to check understanding.

Ask the person giving you feedback to concentrate on:

- the questions you ask
- your body language when doing so (if face to face)
- your listening skills
- the words you use
- your tone of voice
- the overall impact of your behaviour on customers.

It would be useful if your assessor can also observe you.

Remember – Always check back that the customer has understood what you have said. If they haven't heard you, you haven't said it.

The difference between negative and positive language

In much the same way as there is negative and positive body language, there are also negative and positive words. Choosing the right words will be critical to your success! Customers need to trust you and to know you are genuine in what you say and that you care. If you choose negative words you may well create an unwanted situation which could have been avoided with a more positive approach.

Say what you can do rather than what you cannot do, but be honest.

Table 2: Positive and negative words and phrases.

Positive	Negative
Yes	No
How may I help you?	What do you want?
I	They
Definitely	Unlikely
I will find out	I don't know
I will	I can't
Always	Never
I'll be quick	I'll do it when I can
I'll sort that out	It's not my fault

Consider your tone of voice

Getting the words right is only one part of effective communication. Your tone of voice and the way you choose to emphasise certain words matters too. After all, 'It's not what you say, it's the way that you say it' — this phrase has been around for ages and still holds true.

Think about this phrase: 'I love my job.' How many different ways do you think it could be said? Try saying it out loud to a colleague or friend, placing emphasis on the words highlighted.

I love my job

I **love** my job

I love **my** job

I love my **job.**

What reaction did you get to each one?

Your customers will develop an impression of you based on your tone of voice which is an important tool in customer service because it helps you to bring emotion into putting your message across. If your tone is clear and strong, you will come across as confident. If it is halting and softly spoken, you may appear timid and lacking in knowledge. Someone who speaks with a flat tone (that is, with no rise and fall in their voice) may come across as boring and again, possibly lacking in knowledge and confidence.

Some of the emotions people bring into their tone of voice include:

- boredom
- anger
- happiness
- frustration
- sadness
- worry.

You should always aim to speak clearly and with warmth and energy. Speaking whilst smiling will automatically bring warmth to your tone of voice.

Being respectful, helpful and professional on the telephone

Why is dealing with customers on the telephone different from dealing with them face to face? The most obvious answer is you cannot see each other. So you are both unable to observe the other person's body language.

Because customers cannot see what you are doing, never say, 'hold on please' and leave the customer waiting. Explain exactly what you are doing and how long you will be. You need to keep them informed of the actions you are taking.

Secondly, there is such an emphasis in today's world on answering the telephone speedily, so when it rings you might feel tempted to grab each call quickly. If you do this, you might speak far too quickly and blurt out your greeting. Take a deep breath and answer the phone calmly. Put a smile in your voice and be polite and courteous.

Thirdly, the customer will feel time spent waiting (for example, for the call to be answered or for you to find out information), is time spent doing nothing. What might be just a few seconds may well feel like minutes to a customer who is literally hanging on the other end of a line. Customers get impatient and frustrated more quickly than they would in a face-to-face situation.

We look further at dealing with customers on the telephone in **Unit A11 Deal with incoming telephone calls from customers** and **Unit A12 Make telephone calls to customers**.

You can find a link to **Unit A11 Deal with incoming telephone calls from customers** and **Unit A12 Make telephone calls to customers** at www.contentextra.com/customerservice

Being respectful, helpful and professional using the written word

Effective communication happens when information is fully understood after it has been passed on and received. Your customer cannot ask you questions on the spot as you will not be there. It is very important therefore, to use words your customer will understand and to get it right first time. Otherwise, costly errors could be made, your organisation's reputation will suffer and you will waste your customers' time.

Unit A3 Communicate effectively with customers

✓ Checklist – Using the written word

Think carefully what you need to say before you write.

- Answer all questions and comments fully.
- Establish rapport in the opening of your communication.
- Be concise. Keep to the point. Do not waffle.
- Summarise the key points and any actions to be taken.
- Avoid jargon.
- Check your communication for spelling and grammar.

We look further at delivering customer service in writing in **Unit A13 Deal with customers in writing or electronically** which is available on the website.

Portfolio Task

Links to a3.1.7, a3.1.8, a3.1.9, a3c, a3d

If your job involves you using the written word, find some great examples of letters or emails you have written which show you have communicated effectively with customers by considering their needs. Show these to your assessor and discuss why they are best practice examples of your writing skills.

Functional skills

English: Writing and Speaking, listening and communication
You may be able to use your written communications as evidence towards Level 1 Functional English: Writing. If you then discuss with your assessor why these are best practice examples of your writing skills, you will need to put your points across clearly and in appropriate language. You may be able to count this as evidence towards Level 1 Functional English: Speaking, listening and communication.

How to maintain effective communication with customers whose language, accents or dialect are different from yours

You may come across some situations where customers find your accent or dialect hard to understand. In some instances, your first language may differ from theirs. Here are some tips for adapting your speech.

Listen or look for clues

Sometimes customers will tell you that they haven't understood, but sometimes they will keep quiet and pretend all is well, so listening and watching for clues is vital. Clues could include:

- a customer who stays quiet when you are expecting a response
- a customer who gives a response which doesn't fit with the question you have asked
- a customer speaking very loudly
- a customer who fidgets and frowns and looks puzzled.

You will not be able to see puzzled faces when talking to customers by phone. So a key consideration is to try to quickly make sure what you are saying is making sense. Listen out for verbal signs from customers that they do not understand you.

Even silence may be a clue that what you have said is not being understood.

Slow down your voice

It is very important to speak clearly and slowly. That way you stand a good chance of communicating effectively. If you feel you are not being understood, action is required. If a customer tells you your accent is hard to follow, then you must slow your own voice down and ask the customer if they now understand. Keep your tone of voice at a light, slow pace.

Similarly, if *you* do not understand your customer's accent, do not pretend you do. Gently explain you are having a little difficulty saying 'I apologise. I am having a little difficulty understanding you. If you could slow down …just a little bit, I'll be able to make sure I help you properly.' Doing this shows the customer you want to help and get it right.

Keep a smile in your voice

If you think your customer is speaking very loudly to you it could be because they are having trouble with your accent. Keep a smile in your voice. It will show you have the patience to keep trying and it will let the customer know you are there to help. It might take time, but this approach will help.

Avoid using jargon

What you understand as everyday language may be completely alien to your customers regardless of any language difficulties. Jargon is guaranteed to confuse a customer and should be reserved for use between colleagues.

Use silence

Do not be in a hurry! Rushing through what you have to say can be quite threatening and will only serve to make your accent even more difficult to understand. Use silence to give customers thinking time before moving on to your next point.

Match your customer's style

The effectiveness of your conversation with a customer can be helped if you match the style used by your customers. This will help establish rapport and ease difficulties with understanding accents.

Keeping a smile in your voice can help overcome language difficulties.

> ✔ **Checklist – Helping customers whose accents, language or dialects are different from yours**
>
> - Slow down your voice.
> - Keep a smile in your voice.
> - Avoid using jargon.
> - Use silence to allow your customer time to understand and respond.
> - Match your customer's style.
> - Check with customers that any changes to your voice are helping.

Portfolio Task   Links to a3.1.1, a3.1.2, a3.1.3, a3.1.4, a3.1.5, a3.1.7, a3.1.8, a3.1.9, a3i, a3j

Make a list of words or phrases commonly in use where you work which you feel customers might find hard to understand.

For each one write down an alternative which you can use to help customers' understanding.

Make sure you ask for a witness testimony from an appropriate colleague when you help customers who find it hard to follow your language, accent or dialect.

How to manage customers' reactions when you are unable to help

There could be many reasons why you are unable to help a customer. For example:

● your organisation's policies and procedures may require you to say 'no'

● legal reasons

● safety reasons

● to protect confidentiality

● the product required is out of stock

● staffing problems

● your own lack of knowledge.

Some service providers take the easy way out and say things like:

> 'That's not our policy.'
> 'I'm not allowed to do that.'
> 'I have no idea if we can do that for you.'
> 'You'll have to come back another day.'

These types of response are likely to cause offence and will do little to keep your customer on side. It is very important to give reasons why you cannot help. A full explanation will go a long way to helping customers understand. Remember, your tone of voice will be equally important. Make sure you do not take the easy way out by not offering alternatives and by not saying what you can do.

✓ Checklist – Saying 'no' the right way

● Be friendly.

● Show empathy.

● Gain trust.

● Maintain eye contact when face to face.

● Give a clear explanation that shows the reasons for not meeting a need or expectation.

● Discuss options and alternatives.

● Explain what you *can* do.

● Agree the way forward.

Links to a3.1.6, a3c, a3d, a3e, a3f, a3h, a3i, a3k

Portfolio Task

Make a list of the main reasons or situations you face which usually mean you are unable to help a customer.

For each one, discuss with your assessor how you are able to maintain effective communication with customers. Include the skills you use to ensure you are respectful, helpful and professional.

You will also need to be observed dealing with customers you are unable to help.

Functional skills

English: Speaking, listening and communication
If you clearly discuss your thoughts and opinions with your assessor using appropriate language, you may be able to count this as evidence towards Level 1 Functional English: Speaking, listening and communication.

Why effective communication impacts on the customer experience

Get things right and your customer will feel assured that he or she has had a good **customer experience** with you and your organisation. Getting things right does not necessarily mean giving the customers everything they ask for; sometimes you will need to balance the needs of customers with those of your organisation. Therefore, the way in which you say 'no' is also very important.

Customers who have made a complaint sometimes feel better about an organisation than they did before the complaint was made. This is usually because of the way the person dealing with them handled their complaint. It is often more about the way in which they are listened to and what is then said than anything to do with any monetary issue. This is called **service recovery.**

Remember – you need to deal with customers in a respectful, helpful and professional way.

Customers generally need to:
- feel in control
- deal with people, places and things that make them feel good
- understand what is happening and why
- feel valued by you and your organisation.

Customers expect **you** to:
- be fair
- be honest.

Key terms

Customer experience – the feelings a customer has about the service received.

Service recovery – when customers feel better about a company after a problem has been resolved than they did before the problem even arose.

☑ **Checklist – Understanding customer needs and expectations**

To understand customer needs and expectations **you** need to:
- ask questions
- listen
- observe.

Message taking

One reason you may be unable to help is simply because you are not the right person to deal with a question or comment. Perhaps you are covering for a colleague who is off sick or on holiday or at lunch. Your customer will still expect prompt action and so any messages you take must be passed on effectively.

Taking notes will help you to recall what was agreed with a customer, what action needs to be taken and by whom. This is all part of maintaining reliable customer service.

✔ Checklist – Note-taking

- Give the date (and time if appropriate) the message was taken.
- Record relevant customer details, for example, name and reference/account/order numbers.
- Give your name and contact details.
- Show what action is required and by whom.
- Indicate critical points (for example, use highlighting or underlining).
- Be legible.
- Be easy to understand by yourself and others.
- Be brief and specific — contain relevant and important points only.

Make sure you pass on any messages promptly otherwise you will waste valuable time and may even forget to do so.

Your messages must be accurate because your colleagues will use the information to deal with the customer's enquiry. If you have promised someone will call back, then state this on the message.

Portfolio Task
Links to a3.1.10, a3l

Think of times when you have passed messages to colleagues. Ask them to write down how you were able to maintain customer service by doing so. Make sure they include things such as the accuracy of the information you passed on and the timeliness of your message.

Include this in your portfolio.

If you have taken notes, keep copies for your portfolio.

Working Life

Winston works as a handyman in a care home. He was cleaning a water cooler when a resident, Hannah, asked for help with her medication. Winston knew her request was quite simple — all he had to do was help her open a packet of tablets. However, only the nursing staff were authorised to deal with medication and so he had to say he couldn't help. In his usual loud voice he said:

'Not my job. Sorry Hannah. You'll have to find a nurse.'

He carried on with cleaning the water cooler and Hannah eventually walked away.

Later, the duty nurse found Winston and told him Hannah had been found in the conservatory looking quite distressed. She had got confused and thought Winston was a nurse and when he said he wasn't going to help, she had become worried she would not get her painkillers.

Ask the expert

Q How could Winston use his voice to show he cared?

A He should use positive language and speak with a smile in his voice. This would show he cared because his voice would sound warm. He was right to say 'sorry' but because he emphasised it wasn't his job, the impact of saying sorry was lost.

Q What should Winston have said?

A As well as saying he was unable to help, he should have said what he could do especially bearing in mind he was dealing with a potentially confused Hannah:

'I'm the handyman Hannah, so I won't be able to help you with your tablets. Let me go and find the nurse who can.'

Saying what he *could* do would have made all the difference.

Top tips

Although Winston had said sorry, his tone of voice and the language he used were less than helpful. He said what he could not do rather than what he could do. By continuing with his work, he failed to notice that Hannah looked confused.

Check your knowledge

1 What is the difference between listening and hearing?

a. Hearing involves asking questions to check which product is needed.

b. Listening involves ensuring a customer is comfortable when talking.

c. Listening means understanding the true meaning of the words.

d. Hearing means a service deliverer needs a quiet workplace.

2 What does a service deliverer need to do to actively listen to a customer?

a. To listen to words and tone, observe body language and give feedback.

b. To listen to words and tone, offer a private place to talk and ask questions.

c. To listen to words and tone, use appropriate gestures and seek help if needed.

d. To listen to words and tone, offer advice, clarify jargon and seek agreement.

3 Why is it important to listen carefully to customers?

a. To exceed sales or performance targets.

b. To pass messages to colleagues who can help.

c. To show you are an active team player.

d. To ensure customer satisfaction is achieved.

4 How can using positive body language help with effective communication?

a. It helps with clarifying complex information.

b. It helps create and sustain rapport and shows empathy.

c. It shows you are following rules and regulations.

d. It helps colleagues to effectively deal with messages.

5 Why is it important to ensure your body language matches what you say?

a. To ensure the customer does not receive mixed messages.

b. It is a legal requirement to always use positive language.

c. To ensure the needs of the customer are always exceeded.

d. To create a positive and welcoming environment to work in.

6 Which of the following are signs that a customer might not understand you?

a. A request for a discount on a product or service.

b. Lots of smiles and thanks for help given.

c. Long periods of silence followed by lots of questions.

d. A request for a response to be given in writing.

7 Why is tone of voice so important to effective communication?

a. Because legislation requires people to be polite and courteous.

b. Because managers expect staff to exceed sales targets.

c. Because a customer always wants to get more than they ask for.

d. Because a customer will interpret emotions as well as words.

8 What must be done to ensure messages are passed on effectively?

a. Tell the customer somebody will get back to them within 48 hours.

b. Record date, name and contact details plus key action points.

c. Send emails containing the information to more than one colleague.

d. Tell a manager or supervisor a customer was unable to be helped.

9 Which of the following are examples of positive body language?

a. Smiling and giving appropriate eye contact.

b. Keeping queues to a minimum.

c. Yawning and apologising for doing so.

d. Answering the telephone quickly.

10 Why is effective communication so important?

a. To create opportunities for selling additional products or services.

b. To enable staff to achieve maximum potential for pay increases.

c. To ensure the needs of both customer and organisation are met.

d. To let customers see up-to-date and relevant information.

Unit A4

Give customers a positive impression of yourself and your organisation

What you will learn:

- To establish rapport with customers
- To respond appropriately to customers
- To communicate information to customers

Introduction

No matter where you work or what your job role is, if you enjoy dealing with people you are probably well on the way to being able to deliver excellent customer service. You will be good at dealing with people (this is sometimes known as being a 'people person') and your behaviour with customers will come across as positive and reassuring. You will be easy to do business with and this means you will give customers a positive impression of your organisation too.

Your communication with customers may be face to face, in writing, by telephone, text message, email, Internet (including social networking), intranet or any other method your organisation supports.

You will learn how to ensure the customer believes you care by creating the right impression, responding well and giving good information. You need to aim to give a positive impression first time, every time, regardless of the situation. Whether things are routine or you are experiencing things going wrong, and whether you are working through a busy or a quiet time, your behaviour will play a very big part in giving this positive impression. A successful career in customer service depends on you being a 'people person' and consistently:

- establishing an effective rapport with customers
- responding appropriately to customers
- communicating information to customers.

Establish an effective rapport with customers

What you need to know and learn

- What you can do to create a positive impression of yourself and your organisation
- How to build rapport with customers
- How to identify and confirm your customer's expectations

What you can do to create a positive impression of yourself and your organisation

Picture a hot summer's day. Some customers might not worry if you go to work looking as if you were heading for the beach. If customers cannot see you, does it matter? Will your colleagues mind? Some people will not worry what you look like, whilst others will. You need to be aware of the image you create so it would be best to keep to your organisation's standards for appearance. That way, you know you will be doing your best to create the right image for both customers and your colleagues.

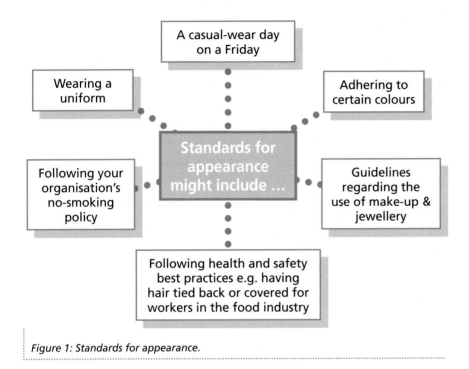

Figure 1: Standards for appearance.

The '3 Vs' of creating a positive impression

Creating the right impression involves three elements: how you are seen, how you sound and what you say. These are the **3 Vs** of creating the right image.

1   **V**ISUAL – how you are seen

2   **V**OCAL – how you sound

3   **V**ERBAL – what you say.

The Visual aspect – how you are seen

How you convey messages to other people through your **body language** is important. The way you dress is also important. Looking sloppy will convey an image that you don't care.

If you pay attention to your posture and 'stand up straight', dress in a style that is appropriate to your job and maintain eye contact, then you are more likely to be creating a positive impression and to appear professional and credible.

We don't always get out of bed feeling full of life before going to work. If you are not careful, your body language will tell your customer you would rather be back at home. This is because your emotional state will show through in your body language.

Key term

Body language – non-verbal signals that we give out and receive when we are communicating with someone.

Think about what impression you give customers if you are doing the following:

- Looking tense, for example, looking stiff, having a wrinkled forehead, or hands clasped tightly to your body. This could give the impression you are lacking in confidence or unduly worried and therefore unable to help. You might feel tense simply because you are aware you have a great deal of work to get through. Whatever the reason, your customer will notice that all is not well.

- Looking away when the customer approaches. This might make the customer feel you are not willing to help.

- Fidgeting, for example, moving around unnecessarily, playing with a pen or jewellery, drumming fingers on the table. Fidgeting can make it look as if you are bored, nervous or losing patience.

- Leaning far back on a chair. Unless you know your customer very well, he or she might feel you want to take control or that you feel you are in a position of power. It is quite an arrogant position to adopt.

- Yawning. This can be seen as a sign of boredom or that you are too tired to do your job.

- No eye contact. This shows you lack confidence or that you do not trust your customer or yourself to do the right thing.

- Wandering eyes. This might look as if you are bored with your customer.

- Sloppy posture – for example, a slumped position. This looks far too casual and as if you do not care. Do something about it. You will feel much better and so will your customer because a good posture shows you care and are confident in your job.

✔ Checklist – Improving your posture

Imagine you have a string coming out from the top of your head and into the ceiling. Now:

- Stand up straight!

  or

- Sit up straight in a chair with your shoulders back – do this without looking false.

- Get yourself comfortable in your new position.

- Regularly check out what you look like in a mirror.

The Vocal aspect – how you sound

You will clearly not create a positive impression if you cannot be heard, if you use inappropriate language and if you do not listen. Here are some tips to improve the way you sound.

Improving how you sound

- Remember to breathe. The deeper you breathe, the firmer your tone will be.

- Try to make sure your facial expression matches what you are saying for example, smile at the right time.

- Vary your voice to avoid speaking in one way. A flat voice is very dull to listen to and your customer will soon switch off. Even though your customer cannot see you when you are on the phone, smile as you speak – this will really make your voice sound much better. Your customers will pick up that you want to talk with them.

- Learn how loudly or how softly you speak. Ask a friend to give you some feedback. Perhaps tape yourself and listen to it.

- Do not drop letters at the start and end of words for example, words starting with 'h' and ending with 'ing'. The sentence 'I am helping you as quickly as I can' should not sound like 'I am 'elpin' you as quickly as I can'. You do not need to sound posh – you simply want to avoid appearing sloppy.

The effectiveness of your communication with a customer can be helped if you match the style used by your customers. This is all about developing rapport – more of this later (see also the key term on page 99).

> ### ☑ Checklist – Improving your vocal skills
>
> Keep to a steady pace.
>
> - Speed up or slow down to emphasise a point.
>
> - Pronounce any technical words very clearly.
>
> - If you think you are going too fast or too slowly – ask!
>
> - Encourage your customer to give you the information you need to help him or her.

The Verbal aspect – what you say

There is little point getting your image and the way you *sound* right if the *words* you use let you down. The *vocal* aspect deals with what you sound like. Whereas the *verbal* aspect deals with the words you use. Below are some tips to help you improve what you say.

Customers will know if you are distracted or bored as they will hear it in your voice

✓ Checklist – Improving *what* you say

- Bring some colour into what you say (but do not go over the top); using dull, nondescript language will make even the most exciting product seem boring or will make you sound as if you do not want to help.

- If you are in a sales role, find different ways of saying the same thing. Instead of saying 'you may be *interested* to know about...' you could try 'you may be *fascinated* to know about...'

- Avoid using jargon. What you understand as everyday language may be completely alien to your customers.

- Do not swear.

- Think about what you really want to say and then say exactly what you mean.

- Ask a friend to tell you if there are any words that you use frequently, for example, 'actually', 'basically' and 'you know'. When used over and over again, these become what are called verbal mannerisms and can be very annoying to the listener.

- Say what you can do, not what you cannot do.

The written word

The impact of your behaviour on the customer through the written word must also be considered, even though your customer will not see or hear you. If your mind is distracted and your attention to detail suffers, you might find yourself sending letters or emails to customers that are not up to your usual standard. The customer will see spelling mistakes and poor grammar as sloppy behaviour.

These three areas combined are what create the image other people have in their minds of you and your organisation. You can influence the image you create.

Appearance (you and your surroundings) **+ Body language + Behaviour =**
Customer Service Professional

Figure 2: Effective communication is not only about what you say, it's also about how you say it.

You can learn more about using your voice and body language in Unit A3 Communicate effectively with customers and Unit A10 Deal with customers face to face.

Portfolio Task   Links to a4.1.1, a4a

Find out what your organisation expects from you in terms of standards for appearance and behaviour.

1   Check out whether there are written guidelines.

2   Check out whether the standards are informal.

3   Write down what you do to ensure you keep to these standards.

4   Keep this for your portfolio.

You and your working environment

Creating the right image is not just about what you look like and your behaviour. It is also about where you work and the tools you work with. Take a look around you and at the tools or equipment you use. How much is visible to customers? What kind of image is created? Think about the following:

- Premises – Are they clean and tidy or is the paint peeling off the walls?

- Equipment – Is it in working order and safe?

- Information – Is it up-to-date or does it look dog-eared?

- Tools – Do the pens provided for customers work?

- Correspondence – When you write to customers do you handwrite or use a computer? What does the letterhead look like – does it convey the right image?

Portfolio Task   Links to a4.1.1, a4a

Make a list of things you do on a daily basis to ensure your working environment creates a positive impression for your customers. Discuss this with your assessor.

> ## ✔ Checklist – creating a good impression in the workplace
>
> - Clean and tidy work areas
> - Up-to-date literature
> - Equipment in working order
> - Accurate signage
> - Noticeboards with helpful information
> - Names/photos of employees
> - Uniforms
> - Natural light
> - Comfortable chairs in a waiting area
> - Crèche facilities
> - Current magazines to read

Meeting and greeting customers

It cannot be stressed enough how important your behaviour is in creating a good image and a good first impression. What your customers think about you in those all-important first few seconds will influence their entire experience of dealing with you and your organisation. This is sometimes referred to as the 'meet and greet' moment.

Little things really do count when it comes to giving a positive impression especially when meeting and greeting your customers. You would be amazed at how many people pay attention to small details. Trying to avoid all the pitfalls we have just mentioned will help you get off to a good start.

You may find yourself doing some of the things below when you meet and greet your customers. Figure 3 illustrates how to meet and greet customers.

Of course, all these behaviours apply just as much throughout a customer transaction as they do at the beginning. However, if you do not get off to a good start, it is much more difficult to recover the situation later.

Portfolio Task
Links to a4.1.2, a4a

1 Find out whether your organisation has a standard greeting for customers that you should use
   a. face to face
   b. on the telephone
   c. when using electronic forms of communication.

2 Check, by asking a colleague to tell you, that you do sound sincere when using a standard greeting.

3 How can you ensure that you sound genuine each time you greet customers?

4 Using the results of your findings to these questions, describe to your assessor your organisation's guidelines for greeting your customers and how you follow them.

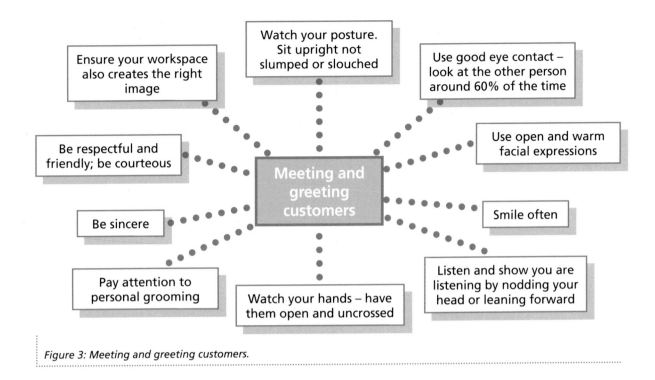

Ensure your workspace also creates the right image

Watch your posture. Sit upright not slumped or slouched

Use good eye contact – look at the other person around 60% of the time

Be respectful and friendly; be courteous

Use open and warm facial expressions

Meeting and greeting customers

Be sincere

Smile often

Pay attention to personal grooming

Watch your hands – have them open and uncrossed

Listen and show you are listening by nodding your head or leaning forward

Figure 3: Meeting and greeting customers.

How to build rapport with customers

We have looked at those first important few seconds when you meet and greet your customers. You need to keep up the good work by building on your good start. This is known as developing and maintaining **rapport**. Without rapport there will be no trust. Without trust, your customer service will not be what it should be.

There will be some people who you meet in both your personal and work life who you instantly hit it off with. You may warm to others over a period of time and there will also be some people who you simply do not like. Much of this 'like/dislike' judgement will stem from those all-important initial impressions and what happens immediately after, to either confirm your judgment or to help you to change your mind.

To maintain your good start it is essential you treat each and every customer as an individual. If you do not, they will not feel that you respect and value them. This involves you recognising that everyone has different needs. Customers will want different things from you, so you will need to adjust the way you behave with each customer.

Building rapport is simply an extension of creating a positive impression. In this section we will look at building rapport face to face and on the telephone, using courtesy to build rapport and maintaining rapport in difficult situations.

Key term

Rapport – a sense of being comfortable with someone whether or not you know him or her well.

Portfolio Task

Links to a4.1.1, a4.1.2, a4.1.3, a4.1.5, a4.1.7

1 Think about how you behave with customers during what you consider to be a normal or routine part of the day:

a. What worked well in the way in that you used your voice?

b. Did what you wear make any difference?

c. What worked well in the way you adapted your behaviour to suit different customers needs?

d. How does your working environment help you?

e. How did you ensure your customers knew you wanted to help?

Write your thoughts down.

2 Now think about how you behave with customers during:

a. a busy time

and

b. a quiet time in your job.

Using the same questions as in question 1, write your thoughts down.

3 Lastly, think about a time when things went wrong (perhaps a power cut, staff shortages or mechanical failure).

Again use the same questions as in question 1 and discuss all three aspects with your assessor.

Functional skills

English: Reading, Writing and Speaking, listening and communication

If you answer the questions in the task in writing, you will have an opportunity to identify a suitable response to the text. This may be able to count as evidence towards Level 1 Functional English: Reading. Your written responses should include sufficient detail to show you have understood the questions and you will need to check them for spelling, grammar and punctuation. Print a copy of your responses as this may count as evidence towards Level 1 Functional English: Writing. If you use your responses as a basis for a discussion with your assessor, you may be able to count this as evidence towards Level 1 Functional English: Speaking, listening and communication.

Building rapport face to face

When you are dealing with customers face to face, there are many opportunities for you to build rapport.

✔ Checklist – Building rapport face to face

- Ensure you give the right amount of **eye contact**. If you use too much, you may appear to be staring; too little and you will come across as uninterested

- **Smile** warmly when it is appropriate for the occasion. But be genuine. Everyone can see through a fake smile.

- Sometimes a **handshake** will be appropriate. If so, make sure it is firm to convey confidence and interest.

- Think about your **posture** and standing up to greet a customer, particularly if you are seeing someone by appointment. Do not invade their personal space though: if you are too close you will make them feel uncomfortable. If you are sitting down, do not slouch. Not only does it look bad, it will also affect the quality of your voice.

- You are really in rapport with someone when you both **mirror** each other's body posture. If you are sitting down, you might find suddenly that you are both leaning towards each other or both nodding at the same time. Do not copy what your customer is doing! That would look as though you were making fun of them. Unless you are a very highly skilled communicator, it is best to let it happen naturally.

Building rapport on the telephone

If you use the phone to deliver customer service you do not have the advantage of being able to observe your customers' behaviour nor they to observe you. You both have to rely solely on what you hear.

> ✓ **Checklist – Building rapport on the telephone**
>
> - Greet callers with courtesy and warmth.
>
> - You may need to use your organisation's standard form of greeting – be sincere in the way that you say it. Do not sound as if you are reading from a script.
>
> - Answer as promptly as possible.
>
> - Remember that you may have said the same thing 50 times that day, but the customer will be hearing it for the first time.
>
> - Watch your posture. Sit upright to sound alert and remember to smile. Your customer will be able to hear if you are smiling or not.
>
> - Be patient.
>
> - Mirror the language your customer uses.
>
> - If you feel under pressure, watch the speed of your voice. If you speak too quickly, you will only end up having to repeat yourself and you may also confuse the customer.

Using courtesy to build rapport

Being courteous is about combining the right attitudes, behaviour and words. Courtesy is a means of showing you care, that you recognise customers' needs and expectations and that you appreciate them doing business with you and your organisation.

Often the only difference between your organisation and its competitors is the people it employs. Do not look on being courteous as something extra you need to do. It is the hallmark of a customer service professional and as such an essential part of your toolkit. You provide the distinctive edge that might make the difference between customers using your organisation or going elsewhere.

Using courtesy is a key factor in establishing and maintaining rapport with customers.

For example, at a market stall a customer might be met with a long queue only to find a hostile assistant who is interested only in getting off to lunch. At the stall across the road, the same customer could easily find a customer service professional who acknowledges the wait the customer has had, by saying, 'I'm very sorry about the wait you have had. Now, what can I do for you?' before going on to explore the customer's needs and expectations. Such a little touch, but it makes all the difference and the wait worthwhile.

True courtesy

A word of warning! False courtesy is easily spotted and will make for poor customer service! When you say 'thank you' you really do need to mean it! If you use the right words with the wrong attitude, the customer will not trust you. For instance saying 'It's nice talking to you' without giving eye contact will give the opposite impression. Similarly, saying 'Thanks for calling' and very quickly cutting the customer off will not make him or her feel very welcome.

Using courtesy is a key factor in establishing and maintaining rapport with customers. Courtesy also helps to build confidence in the level of service you and your organisation provide.

✓ Checklist – using courteous behaviour to build rapport

- Show you want to help and that the customer is not interrupting you
- Keep your workspace clean, tidy and prepared for your role
- Show you remember regular customers
- Acknowledge customers immediately
- Say 'please' and 'thank you' when appropriate
- Volunteer to help others when you can
- Make eye contact
- Do not shout or talk to customers from too far away
- Keep customers informed.

Maintaining rapport in difficult situations

During the meeting and greeting stage with customers, rapport needs to happen in just a few seconds. That is the whole point of creating the right atmosphere to do business with customers; it should not be something which takes ages and ages to build.

It can be quite easy to lose rapport even when the customer appears to want to do business with you. It is even easier to lose rapport if a customer becomes angry or confused. You can spot this happening by observing a customer's facial expressions and listening to their tone of voice. Whilst you can never be 100 per cent sure what a customer is feeling by doing this, it is a good indication of what might be happening.

Unit A4 Give customers a positive impression of yourself

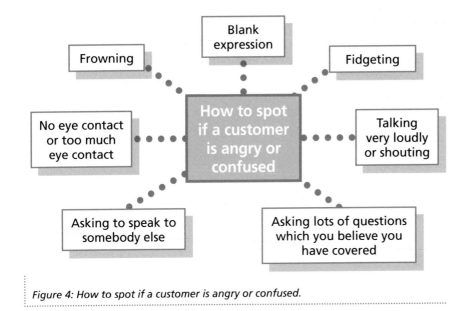

Figure 4: How to spot if a customer is angry or confused.

You should avoid talking more than you listen to a customer, arguing with him or her and using complicated language or jargon. Instead, build confidence in yourself and your organisation despite being involved with a difficult situation.

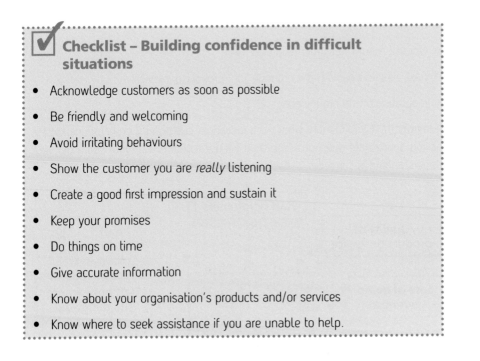

✓ Checklist – Building confidence in difficult situations

- Acknowledge customers as soon as possible
- Be friendly and welcoming
- Avoid irritating behaviours
- Show the customer you are *really* listening
- Create a good first impression and sustain it
- Keep your promises
- Do things on time
- Give accurate information
- Know about your organisation's products and/or services
- Know where to seek assistance if you are unable to help.

Portfolio Task

Links to a4.1.1, a4.1.5, a4.1.6, a4.1.7, a4a, a4d

Think about an occasion when you dealt with a customer who was angry or confused. What was it about the customer's behaviour which made you think they were angry or confused?

1 Were they angry or confused before you had started to deal with them?

2 Was it something *they* said or did that caused their anger/confusion?

3 Was it something *you* said or did that caused their anger/confusion?

4 What did you do to adapt your behaviour?

5 What did they do or say which helped you to understand how they felt?

6 Using your answers to these questions, explain to your assessor how you can recognise when a customer is angry or confused.

How to identify and confirm your customer's expectations

What makes your organisation different from its competitors? **You do!** Service failings frequently revolve around employees and their attitudes and behaviour, for example, staff who are helpful, willing to take responsibility and have the right level of knowledge to help customers will be on their way to providing the right level of customer service.

Each customer will have their own ideas as to what to expect from your organisation. These **customer expectations** are based on a number of factors, including:

● advertising and marketing

● word of mouth from friends or family

● past experiences with the organisation, product or service

● reputation of the organisation.

It is important you identify what each individual customer's expectations are by asking appropriate questions. You then need to confirm with your customer your understanding is correct.

Key term

Customer expectations – what customers think should happen and how they think they should be treated when asking for or receiving customer service.

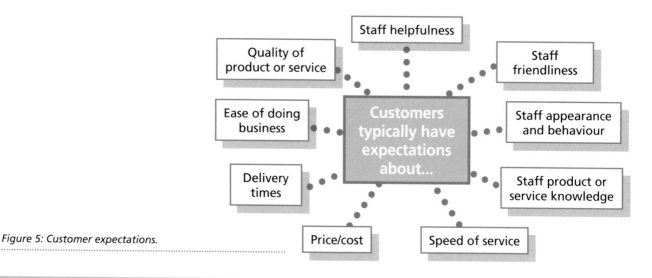

Figure 5: Customer expectations.

Portfolio Task   Links to a4.1.4, a4.1.5, a4b

Find out if your organisation has guidelines on how to recognise what your customer wants and explain to your assessor:

1 how you ensure you follow these guidelines

2 what you do personally to spot what your customer wants.

Respond appropriately to customers

What you need to know and learn

- What your organisation expects from you when recognising customers' needs and expectations
- How to choose the most appropriate way to communicate with customers
- How to deal with customers' questions and comments

What your organisation expects from you when recognising customers' needs and expectations

Organisations will differ in what they expect by way of standards from their customer service employees. Some organisations tell employees what should be said when answering the telephone, while others will leave it up to employees. Some expect calls to be answered within five rings or have a dress code or uniform.

What will be similar across all organisations are the behaviours and attitudes expected from employees. Most organisations will expect employees to display the behaviour shown in Figure 6.

Of course, it is not just *what* you do that counts when responding to customers' needs and expectations, it's the *way* in which you do it. For example, if you are answering a query from a customer who is anxious to sort out a problem, not only should you sort the problem out but you should also consider your customer's feelings in doing so and adapt your behaviour accordingly. A doctor would need to adapt his or her behaviour to behave differently towards a patient who is asking advice about injections needed when travelling abroad and a patient who needs advice about dealing with a terminal illness.

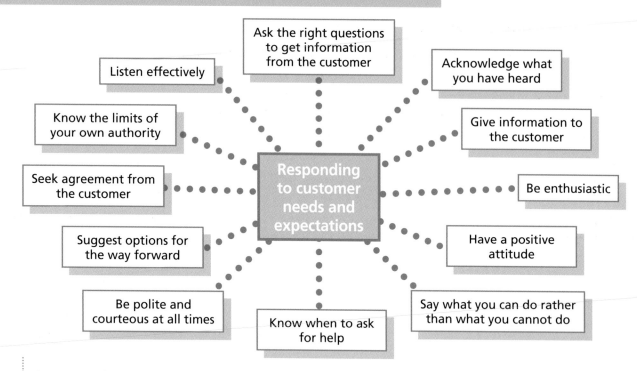

Listen effectively

Ask the right questions to get information from the customer

Acknowledge what you have heard

Know the limits of your own authority

Give information to the customer

Seek agreement from the customer

Responding to customer needs and expectations

Be enthusiastic

Suggest options for the way forward

Have a positive attitude

Be polite and courteous at all times

Know when to ask for help

Say what you can do rather than what you cannot do

Figure 6: Responding to customer needs and expectations.

Your call is important to us, so please hold ....

Figure 7: Customers will quickly end a phone call when they hear automated responses.

There is a key expectation which customers of all organisations are increasingly showing and that is around waiting times. Customers are no longer prepared to wait whether face to face, on the phone or in response to an email or letter. For example, customers will quickly end a phone call when they hear automated responses saying 'You are in a queue but your call is important to us. Please hold until one of our agents is free.'

Your organisation may have guidelines to follow when responding to a customer. These might include the guidelines in Table 1 but they will vary between organisations.

Table 1: Possible guidelines to follow when responding to a customer

Time	• The maximum number of rings before a telephone *must* be answered • Waiting time in a queue
Acknowledgements	• Acknowledging letters/emails within a set timescale • Sending an acknowledgement e.g. a letter/email to confirm safe receipt with a full response to follow
Use of names	• What to call the customer – first name, surname or neither • Giving your own name to the customer
Legislation and regulations	• What you are permitted to do and what NOT to do under law • The nature of any contract your customer has with your organisation
Method of communication	• When to use telephone/email/ letters/text/internet/intranet and when you need to deal with the customer face to face.

Portfolio Task

Links to a4.2.1, a4.2.2, a.4.2.3, a4.2.4, a4.2.5, a4b, a4c, a4e

Find out whether your organisation has guidelines that you need to follow when responding to customers with respect to:

1 Time – on the telephone or in a queue

2 Sending holding letters/emails if you are unable to action a full response on the spot

3 Use of names – your own and what to call the customer

4 When to use written communications, for example, emails or letters

5 What situations must always be dealt with face to face.

Discuss your findings with your assessor and ensure you are observed responding to customers using your organisation's guidelines.

Functional skills

English: Speaking, listening and communication
If you clearly discuss your findings with your assessor using appropriate language, you may be able to count this as evidence towards Level 1 Functional English: Speaking, listening and communication.

You can learn more about responding to customers in **Unit A3 Communicate effectively with customers** and **Unit A10 Deal with customers face to face.**

How to choose the most appropriate way to communicate with customers

Have you ever received a text message or 'junk mail' claiming you had won a fantastic prize but you need to call a number at an expensive rate in order to claim it? Did you think 'WOW, I'll phone right now!' Did you actually do this? How do you think you would feel (or how did you feel) when you had to wait for a couple of minutes when you knew it was costing you £5 a minute to be kept waiting? Why do you think this company chose to ask you to communicate with them via a phone call? Why could you just not post back a letter? Yes, you've got it! This company wanted you to phone as they could collect the phone charges from you. Posting a letter would not enable them to receive any income.

Your organisation may have set guidelines it wishes you to follow about when to use the phone, letter, email (or other form of electronic communication)

and when to deal with customers face to face. These guidelines may also state when the telephone must always be used to talk to a customer. For example, a guideline might state a customer should be telephoned within 24 hours of receipt of a complaint. Table 2 shows ways in which each method of communication might be used.

Table 2: Choosing the most appropriate method of communication

Method of communication	When to use
Face to face	• When the customer is on your premises • When delivering 'bad' news • When delivering 'good' news – perhaps to support and add weight to a congratulatory letter • When a permanent record is not required
Letter	• When a permanent record is needed • In formal situations, e.g. where a letterhead showing the company brand/logo adds credibility and confidence • When you have the time to allow for a letter to be received • When you are sending out product or service information
Telephone	• When instant communication is required • When you need to ask questions and get a quick response • When the customer is expecting you to call them back • In situations when personal contact is important
Email	• To act as confirmation of what you have said on the phone • To promote a product or service especially to an existing customer • Internally to colleagues but not for 'bad' or 'sensitive' news • When you cannot get hold of someone on the phone • When you are responding to someone who has contacted you by email

Portfolio Task

Links to a4.2.2, a4b, a4c, a4e

1 a. Find out if your organisation has any guidelines for selecting the methods of communication within your job role.

   b. Are there any other methods available to you not mentioned above?

   c. If so, in what situations is it appropriate to use them?

   Make a list of the guidelines and describe how you use them.

2 a. If you are involved in writing to customers, in what other situations do you need to write or email customers?

   b. Find some recent letters/emails you have written and make a list of them.

   c. For each one why did you choose to write rather than telephone or perhaps meet the customer?

3 Discuss with your S/NVQ advisers and your line manager whether it is appropriate to include copies of these within your portfolio. If you do so, ask what you need to do to protect customer confidentiality.

Functional skills

English: Writing
Copies of your written communications may be counted as evidence towards Level 1 Functional English: Writing.

How to deal with customers' questions and comments

If you listen effectively and ask the right questions, misunderstandings are less likely to occur. You need to develop certain skills that will help you to ensure you have understood the customer and the customer has understood you. Getting it right first time is all part of providing the right level of customer service and helps to establish an effective relationship with customers. The skills you need to develop include the following:

● effective listening

● asking the right questions

● repeating information back

● summarising what has been agreed.

Active listening

As a customer service professional, you should not always be doing the talking. Part of being polite with customers is to show them you are *really* listening when *they* are talking. This is called **active listening** and it applies both on the telephone and in face-to-face situations.

If you listen well you are going to get things right first time and not have to return to your customer later for clarification. Listening effectively also means you are more likely to be able to meet or exceed your customers' expectations. If you go into a fish and chip shop and order haddock and chips that is what you want not chicken and chips!

Effective listening is all about showing your customers that you care. It means that you take notice of the words you hear *and* the tone in which they are said and the body language of the customer.

The same words can be said in different ways, for example:

● by someone with a smile on their face who says the words enthusiastically

● by someone with a smile on their face who hesitates when speaking

● by someone who is red in the face and shouts out the words.

In Figure 8 you can see you have a satisfied, a confused and an angry customer. Yet all three said the same words.

> **Key term**
>
> **Active listening** – paying careful attention to understand more than the words being spoken.

Figure 8: You will need to listen effectively to determine whether you have Mr Happy or Mrs Confused or Mr Angry.

Communicate information to customers

What you need to know and learn

- How to use the information your organisation supplies to help you deliver fantastic customer service
- How to explain to customers the reasons you are unable to meet their needs or expectations

How to use the information your organisation supplies to help you deliver fantastic customer service

We will now build on your good start with customers to show you how to communicate information. Customers need to be able to understand what you and your organisation are offering in as clear a way as possible. If there is any confusion, mistakes can happen, customers will be dissatisfied and complaints may follow. There may also be legal reasons why you need to communicate information to customers, such as changes to terms and conditions of a bank account.

Customers need to be able to understand what you and your organisation are offering in as clear a way as possible.

You need to know where to find information relating to your organisation's products or services. Finding information quickly and efficiently helps you answer customers' questions and queries promptly. It will also instil confidence in your customers that you know what you are talking about.

You will not need to know in detail about *all* the products and services your organisation offers, just those that are relevant to you and your role. You do need to know where to go to for help if there are questions and queries about a product or service that is outside your own area of responsibility. Do not feel shy about asking for help, it will help you enjoy your job more and you may even learn something new.

Giving incorrect information to customers is a serious issue. You will annoy and frustrate a customer by doing so and, in the worst case scenario, giving incorrect information could even be dangerous.

✓ Checklist – Finding out about your organisation's products and services

Talk to colleagues.

- Ask your supervisor, line manager or team leader.
- Read catalogues/brochures/price lists/websites including the company intranet.
- Attend training sessions, briefings and meetings.
- Read specially designed company product or service information books.
- Keep up to date by:
  - ensuring all the product and service information you give to customers is current
  - looking at dates on any paper-based information you give to customers.
- Find information quickly by:
  - knowing how to access computer-based information
  - ensuring you never run out of paper-based information
  - knowing who to ask for help.

Portfolio Task   Links to a4.3.1, a4.3.2, a4b, a4c, a4e

1 a. Find out how many products or services your organisation offers.

   b. Which of these are relevant to you and your role?

   c. Where will you find the best source of information for products or services?

   d. Are there any products or services you are asked about for which you struggle to find out the required details? Sort out now what you need to know and understand about these.

   Write down your thoughts.

2 Look back to the work you have done for Unit F1 Communicate using customer service language, and recap the key products or services you deal with by making a list.

   Discuss with your assessor how you ensure you can quickly find information about these. Describe a time when you created a positive impression with a customer by providing him or her with information.

113

Identifying the right information

It is very important to understand exactly what your customer needs before you give out any information. We have written about how to communicate effectively with your customer using the skills of asking questions, confirming your understanding and summarising what you have heard. Never be afraid to go back over areas that seem to confuse a customer. Accuracy is very important.

Remember – Helping people is not only about doing or saying the right things. It is also about making sure you do so in a way that best suits the individual customer's needs and expectations.

Before you can answer any of the questions or provide information to customers about products or services you must make some decisions. These could include:

● ...What sort of information should I give?

● ...How much information should I give?

● ...What method of communication should I use?

● ...What words should I use?

Essentially what you need to do is tell your customer all the information he or she needs to answer their questions. When dealing in facts and figures, always be accurate. Gather all the information you need from the customer before answering a question. For example, if a customer asks what time a bus leaves, you will first need to check where they will be leaving from before offering information.

Think too about giving any information about a product or service that you feel the customer needs to know, such as warning them of any possible problems affecting a service, imminent product changes or special offers.

Always remember the supply of information is affected by legislation. Refer back to **Unit F2 Follow the rules to deliver customer service** (pages 48 – 70) where we deal with what this means to you.

Check your customer has understood the information you have given

Firstly, you need to decide how much information to give. Some customers will want to know everything there is to know about a product or service. Others will want only the bare details. For those who seem to want to know everything, do remember that people can only absorb so much information at a time. When appropriate, remember to use company leaflets and brochures so that customers can read them in their own time. It does not pay to overload customers with so much information that they become confused.

Figure 9: Asking questions will help you tell if you have given the customer enough information.

You can test whether you have given enough information by asking if there is anything else the customer wants to know, or if you have answered their question. For example:

- 'Does that answer your question?'
- 'Would you like to know more about the product?'
- 'Have I covered everything you need to know?'
- 'Are you able to come to a decision now?'

If dealing face to face with a customer, look for any non-verbal signals the customer may give. If the expression is open and smiling you have probably said enough. If there is a frown present you may have a confused customer. If you are on the phone, silence may indicate there is a problem. Check this out by asking questions.

This will enable your customer to get some breathing space and for you to try once more. Be very careful you do not patronise or insult the customer — they might think you are implying they are not very clever.

✓ **Checklist – Giving information to customers**

- Ask questions to find out what the needs and expectations of the customer are.
- Check you have fully understood what the customer wants.
- Give enough information to answer questions.
- Avoid using jargon.
- Explain any technical or specialist language — or find another way of saying it.
- Choose your method of communication to suit the type of information you are giving.
- Consider how fast a response is required.
- Make sure the information you give is accurate and up-to-date.
- If appropriate, check you have met the customer's needs and expectations.
- If appropriate, advise the customer how he or she can take things forward.

Portfolio Task

Link to a4.3.3, a4d

Think back to a time when a customer appeared confused with information you had given him or her. Write down your answers to these questions.

1 What was the product or service involved?

2 Does explaining this product or service always cause problems?

3 What sort of information do customers find hard to understand?

4 What have you done to ensure clear explanations are given?

Functional skills

English: Reading and Writing

If you answer the questions in the task in writing, you will have an opportunity to identify a suitable response to the text. This may count as evidence towards Level 1 Functional English: Reading. Your written responses should include sufficient detail to show you have understood the questions and you will need to check them for spelling, grammar and punctuation. Print a copy of your responses as this may count as evidence towards Level 1 Functional English: Writing.

How to explain to customers the reasons you are unable to meet their needs or expectations

We would all like to get what we want at the price we want to pay, when we want it. However, it is not always right or possible to say 'yes' to customers. This is because you need to balance the needs of your customer with those of your organisation. If you said 'yes' to every customer request, your organisation might go out of business.

Customers whose needs or expectations are not met are likely to feel disappointed or even angry and frustrated. So, it is important that you do all that you can to explain *why* you cannot do what he or she wants.

When you cannot meet customers' needs or expectations

Saying 'no' is not about refusing to help. It's more a case of helping the customer to understand that on this occasion you are unable to help with X but you can offer Y. You should try to offer options and alternatives and do this in a way that recognises the first choice has not been met.

This means showing empathy and understanding. Customers need to feel you appreciate the position they are in and that you have recognised their feelings at not having their needs or expectations met. By offering options and alternatives the customer will feel valued because you have not closed the door on him or her.

Reasons why you might have to say 'no'

Your organisation's policies and procedures

There will be times when your organisation's policy requires you to say 'no'. For example, it may not be cost effective for large stocks of bulky items to be kept on the premises meaning there might be a longer wait for a customer to get what he or she wants. A hairdresser might have a policy which states that children under 10 must be accompanied by a parent or guardian.

Legal reasons

Organisations and their employees must comply with the law. For instance, in a shop selling fake leather coats, a customer might ask to try one on. Under The Trade Descriptions Act, it would be wrong of the sales assistant helping him or her to say that the coat is leather; they must explain that the coats are, in fact, fake leather.

Safety reasons

If small children are in the queue for the new roller-coaster at the adventure park, it would be wrong to let them on the ride if they are shorter than the minimum height restriction.

Protecting confidentiality

Protecting information you have about a customer is another reason why you might have to say 'no'. Protecting customers' confidentiality is part of your legal obligations, so it is very important not to give out personal information to unauthorised people.

Out of stock

Sometimes, you may simply not have in stock the product your customer requires.

Staffing problems

If a customer asks to deal with a person by name, this may not always be possible as the person in question might be on holiday or on sick leave.

In all these instances, having to say 'no' doesn't necessarily have to mean you will get an unhappy customer at the end. However, bear in mind that sometimes you might be saying 'no' in sensitive situations and you must therefore be particularly careful about how you say it.

Saying 'no' the right way

Customers hate the 'I don't care' attitude of some service providers. Unfortunately, there are a few people who will take the easy way out and say things like:

- 'That's not our policy.'

- 'I'm not allowed to do that.'

- 'I have no idea if we can do that for you.'

Make sure you do not take the easy way out by not offering alternatives and by not saying what you can do.

✔ Checklist – Saying 'no' the right way

- Be friendly.

- Show empathy.

- Maintain eye contact when face to face.

- Give a clear explanation that shows the reasons for not meeting a need or expectation.

- Discuss options and alternatives.

- Explain what you *can* do.

- Agree the way forward.

Portfolio Task   a.4.3.4, a4b a4d

With a colleague list the four main customer needs that seem to appear frequently that you and your organisation are consistently unable to meet.

1 Discuss why this is.

2 Discuss the reaction you get from customers when you are unable to meet these needs or expectations.

3 Using the outcome of these discussions, talk to your assessor about a specific time when this happened.

Working Life – Brian's story

I'm Brian and I work as a foreman in a brick-making yard. Last week a woman was looking around and asked for some samples of 'Reigate bricks' to take home to her husband who was project managing an extension to their house. This really made me laugh because our yard is not in Reigate (which is 25 miles away), therefore we do not make Reigate bricks. I told her she would have to go to Reigate to get them and I guess I made her feel pretty small by the way in which I said it. Her face turned red and it was difficult to know if she was angry or confused or both.

I had fallen into the trap of thinking 'a woman just won't understand' so I failed to give her any detailed information or to question her as to why she particularly wanted Reigate bricks.

Her response was 'I also wanted to order a load of cement but as you think this is so funny, I'll get it somewhere else!'. Off she went looking quite embarrassed and I realised I had lost what might have been a good order.

Ask the expert

Q Why did the customer not see the funny side of the situation?

A Rapport did not exist because the foreman's immediate reaction was to laugh at the customer before any explanation was given.

Q Why wasn't rapport established after Brian realised the customer was not happy?

A Brian failed to say 'sorry' and did not offer an explanation as to why the geographical location of a brickyard affects the type of bricks produced. He showed no respect to the customer even though he realised he had made a mistake.

Q What was the likely impact on the brickyard of Brian's mistake?

A This customer is unlikely to go back and will probably tell friends and family what happened. Reputation will suffer.

Top tips

Always treat your customer with respect and make sure rapport is established by adapting your behaviour to suit the individual customer's needs. Avoid jumping to conclusions and ask questions to assess what the customer wants. Check you have fully understood and give sufficient information to enable the customer to make a decision. Say what you can do instead of what you cannot do. Humour should be used with great care and, usually, only when you know the customer well enough to not offend.

Check your knowledge

1 List three ways in which you can create a positive impression with customers.

2 What can you do to convey a positive attitude when on the telephone?

3 Why is eye contact important when dealing with a customer face to face?

a. To check the customer's identity.

b. To establish rapport with the customer.

c. To help the customer understand.

d. To distract the customer from a queue.

4 When would you choose to write a letter to a customer rather than use email?

a. When a written response is required to a query.

b. When replying to a complaint or a compliment.

c. When colleagues are using the phone or computer.

d. When wanting a permanent record and proof of receipt.

5 List four key points to remember when greeting customers.

6 What should you *always* offer customers when you cannot meet their needs or expectations?

a. A refund.

b. An apology.

c. An explanation.

d. A referral.

7 Why is it important to customers that you meet your organisation's standards for appearance and behaviour?

a. To instil confidence and create a positive impression.

b. To beat the competition and win new business.

c. To comply with codes of conduct and legislation.

d. To create a happy working environment.

8 Why is establishing rapport important to a customer?

a. It allows me to exceed sales targets.

b. It tells everyone we are the best.

c. It shows I want to help and am caring.

d. It is a requirement under law.

9 How can you check your customer has understood you?

a. By monitoring my own performance.

b. By listening and taking notes.

c. By involving colleagues and listening.

d. By listening and asking questions.

10 Why is a neat and tidy working environment an important factor in creating a good impression when dealing with customers face to face?

a. It shows the customer we have effective maintenance staff.

b. It shows the customer we care about the experience they receive.

c. It shows the customer we look after their health and safety.

d. It shows the customer staff are looked after well and get training.

Unit A10

Deal with customers face to face

What you will learn:

- To communicate effectively with your customer
- To improve the rapport with your customer through body language

Introduction

This unit is all about the skills and behaviours you need to demonstrate to be successful when dealing with customers face to face. The impression you create will have a significant impact on what your customers feel about you and the service you deliver.

Customers will be able to see the image you create as well as hear what you say to them. This means you need to think about your verbal and non-verbal communication skills. The way you look and behave, together with what you say to customers need to fit together like a jigsaw — if any pieces are missing you will probably not achieve customer satisfaction.

When you prepare to deal with customers face to face you must consistently show you:

- communicate effectively with your customer
- improve the rapport with your customer through body language.

In particular, this unit looks at creating rapport with customers in face-to-face situations. This area is also covered in **Unit A3 Communicate effectively with customers** and **Unit A4 Give customers a positive impression of yourself and your organisation**. The key knowledge and understanding covered by these two units is recapped here. If Units A3 and/or A4 are not included as some of your Optional Units, we recommend you take a look at them in this book to support your learning and development for this unit.

Communicate effectively with your customer.

Communicate effectively with your customer

What you need to know or learn

- How to hold a face-to-face conversation with customers which establishes rapport
- How to give explanations to customers about your organisation's products or services
- How to manage difficult situations

How to hold a face-to-face conversation with customers which establishes rapport

Face-to-face behaviour occurs when your customer can see you and you can see them. Even if you work in a call centre you will still be in situations where this is important, for example, with your colleagues and with your internal customers. This means people have access to all your behaviour patterns. You can be both seen and heard.

In both your personal and work life, you will instantly hit it off with some people. There will be other people whom you warm to over a period of time and there will also be some people whom you simply do not like. In all of these cases you need to develop **rapport** to ensure conversations work. Without rapport there will be no trust. Without trust, your customer service will not be what it should be.

To establish rapport when holding a conversation, it is essential you treat each and every customer as an individual. If you do not, he or she will not feel you respect and value them. This involves you recognising that everyone has different needs. Customers want different things from you, so you will need to adjust the way you behave with each customer.

Holding conversations face to face gives both you and your customer opportunities to create rapport or ruin it very easily! Communication will only be effective when you are aware of the importance of your appearance, body language and behaviour. You need to understand the potential impact of all three areas on your customers.

Appearance

You and your surroundings are clearly visible, so there is perhaps more for you to think about getting right than there might be when speaking on the telephone. Nobody wants to work in dirty surroundings. It shows you and your organisation do not care. Nobody wants to talk to a customer service assistant who does not take care over his or her own personal appearance. Get this wrong and it really does not matter what you say; the customer will have already lost confidence in you and you will not be able to hold a conversation with rapport.

> **Key term**
>
> **Rapport** – a sense of being comfortable with someone, whether or not you know him or her well.

Table 1 gives some suggestions for what you can do to hold a conversation which establishes rapport.

Table 1: Establishing rapport when holding a conversation

Positive behaviour	Potential impact in face-to-face situations
Handshakes – formal situations	• Shows respect and builds confidence. • Not shaking hands in formal situations might create unnecessary distance and lead to a lack of confidence.
Handshakes – informal situations	• Shows you are willing to help. Creates an air of professionalism.
Moving closer to your customer	• Shows interest and caring. • Helps people to hear you in noisy or distracting situations. • Creates an air of privacy.
Facing your customer	• Both you and your customer can see each other properly. • Aids listening. • More formal than sitting next to a customer which some people will feel is too casual. • Nodding your head indicates you are listening.
Eye contact	• Looking directly into your customer's eyes (without staring) is a must. • The conversation will flow because you are showing interest. • Customers will be able to see how you move the little creases that form when your eyes smile. Rapport is created.
Smiling	• You know how *you* feel when someone smiles at you. Used at the right time a smile can make the difference between a conversation going well and one that goes nowhere.
Voice	• Speaking loudly or softly, very quickly or very slowly or just keeping quiet – all these ways of speaking have their place in holding a conversation with rapport. Your voice is very important.
Physical appearance	• Create a professional image. Being clean and tidy is always better than being scruffy, no matter what your job involves.

Establishing rapport when holding a conversation face to face is simply an extension of creating a positive impression.

Table 2 gives some situations and behaviours which have the potential to cause unnecessary problems when talking face to face with customers.

Table 2: Potential barriers to holding an effective conversation

Potentially negative situations	Impact on conversation
Standing when a customer is sitting	• You appear dominant – could be confrontational for your customers. • Acts as a barrier to rapport.
Facing the customer from behind a desk, screen or other barrier	• The barrier will not help the flow of conversation. Your voice may be difficult to hear. Distance is created. • Most customers accept security screens are a fact of life. You will though need to work harder to develop rapport because the screen has the effect of putting a wall between you and your customer.
Making no eye contact	• Customers will read a great deal from your eyes. If you do not make eye contact, you run the risk of being seen as untrustworthy, lacking in confidence or simply uncaring. Conversation will not flow.
Frowning	• Conversation will be stilted. Who wants to talk with someone who appears unhappy or angry?

Portfolio Task
Links to a10.1.1, a10.1.2, a10.1.3, a10.1.5, a10.2.1, a10a, a10b, a10e

Ensure you are observed by your assessor in your face-to-face dealings with customers. If this is not possible, ask for a witness testimony from an appropriate person and seek feedback on:

- how you established rapport

- what went well

- what did not go quite so well.

Discuss with your assessor how your working environment helps or hinders you when dealing face to face with customers.

✔ Checklist – Holding a conversation which establishes rapport when face to face with customers

- Ensure you give the right amount of **eye contact**. If you give too much, you may appear to be staring; too little and you will come across as uninterested.

- **Smile** warmly when it is appropriate for the occasion. But, be genuine. Everyone can see through a smile that is fake.

- Sometimes a **handshake** will be appropriate. If so, make sure it is firm to convey confidence and interest.

- Think about your **posture** and standing up to greet a customer, particularly if you are seeing someone by appointment. Do not invade their personal space, though.

- Do not slouch if you are sitting down. Not only does it look bad, it will also affect the quality of your voice.

- Be clean and tidy and think about your **personal image**. Keep the environment you work in looking professional too.

Portfolio Task
Links to a10c, a10e

Find out whether your organisation has a standard greeting for customers that you should use face to face.

1 Check, by asking a colleague to tell you, that you do sound sincere when using a standard greeting.

2 How can you ensure each time you greet customers that you sound genuine?

3 Your organisation may also have guidelines which include dealing with difficult situations and when it is permissible to remove any security barriers. Find these out now.

4 Write a personal statement which explains your findings.

Using courtesy to build rapport

Being courteous is about combining the right attitudes, behaviour and words. Courtesy is a means of showing you care, that you recognise customers' needs and expectations and that you appreciate them doing business with you and your organisation.

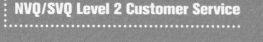
Unit A10 Deal with customers face to face

Figure 1: Look for opportunities to impress your customers.

Often the only difference between your organisation and its competitors is the people it employs. Do not look on being courteous as something extra you need to do. It is the hallmark of a customer service professional and as such an essential part of your toolkit. You provide the distinctive edge that might make the difference between customers using your organisation or going elsewhere.

When holding conversations face to face you will have many opportunities to establish rapport through courteous behaviour. This could range from offering refreshments, a comfortable seat, a reassuring hand and opening doors for your customers.

Take advantage of the many opportunities you will have to impress your customers when dealing with them in person.

✓ Checklist – Using courteous behaviour to hold effective conversations

- Show you want to help and that the customer is not interrupting you.
- Keep your workspace clean, tidy and prepared for your role.
- Show you remember regular customers.
- Speak clearly and slowly.
- Listen carefully.
- Say 'please' and 'thank you' appropriately.
- Make eye contact.
- Do not shout or talk to customers from too far away.
- Be polite by offering practical help before it has been requested.

Key term

Service offer – what the organisation promises to do for its customers

Portfolio Task   Links to a10.1.2, a10.1.3, a10.1.5, a10.1.7, a10.2.1, a10.2.2, a10.2.3, a10a, a10b, a10c, a10e

Think about situations where using courteous behaviour really helped you deliver great customer service. Remember times when you were busy; how did being courteous help?

Write down examples of what you do and include the impact of each action on your customer.

Discuss with your assessor:

1 How the conversation with a customer is helped by your actions.

2 How your organisation's **service offer** to customers is met by what you do.

You will also need to be observed.

The power of your voice

You will clearly not be able to hold an effective conversation if you cannot be heard or are not clear with your choice of words. Look at the advice in **Unit A4 Give customers a positive impression of yourself and your organisation**, pages 95 – 96 on Improving how you sound and Improving what you say.

> ☑ **Checklist – Improving your vocal skills**
>
> • Keep to a steady pace.
>
> • Speed up or slow down to emphasise a point.
>
> • Pronounce any technical words very clearly.
>
> • If you think you are going too fast or too slow – ask!
>
> • Encourage your customers to give you the information you need to help them.

Choosing your words to help the conversation go smoothly

To make your conversation effective, choose your words carefully. It will help your customer have confidence in you. If a customer sees or hears you are confident, he or she will be more likely to trust you.

This trust will only be there if you are genuine and honest in your approach. Emphasising what you can do for customers rather than what you cannot do, will demonstrate you are confident in what you are saying. If you can back this up by saying what specific action you will take, this will continue to instil confidence in your customers.

You will convey messages simply through the words you use. Your choice of words is therefore very important. Words fall into three main categories:

• positive   • neutral   • negative.

Table 3: Positive, neutral and negative words and phrases

Positive	Neutral	Negative
Yes	Perhaps	No
How may I help you?	How can I help?	What do you want?
I	We	They
Definitely	Possibly	Unlikely
I will find out	I'm not sure	I don't know
I will	I'll do my best	I can't do that
Always	Sometimes	Never
I'll be quick	As quickly as I can	I'll do it when I can
I will sort that out	I'll find out who can help	It's not my fault

Jargon

Jargon is guaranteed to confuse a customer. Jargon should be reserved for use between colleagues. Even then, you will need to be sure your colleagues understand you.

Portfolio Task   Links to a10.1.1, a10.1.2, a10.1.4, a10.1.5, a10a

1   Make a list of words, phrases or potential jargon which are routinely used where you work but which you feel might confuse customers.

2   For each one write down an alternative which you have used to help customers' understanding.

Keep this list for your portfolio. Your assessor will consider your choice of words when observing you.

You will also need to make sure your choice of words is appropriate.

You will clearly not be able to hold an effective conversation if you cannot be heard or are not clear with your choice of words.

Establishing and maintaining rapport with people with disabilities

When working through **Unit F2 Follow the rules to deliver customer service**, you will have learnt that there are rules which help to ensure people with disabilities are treated fairly and equally. Whilst we would all hope legislation is not needed for this to happen, unfortunately, many people are unaware how their own behaviour alters simply because they are dealing with a customer with a disability.

Here are some pointers to help build and sustain rapport:

- When talking to a person with a disability, look at and speak directly to that person, rather than through a companion who may be with your customer.

- Relax. Do not be embarrassed if you happen to use accepted common expressions such as 'see you later' that seem to relate to the customer's disability.

- When greeting a person with a severe loss of vision, always identify yourself and others who may be with you, for example, 'I'm Darryl Tweed, and on my right is my colleague Allan Churchward. We are both here to help you decide which item to choose.'

- If a customer with a sight impairment is part of a larger group of people, give a vocal cue by announcing the name of the customer to whom you are speaking. Speak in a normal tone of voice, indicate in advance when you will be moving from one place to another and let it be known when the conversation is at an end.

- Many people find themselves raising their voices to customers who are visually impaired. Do not shout – your customer can hear you!

- Look directly at customers who appear to have a hearing impairment. Speak clearly, naturally and slowly to help those who can lip-read. If you shout, you may appear rude and it will not help as shouting distorts sound. Customers who cannot lip-read will look at your facial expressions and other body language to help understand you.

- If you have technical or complicated information to explain to a customer with a hearing impairment try writing it down.

- If you can, sit in a chair when talking with a person in a wheelchair for more than a few minutes. This means eye contact will be at the same level, which will help with rapport.

- If your customer has a speech impairment, you will need to listen carefully. Show patience and avoid putting words into your customer's mouth; you might make wrong assumptions and it can appear rude. Repeat back your understanding of what your customer has said.

How to give explanations to customers about your organisation's products or services

Irrespective of the nature of your job, you will always need to listen effectively to what customers say to you. If you do not, you won't be able to tell if you are helping them appropriately. Listening provides much useful information, yet good listening skills are not particularly common.

Why it is important to listen

To build trust: People who listen are trusted more than those who do all the talking whilst others are trying to talk too. Building trust will inspire confidence in you and your organisation's products or services.

To achieve credibility: If you listen well, you stand more of a chance of responding well to customers' comments and queries about your products or services.

To show support: Listening reassures people, especially when they are upset, have a problem or are concerned. Listening shows respect and empathy for other people. By listening, you are sending a message that says 'You are important to me. I respect you.' Your customers will feel valued.

To gather information: Listening gives you lots of information that can be useful to help customers both now and in the future. For example, you can use the facts you obtain by listening to match a product or service to customers' needs.

Using active listening to explain products or services

Active listening is all about connecting with your customers' emotions and using body language which will indicate to customers you have heard and understood what has been said. This means you need to listen for total meaning and respond to feelings i.e. listen both for content and also for the underlying emotions.

What we say can have more than one meaning depending on how we say it. For example, if someone says: 'Please help stop this happening again' in a sad voice, it could mean 'I am really unhappy'. But, if said in an angry tone it could mean 'I am going to complain to your boss'.

> **Key term**
>
> **Active listening** – paying careful attention to understand more than the words being spoken.

The real message is in the emotion rather than the words themselves. As a customer service professional you need to respond to the emotional message that lies beneath the words. Using the above example, this would mean saying to Miss Sad:

'I can see you are really upset. I will do everything I can to put this right.'

To Miss Angry, you might say:

'I do apologise for the inconvenience this has caused you. I would like to help you sort this out now if that's OK?'

Non-verbal cues

Remember, not all communication is verbal, so watch for the non-verbal messages too. It is vital you take the time to listen carefully to what the customer has to say even when you are busy. If you do not, misunderstandings can occur and mistakes might be made. Inappropriate products or services could be discussed.

We look more at body language in the next section in this unit, Improve the rapport with your customer through body language, on pages 140 – 150.

Working environment or workspace

Your working environment or workspace could cause a distraction and make it hard for everyone to concentrate. People milling about, and even a picture on a wall or a clock that has stopped can also be distracting. A noisy environment will clearly make voices hard to hear and it is difficult to talk comfortably if it is too hot, too cold or too humid. If you are going to be talking and listening for a while, a comfortable environment can be important; have sufficient comfortable seating available. Do everything you can to minimise environmental distractions including working in a clean and tidy way.

Paying attention

Pay attention to your customers by visibly focusing on them. Face your customer so that non-verbal cues can be spotted by both of you. The trick to giving full attention is to do it from inside your head, not just by moving your body. If you can be truly interested (which is often just a matter of attitude) then your body will happily follow your mind

Managing your reactions

Manage your reactions by being careful how you react to what your customer says. It is easy to be put off by someone who shows a marked lack of interest or who does not seem to understand what they are saying. Pause before you dive into a response. Think about what you would say and the effect that it would have. Consider if this is what you want to achieve.

Figure 2: Active listening means you'll find out what the customer really wants.

> ☑ **Checklist – Active listening skills**
>
> - Make your working environment as comfortable as possible for customers.
>
> - Minimise noise and distractions.
>
> - Give your customer your full attention.
>
> - Manage your reactions.
>
> - Confirm you have understood by nodding or using phrases like 'I see', 'I understand', 'oh yes', and 'OK'.
>
> - If you do not understand, say so by asking for clarification — e.g. 'Could you tell me a little more about that?', 'Do you mean abc or xyz?'
>
> Remember to read your customers' emotions as well as listening to the words they say.

Check for understanding

When explaining your organisation's products or services to customers you should ask questions to check for understanding.

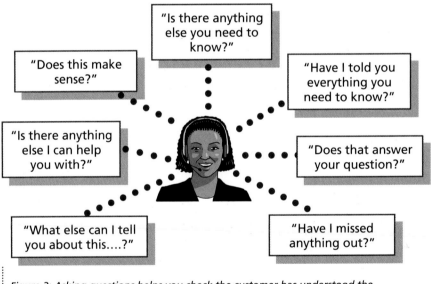

Figure 3: Asking questions helps you check the customer has understood the information you've given.

Explaining *why* you have said something also helps to make sure a customer has understood complicated information. For example, if you were helping a customer understand how to fill out a form to open a savings account, you could explain that Part A needs to be completed first to ensure the customer has the necessary proof of identity.

You can also use any supporting literature, information leaflets etc. that your organisation provides to help you explain things to customers. If a product is involved, perhaps you can have it with you and give a demonstration to support your explanation.

Unit A10 Deal with customers face to face

> ☑️ **Checklist – Giving explanations**
>
> • Give customers a full and clear explanation.
>
> • Act with confidence to inspire your customers.
>
> • Talk in terms of benefits rather than features.
>
> • Avoid jargon and technical terms.
>
> • Do not make assumptions that customers will automatically understand.
>
> • Ask questions to check for understanding.
>
> • Clarify any points where necessary.
>
> • Use supporting literature, information leaflets.
>
> • Agree on the way forward.

How to answer customer questions about your organisation's products or services

Too much or too little information could leave your customer feeling confused. What customers want is to leave you feeling their needs have been met. It is even better if you have managed to exceed their expectations.

It is all about identifying each customer's individual needs and then matching your products or services closely to them.

People buy products or services for different reasons – we all have our individual preferences. It is important you identify what your customer needs by asking questions and listening carefully to what you are told. You can then match the best product or service to your customer's needs.

To do this, you will need to know the **features** and **benefits** of your products or services. This will help you to answer simple questions and to give great customer service.

Features describe characteristics, for example,size, colour, shape, speed, accessibility. A benefit describes what the feature will do for a customer. The best explanation you can give to a customer is to talk about both, for example:

> *"Our skirts have elasticated waistbands so it doesn't matter how much you eat at Christmas!"*
>
> *"This chair has a built-in lumbar support to help prevent backache."*
>
> *"We always phone you before arranging delivery to make sure the time is convenient."*
>
> *"This broadband connection is ultra-fast; you will save time."*

When listening to what your customer wants always keep in mind the ten key customer benefits shown in Figure 4.

Key terms

Feature – what a product or service does.

Benefit – how the product or service can help a customer.

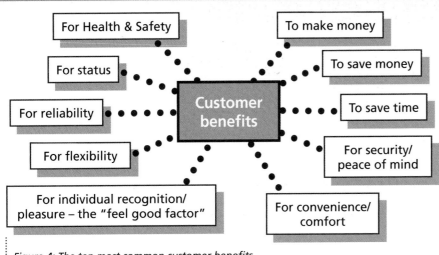

Figure 4: The ten most common customer benefits.

How to manage difficult situations

For the purposes of achieving this unit, you are required to demonstrate you can:

● balance conflicting demands for your attention whilst maintaining rapport with your current customer

● calm down situations when one customer is adversely affecting the customer service enjoyed by other customers.

We are going to concentrate on showing you the skills you need to calm customers down. It is important you also recognise the skills are very useful in a number of other difficult situations. These might include:

● dealing with customers who do not know what they want

● having to say 'no' to customers, that is, when you are unable to meet customers' expectations

● dealing with customers who are affected by people, resources or systems letting you down.

Portfolio Task
Links to a10.1.8, a10c, a10e, a10i

1 Discuss with your assessor two or three situations which occur in your workplace which mean you are face to face with customers who are not calm. Now think about times when you have used your skills to calm customers down. This might include calming an angry customer, an abusive customer or a frightened customer.

2 Describe how you have used any organisational guidelines to deal with these situations.

Applying HEAT to calm dissatisfied customers

There is a technique you can use called HEAT to help with calming down dissatisfied customers.

Hear
Empathise
Apologise
Take ownership.

Hear

In situations where a customer is dissatisfied it will always be important to show you are listening. Be quiet, focus your attention on the customer by not being distracted by what is going on around you both. Most importantly, do not interrupt.

Empathise

After being given the chance to let off steam, the customer will want to know you understand and care. Listen and respond with empathy to acknowledge the customers' feelings (for example, unhappiness, anger, frustration, disappointment). Also acknowledge you understand the facts which have caused the situation to occur. To empathise you will need to:

- acknowledge the customer's feelings

- acknowledge the facts of the situation

- let the customer know you heard him or her

- let the customer know you understand how he or she feels and why he or she is upset.

Apologise

The customer will want to hear you are sorry about what has happened to him or her. Expressing empathy before apologising shows the customer you understand why he or she is not calm. Unless the problem is your fault, you can apologise without accepting blame. You could say 'I am really sorry you feel you were sent the wrong information, or 'I am sorry we are so busy you have had to wait for so long'. However, strike the right balance: apologising too much might make your organisation appear incompetent; admit fault only if it is obvious the organisation is to blame.

Take ownership

Usually some action will be required so if the issue can be fixed on the spot, do so. If it is not something you can do immediately, do let the customer see something has been done. This might mean referring to a supervisor, taking notes or making promises. Your promise might include saying you will let the customer know the outcome so make sure you do follow this up.

✓ **Checklist – Using HEAT to calm customers**

- Hear what your customer is saying by actively listening. Acknowledge what he or she says.

- Empathise: 'I am sure this was upsetting for you to see. It would upset me too.' Put yourself in the customer's shoes.

- Apologise: 'I apologise for the inconvenience our late opening has caused you.'

- Take ownership: 'I am going to speak with my supervisor to get you a refund.' Say what is going to happen. Then do it.

How to behave assertively

It is not just dissatisfaction with service which causes customers to not be calm. There could also be personal problems or fear of a situation (for example, fear of flying or of dentists) which impact upon their behaviour with you. Different customers will react in different ways to the cause of their dissatisfaction or unhappiness. However, there are ways of minimising the impact of their emotions and the effect they have on other customers. This involves you behaving *assertively* and professionally in order to deal with a difficult situation and to stop the situations from getting worse.

When under pressure, humans will literally heat up; faces will turn red, collars will feel tight, the temperature rises until boiling point is reached and an explosion occurs. **Assertive behaviour** means turning the heat down; not just your temperature but your customers' too. You can do this by learning how to be assertive.

Key term

Assertive behaviour – standing up for your rights without violating the rights of your customer.

Assertive behaviour

Some people confuse assertiveness with aggression. Behaving assertively is *not* about being forceful, shouting at customers or doing absolutely anything to get your way. It is about behaving in a calm and professional way to defuse a difficult situation.

To behave in an assertive way you need to:

- remain calm
- listen
- demonstrate that you understand
- consider the consequences for all parties of getting what you want/need
- ask for what you want/need without offending others.

Figure 5: By behaving assertively you can turn down the heat.

How do you react in situations where customers are angry? Which of the behaviours shown in Table 4 do you show?

Table 4: Behaviours when reacting to angry customers.

Do you fight back by attacking?	Do you give in and submit to demands or listen and do nothing?	Do you stand up for yourself and your rights without giving offence?
AGGRESSIVE behaviour	**PASSIVE** behaviour	**ASSERTIVE** behaviour

Notice all these words relate to your *behaviour*. Remember that behaviour breeds behaviour so if you are dealing with an angry customer you may be tempted to react in a similar fashion and become aggressive. What you need to aim for is *assertive behaviour*.

Table 5 illustrates how assertive behaviour differs from aggressive or passive behaviour.

Table 5: How assertive behaviour differs from aggressive or passive behaviour.

Assertive behaviour	Aggressive behaviour	Passive behaviour
Discuss calmly	Use threats	Be humble and apologetic
Listen	Interrupt	Say nothing
Make brief statements	Use 'I' a lot	Ramble and waffle
Ask open questions to seek information	Ignore what the customer wants	Simply accept what the customer wants
Stand up for your rights whilst respecting the customers' rights	Stand up for your rights but violate the customers' rights	Give in and don't stand up for your rights
State your views	Demand acceptance of your views	Fail to state your views
Show you understand the customers' views	Show you are not interested in the customers' views	Show an interest in your customers' views but hide your own
Don't blame; seek the right solution	Blame others	Blame yourself

How to adapt your behaviour to calm customers down

As we have seen, behaviours are expressed in various ways through your voice, body language, your use of eye contact and the way that you express yourself. Table 6 shows how people's voice and body language change depending on whether they are showing assertive, aggressive or passive behaviour.

Table 6: Using voice and body language in an assertive, aggressive or passive manner.

	Assertive behaviour	Aggressive behaviour	Passive behaviour
Voice	Sincere, steady pace, calm	Harsh, loud, shouting	Quiet, flat, dull,
Speech	Fluent, emphasises key words or points	Fluent, abrupt, interrupting, emphasises blame, sarcasm	Hesitant, struggles to find right words
Eye contact	Steady	Stares	Shifting or little direct contact
Facial expression	Open, steady, genuine smile	Rigid, chin out, scowling, eyebrows raised in disbelief, frowning, no smiles or false smile	False smile
Other body language	Head up, hands open	Moving around unnecessarily, thumping fists, pointing fingers	Head down, hands fiddling with things

Portfolio Task

Links to a10.1.7, a10.1.8, a10f, a10g, a10i

1 Over a one-week period, notice how those customers who have experienced difficulties with your organisation's customer service, behave with you. Keep a diary of what happens. Think especially about body language, tone of voice and words used. Use the headings in Table 6 to help you.

2 Discuss with your assessor how their behaviour affected other customers and what you did to calm the situation down.

You will also need to be observed.

The advantages of adopting assertive behaviour

Aggressive and passive behaviours are both automatic. In other words, you are most likely to react to a difficult situation by being aggressive or passive. This is because our bodies naturally react to a stressful situation by wanting to fight back (aggressive behaviour) or run away (passive or submissive behaviour).

You need to *learn* how to be assertive and make a conscious effort to adopt this style of behaviour if you are to make the most of the advantages of dealing with people in an assertive way. The advantages are clear; you will be dealing with people in an open and honest way whilst at the same time showing them you understand.

By adopting an assertive and professional approach you will help to calm the situation down. This will help you deal with those customers who are frustrated, disappointed and angry.

If you can develop the skill of being assertive without being aggressive, you will be able to turn a negative experience into a win—win situation. In other words, you and your organisation win and the customer also wins.

The main advantage for *you* adopting assertive behaviour is: your job will be made much easier if you are assertive during difficult times. This is because you will not be using behaviours which only serve to make a bad situation worse. For example, when you hear someone shout at you, your natural inclination might be to raise your voice back. However, this will mean the shouting continues and everyone comes out of the situation feeling unhappy.

Your own confidence will increase because you will be able to control a difficult situation to ensure that both your customer and yourself come out feeling understood and with a solution which both parties find acceptable.

Checklist – Using assertive behaviour to calm customers down

- Take control by adopting assertive behaviours.
- Remain calm yourself.
- Always listen and acknowledge you have heard the customer.
- Demonstrate that you understand.
- Find solutions without heated arguments.
- Do not blame others.
- Avoid overusing the word 'sorry'.
- Work towards a win—win situation.

✔ Checklist – calming down a difficult situation

- Put yourself in the customer's shoes and remember that emotions will be running high. You will not have long to recover the situation.

- Listen actively.

- Control your tone of voice and body language – do not glare.

- Show some understanding of the situation.

- Show you want to help.

- Ask questions to get to the facts.

- Be factual – do not be tempted to express your own opinions or emotions.

- Summarise the situation.

- Say what you can do.

- Suggest options to your customer.

- Follow things through to completion.

- Check the customer is satisfied.

- If any anger goes beyond your capabilities, get help from somebody in authority.

Improve the rapport with your customer through body language

What you need to know or learn

- How to interpret body language

Key term

Body language – non-verbal signals that we give out and receive when we are communicating with someone.

You will find it useful to look at **Unit A4 Give customers a positive impression of yourself and your organisation** in this book to learn or recap the importance of giving customers a positive impression of yourself and your organisation. Building on the theme of Unit A4, we will now look at **body language** and its impact on customer satisfaction.

Slumped shoulders while you walk, hands in pockets and slouching at your desk are all postures that will contribute to a negative image. Sadly, there is no air-brush technique which is going to help you. Make the effort to use body language effectively and it will make life easier for you and your customer. It will help if you know about the impact of body language on your ability to communicate well with customers.

Body language or, as it is also known, non-verbal communication, is about all the things that people 'say' without using words. This means what you do with your hands, face and other parts of your body also convey messages to your customers. Since many of you will spend much of your working lives communicating with other people, it makes sense to make the most of all your communication skills including body language. This will help to ensure you put across the right messages since words are just one part of the way in which people communicate.

Get your body language wrong and you could be in trouble — customers may misunderstand the true meaning of what you are trying to say. Equally, if you misinterpret your customers' body language, then you too are at risk of misunderstanding what your customer wants and expects.

How to interpret body language

There are six major emotions we all feel from time to time. They are: anger, fear, disgust, sadness, happiness and surprise. Each one of these can be displayed through body language. Body language is often subconscious, that is, we don't realise we are doing it. Our body language can support what we are saying verbally (for example, smiling when giving good news) or it can show that what we are saying is not genuine (for example, frowning when giving good news; this might show we are not really happy with what we are saying).

Figure 6: You cannot please everyone all of the time.

Interpreting body language can be quite complicated and should not be done without considering all the postures, signals and behaviours someone is exhibiting, together with the situation. For example, staring on its own could mean a lot of things, but when combined with a frown, sneer and clenched fists, it is quite likely that the person will be aggressive towards you. You also need to take into account what the person is saying and see the whole context of the situation.

Aggressive body language

We hope that you will not encounter customers who become aggressive. However, it is a fact of life that aggression does sometimes occur, particularly in certain types of work where customers are likely to be under stress. For example, hospitals and doctors' surgeries often display notices which state, 'Aggressive behaviour towards our staff will not be tolerated'.

Aggressive behaviour is often very easy to spot because of the verbal language used and because the body language associated with aggression is very distinctive too. Invading someone's personal space could also be an act of aggression, especially when accompanied by other aggressive signals. Going inside someone's personal space without permission is interpreted as invading their territory. We talk more about personal space on page 149.

Bored body language

Why do customers get bored? Well, it may be because their expectations and questions are not getting answered. If so, boredom could soon turn to frustration and anger. Sometimes, listening to a monotonous tone of voice can be very boring, even if the words give good advice. Speaking in an upbeat manner will help and so will involving the customer more in the conversation.

It is also important to realise when you have said enough to satisfy customers' expectations. You need to spot signs that customers are getting bored, so that you do not go over the same information and waste time by continuing to talk when you have actually said enough.

What to do if your job is repetitive

If you are in a very repetitive job where customers ask you the same things time and time again you might not realise you are giving away the fact that you are bored through your own body language. This also can happen if you go through a spell where you are not busy and are literally waiting for the next customer to turn up. Tapping of feet and gazing around at what is on the wall will make it look like you are bored.

Make sure you focus your attention on your customer to avoid appearing bored and uninterested. Give appropriate eye contact and show you are listening by nodding.

Table 8: Examples of body language showing different attitudes.

Type of behaviour	Examples of body language
Aggressive	• frowns • pursed lips • sneering • snarling • staring • red face • clenched fists • leaning forward • invading personal space
Bored	• looking around the room • looking at your watch • blank face • scratching face • tapping toes or fingers • leaning back in chair • yawning
Closed	• crossed arms (protecting the body) • crossed legs, perhaps twisted around each other • head turning away from customer, perhaps looking down • hand over mouth
Open	• arms open • gesturing with hands whilst speaking • head leaning towards customer • legs not crossed • plenty of eye contact • nodding to show agreement
Relaxed	• steady slow breathing • relaxed arms and hands • hand and arm gestures which are open and smooth • voice relaxed and even • smiling with mouth and eyes • direct eye contact without staring
Deceptive	• twitching • fidgeting • licking lips • false smiles • avoiding eye contact • speaking quickly • hesitating • swearing

Using body language to ensure your customers feel valued

While you are dealing with a customer, you may have others waiting for your attention. This can be awkward — who do you help first? Do you leave your customer or do you ignore the people calling for help? What about all those customers staring at you in the queue behind the customer you are currently dealing with?

Balancing different customers' needs

You need to be able to balance the need to be friendly and efficient with your immediate customer with the needs of people waiting for your attention. You could try using body language to do that. The most important emotion you could try to portray through body language is enthusiasm. If you could achieve that, customers waiting to see you are at least going to know the wait is worth their while. Try looking at the queue briefly, nodding your head to acknowledge you can see what is happening and give eye contact to as many people as possible. After you have done that, return to your customer by giving him or her eye contact and continue your conversation

Dealing with interruptions from colleagues

Dealing with colleagues who are trying to get your attention is slightly different. Customers definitely do not want their time talking with you disrupted by your colleagues.

Unless there is an urgent health and safety issue you should indicate to your colleague you are temporarily unavailable. You do not need words to achieve this. Try holding your hand up with the palm facing outwards and shake your head at the same time to indicate 'no'. Your colleagues should soon get the message.

If your colleagues are genuinely in need of your help, try to give it as soon as customers have been dealt with; remember to go back to colleagues as soon as you can to see what they need from you.

Portfolio Task

Links to a10.2.4, a10.2.5

1   Ask your colleagues and/or your supervisor or team leader to give you some feedback on how you ensure customer service is unaffected when they ask you for help or interrupt you in any way.

2   Now ask for feedback on what happens when you are dealing with several customers who want your attention.

Summarise the feedback you get into a report.

Functional skills

English: Writing

Your report should be structured so as to present the feedback you received in summary format. Think about using headings and sub-headings or some other format which makes it logical for the reader to follow. You may be able to use your report towards evidence for Level 1 Functional English: Writing. Make sure you check for grammar, punctuation and spelling and include an appropriate level of detail.

Working Life

I am Jamal and I work in a beachside café. Last week I noticed a woman come in shortly before we were due to close and she had a broad grin across her face and was looking all around the premises and especially at the photos of the café which were taken in the sixties. We got talking and she was telling me that, as a child she regularly came on holiday here and that she was delighted the café hadn't changed very much. She was just about to order when a regular customer came in and I could feel him staring at me. I decided I ought to deal with him first. The woman seemed surprised; she stopped smiling and took a step back. Shortly afterwards she walked out. I did call out to her but she ignored me.

Ask the expert

Q As keeping the regular customer loyal would be considered a priority, wasn't Jamal right to deal with him first?

A No! Jamal did need to juggle demands for his attention but he should avoid being tricked into doing something by one customer which is likely to upset another customer.

Q How could Jamal use body language to help keep both customers happy?

A Firstly, he needs to learn to interpret body language. When the woman stopped smiling and took a step back, it was a warning sign that all may not be well.

Secondly, he should use his own body language skills. He could acknowledge he had noticed the regular customer by nodding his head and giving eye contact to him. He should then have returned quickly to the customer who was first in the queue.

An alternative would be for Jamal to ask the woman if she minded him quickly dealing with the man as he would love to talk more with her about the café. However, he chose to ensure the regular customer was served first. Neither Jamal nor this customer showed the woman any courtesy. As there are likely to be other places nearby where she could eat and drink, business was lost.

Top tips

Jamal was torn between ensuring the regular customer was kept happy and dealing with the new customer. He allowed himself to be intimidated by a regular customer. Careful use of his own body language skills may well have helped to keep both customers happy. Instead, he allowed one customer's behaviour to disrupt service to other customers.

Always act with confidence. Learn how to interpret body language and then use your own body language in a way which ensures customer satisfaction is achieved.

Although the woman was not a regular customer, she may well have become one in the future. Act with confidence.

Check your knowledge

1 List 4 ways of creating rapport with a customer in a face-to-face situation.

2 Why is eye contact important?

a. It is a health and safety requirement.

b. It enables people to build confidence.

c. It is a legal requirement to show respect.

d. It helps to build and sustain rapport.

3 How can you use a customer's facial expressions to understand how he or she is feeling?

a. By interpreting them together with the words they use.

b. By copying what they do to show respect and courtesy.

c. By asking questions about what he or she is doing.

d. By offering to provide a comfortable space to talk.

4 How does active listening help with delivering great customer service?

a. It enables additional products to be offered.

b. It ensures needs and expectations are met.

c. It ensures queuing is kept to a minimum.

d. It enables colleagues to work efficiently.

5 Describe what HEAT stands for and how you can use it to calm down a situation where a customer is upsetting another customer.

6 Why is personal space important when face to face with a customer?

a. To show respect and courtesy.

b. It is a health and safety matter.

c. To protect confidentiality.

d. To help with giving explanations.

7 How can you balance the needs of one customer with those of another?

a. By speaking quickly and avoiding long conversations.

b. By using teamwork to minimise queues and complaints.

c. By using body language to let all customers know you care.

d. By requesting customers visit outside of the lunch period.

8 Why is assertive behaviour important?

a. The organisation will get what it wants.

b. The customer will always be in control.

c. It helps to achieve a win–win situation.

d. It enables products or services to be sold.

9 Describe what body language a customer might be showing if he or she is unhappy.

10 Describe what body language a customer might be showing if he or she is happy.

Unit B2

Deliver reliable customer service

What you will learn:

- To prepare to deal with your customers
- To give consistent service to customers
- To check customer service delivery

Key term

Customer expectations – what customers think should happen and how they think they should be treated when asking for or receiving customer service.

Internal customer – somebody from the same organisation as the service provider.

External customer – somebody from outside the organisation which is providing him or her with a service or product.

Introduction

This unit is all about how you deliver consistent and reliable customer service. You will need to show you are consistently good with people and can use your organisation's procedures and service systems to help meet and, if possible, exceed **customers' expectations**.

You will prove you are a customer service professional by consistently delivering excellent customer service. You will show that you prepare well to deal with customers; that you deal with different types of customers in different circumstances; and that you check the service you have given is indeed reliable and has met customer expectations. You will be expected to show you can do this time and time again. Your customers include everyone you provide a service to and may be **internal** or **external** to your organisation.

When you deliver reliable customer service you must consistently show you

- prepare to deal with your customers
- give consistent service to customers
- check customer service delivery.

What is meant by 'being reliable'?

Different people will want different things and expect different forms of customer service and reliability from different organisations. Below are some examples of what delivering reliable customer service might include:

- being trustworthy
- keeping promises
- being accurate
- doing things on time

- being efficient
- being professional
- being dependable
- meeting expectations.

All this might sound familiar and, clearly, delivering reliable customer service underpins everything you need to do to be a customer service professional. You might even be thinking you have shown you deliver reliable customer service by meeting the requirements of some of the other units. In particular, you should consider how the mandatory **Unit F1 Communicate using customer service language** and **F2 Follow the rules to deliver customer service** provide you with opportunities to meet the requirements of this unit. It follows that the knowledge and understanding you need to apply in your daily work to provide evidence for other units may also be useful for this unit. In these situations, we refer you to the relevant section in this book, rather than repeat subject matter covered in other units.

You show you are a customer service professional by consistently delivering excellent customer service.

Portfolio Task

Links to b2b

1 Think back to a recent transaction you were involved in as a customer. Perhaps booking a holiday, doing the weekly shop, having the car serviced...

What did you expect from your service provider in terms of reliability?

2 Now think about your own organisation.

a. Make a list of the things you think your customers expect from you and your organisation in terms of customer service and reliability. How does this compare with what you personally expect from people and organisations you do business with?

b. What do you do to ensure you are providing a reliable service to customers?

c. How does your organisation support you in providing reliable customer service?

3 Discuss your responses to these questions with your assessor.

Functional skills

English: Speaking, listening and communication
If you clearly discuss your findings with your assessor using appropriate language, you may be able to count this as evidence towards Level 1 Functional English: Speaking, listening and communication.

If you can truly consider yourself to be a reliable person, your career can only benefit. You will be seen as someone who always performs well and who can be depended on by both customers and colleagues to do a good job. It will make your working life a great deal easier too, because you will get things right at the first time of asking. The **customer experience** will be a good one.

Prepare to deal with your customers

Key terms

Customer experience – what a customer feels and remembers about their dealings with you.

Preparation for service – being ready and able to achieve customer satisfaction before dealing with customers.

What you need to know and learn

- What your organisation's procedures and systems are for delivering customer service
- How to develop your knowledge of your organisation's services or products
- What preparation you need to do to help you deal with customers
- What you need to consider for health and safety in your area of work.

Preparation for service is everything. You cannot even begin to deliver reliable customer service if you have not got yourself ready and made sure you have all the basic requirements in place. If you do all the correct preparations before you deal with customers, it not only helps you deliver efficient, reliable consistent service, but also ensures that your experience of your job is enjoyable and rewarding.

This includes making sure:

- your product or service knowledge is up-to-date
- any equipment you use is in good and safe working order
- your working environment creates the right impression
- you have got everything ready before you deal with your customers
- you know your organisation's requirements for health and safety in your area of work.

What your organisation's procedures and systems are for delivering customer service

Along with needing to know all about your organisation's services and products is the need for you to know and understand what procedures and systems your organisation has in place to help you deliver reliable customer service. Procedures exist to help you and your customers know what to expect. They assist everyone by stating what happens, when it happens and how it should happen.

Organisations will have many systems and procedures in place, including:

- feedback systems
- complaints procedures
- service standards
- emergency procedures.

Please refer to **Unit F2 Follow the rules to deliver customer service**, and the section entitled Follow your organisation's customer service practices and procedures, on pages 37 – 44.

Portfolio Task

Links to b2b

1   Find out now about the procedures and systems your organisation has in place in relation to:

 a. customer feedback

 b. complaints handling

 c. service standards

 d. emergency procedures

 e. any other system or procedure that affects your job.

2   Write a personal statement (report) which shows the part you play in following company procedures. Ensure you include real life examples of where and when you have used procedures and systems.

Functional skills

English: Writing

You may be able to use your written report as evidence towards Level 1 Functional English: Writing. Make sure you check for grammar, punctuation and spelling and include an appropriate level of detail. Think carefully about the format of your report and ensure it is presented in a logical format.

How to develop your knowledge of your organisation's services or products

You have already started to look at your organisation's services and products when working through mandatory unit **F1 Communicate using customer service language**. Refresh yourself on the services or products applicable to your role by referring to the section entitled *What services or products your organisation provides*, see pages 22 – 24.

Think how knowing all about services and products links into delivering reliable customer service. What would happen if you went to the supermarket and found the shelves empty, or phoned a call centre and were told the wrong information or went to the pharmacy and were given somebody else's prescription? Being unreliable can sometimes be dangerous.

Links to b2.1.1, b2a

Portfolio Task

Complete these sentences on a separate piece of paper and keep it for your portfolio.

1 It is important to keep my service or service knowledge up to date because…

2 The risks associated with giving customers incorrect service or product information are…

3 The impact on my organisation of giving out wrong service or product information is…

4 I know I give out reliable service or product information because I make sure I…

Keeping your product or service knowledge up to date

The technology industry is one of the fastest-moving around. Whether it be TVs, audio equipment or mobile phone technology, as soon as one new product or service is introduced it goes out of date!

However, you do not need to be working with technology to need to keep yourself up to speed with changes; all organisations look to improve what they offer. They need to do this to keep ahead of the competition and to provide variety for their customers. Other changes may occur to comply with legislation, or for safety reasons. So, once you have tracked down the most suitable source of information available to you, it is vital that you regularly keep up-to-date with changes your organisation might make to the service or product.

It will help you if you keep your own store of information about key products or services. Keep everything in one place, for example, in a binder, on your hard drive or simply in the top drawer. If it is all in one easily accessible place you can refer to it often, keep it up to date and know that you can do your work with the answers easily available to you.

This information store will also help you to keep on top of any new products or services your organisation introduces. Let's call this *My Product or Service Guide*. You will be able to compare what is in your own guide with your organisation's information.

Figure 1: It is important to keep product or service knowledge up to date.

You need to make sure you are always up to date so the information you give to customers is accurate. Customers must be able to trust what you tell them! If you are not up to date you will not be giving a reliable service.

✔ Checklist – Keeping your service or product knowledge up to date

- Use your own Service or Product Guide.
- Regularly check your information is current.
- Look for updates on company bulletins/newsletters/intranet.
- Ask colleagues.
- Listen to customer comments.

- Think about things you have read in the press or seen on TV and how they might affect the services or products you deal with.
- Check if any new or additional products or services have been introduced.
- Always look for ways to improve your knowledge of products or services.

Portfolio Task

Links to b2.1.1, b2a

1 Find out what procedures your organisation has for advising staff of changes to services or products. What do you need to do to ensure your knowledge is kept up to date? Write a personal statement covering this.

2 Thinking about your organisation's own services or products, collect copies of adverts, articles from newspapers, in-house magazines, emails and the intranet/Internet. Do this for a month or so and then read them to see how products or services have changed.

Check back in your own Services and Products Guide to see if you have already noticed any changes. If necessary, make any amendments.

3 Keep your personal statement for your portfolio and discuss with your assessor how you use your guide.

Functional skills

English: Reading and Speaking, listening and communication

You will need to do some reading both of your own Services and Products Guide and also other service and product information sources. You will therefore need to read and understand a variety of texts. You may be able to count this as evidence towards Level 1 Functional English: Reading. If you then use this information as a basis of discussion with your assessor, you may be able to count this as evidence towards Level 1 Functional English: Speaking, listening and communication.

What preparation you need to do to help you deal with customers

Your preparation should include making sure that:

- any equipment you use is in good and safe working order
- your working environment creates the right impression
- you have got everything ready before you deal with your customers.

Equipment – making sure it is reliable and safe

Remember, you want to deliver reliable customer service. This is an impossible task if the equipment you use lets you down. It must be in good and safe working order. Equipment includes everything you need to deliver customer service. For example, the photocopier, vehicles, computers, point of sale machines, kitchen equipment, answerphone, stationery, etc.

To ensure that your equipment is in good and safe working order, you must check it regularly and before you deal with a customer. In other words, you must *prepare* it so that a customer does not see or hear you trying to sort something out whilst he or she is waiting for you. That is intensely frustrating for a customer and also could cause an unnecessary delay or even be dangerous. It creates the wrong impression too and your customer will soon lose confidence in you and your organisation.

You do not necessarily have to perform a detailed check every day. That does not mean you should not check out any essential items of equipment. Think about the types of equipment you use and work out a reasonable timescale for carrying out checks. Carry out daily checks of any equipment you simply cannot be without. A quick look over the equipment may be all that is needed.

Portfolio Task   Links to b2.1.3

1   Make a list of the types of equipment you deal with.

2   Create a diary note to remind you to check the equipment is in good and safe working order.

Keep these for your portfolio.

Your work area and its impact

In **Unit A4 Give customers a positive impression of yourself and your organisation** we looked at how you can give the right impression through the image you create. This image will be dramatically affected for good or for bad by the conditions you work in and what your work area looks like. Does being neat matter? Yes, it does, especially if your customers can see your work area. Customers often make decisions about how professional and reliable you are by looking at the conditions in which you work.

Neatness is not only about your appearance, but also about having an organised work area. Even if you are dealing with a customer on the phone or over the Internet, you will find that you cannot find things easily if your desk or work area is untidy. In most cases, being untidy means you are disorganised. This will make you inefficient and causes delays!

Working surrounded by clutter could add to the amount of time you take to do even routine tasks. Taking the time now to clean out your desk, sort out any paperwork and organise your filing system will help you to deliver reliable customer service and reduce your stress levels.

For those of you who use a desk, you might like to consider operating a clear desk policy. A clear desk policy means just that — keeping your desk clear.

Figure 2: In most cases being untidy means you are disorganised.

You need to store away files, papers and IT software when not in use in order to maintain a clean and tidy working environment. This means putting things away when you are away from your desk for a long period of time and at the end of your working day. Doing this also has the advantage of protecting information and office equipment from unauthorised access, loss or damage.

It may help you to have a daily checklist to refer to when preparing to deliver service. We have provided an example here in Table 1.

If you check these issues out you can be sure you are creating the right image to welcome customers in a warm and caring manner. In doing this you will also be well on the way to delivering reliable customer service.

Remember that your job role may not require you to water the plants, or make sure all the computers in the organisation are working, but it is important to be aware of your whole workspace and make sure that you maintain your personal area, and report problems in general areas.

If you are part of a team – you all need to be proud of your workspace; this is all part of delivering professional and reliable customer service.

Table 1: A daily checklist

Area to be checked	Check:	Action needed
Car park	• litter free • no obstacles to easy parking	
Shopfront/building frontage	• no litter in doorway • plants in hanging baskets/window boxes OK • windows are clean	
Entrance	• steps are clean and clear • no litter • doormats are clean	
Signage	• signs are in place • wording is clear and legible	
Customer space	• plants (artificial or real) are clean and healthy • furniture is in a good state of repair • leaflet dispensers etc. are well stocked and up to date • work surfaces, fittings, toilets, bins, all clean • lighting works • heating and ventilation works • cupboard doors/drawers are shut • equipment is in good and safe working order • clocks show the right time	
My workspace	• product and service information is well stocked and up to date • stationery tidy replenished • work area is clean and tidy • equipment is in good and safe working order • internal contact list is up to date	

Portfolio Task

Links to b2.1.2, b2.1.3

1 In the context of your working environment, complete these sentences on a separate piece of paper and keep it for your portfolio.

My work area can be kept tidy by...

The things I need to do to make my work area safe for my customers to use are...

For my colleagues to be safe, I should make sure...

The impact and benefit of being well organised in my working environment is...

2 Create your own daily checklist based on Table 1, use it and keep it for your portfolio.

What you need to consider for health and safety in your area of work

The basis of British health and safety law is the **Health & Safety at Work Act 1974.** Please remind yourself of the impact of this legislation on your ability to deliver reliable customer service by referring to pages 48 – 51 in **Unit F2 Follow the rules to deliver customer service**.

Other regulations you should remind yourself about include:

● **Workplace (Health, Safety and Welfare) Regulations 1992** cover a wide range of health and safety issues such as ventilation, heating, lighting, workstations, seating and welfare facilities.

● **Manual Handling Operations Regulations 1992** which deal with the manual handling of equipment, stocks and materials. Where reasonably practicable an employer should avoid the need for his or her employees to undertake manual handling involving risk of injury.

● **Personal Protective Equipment at Work Regulations 1992** which deal with protective clothing or equipment which must be worn or held by an employee to protect against health and safety risks.

● **Health and Safety (Display Screen Equipment) Regulations 1992** introduced measures to prevent repetitive strain injury, fatigue and eye problems in the use of technological equipment. This includes eyesight tests on request, breaks from using the equipment and provision of health and safety information about the equipment to the employee.

You also need to know about health and safety issues that apply if your customer has an accident whilst with you. Something as simple as someone spilling a cup of hot tea can escalate into a full-blown emergency if you do not know what emergency procedures are in place to help you.

For more information, refer to the section on emergency procedures on pages 44 – 46 in **Unit F2 Follow the rules to deliver customer service**.

Key term

Health & Safety at Work Act 1974 – covers the responsibilities employers have to employees and also to customers who are on their premises.

Portfolio Task

Links to b2.1.2, b2.1.3, b2b

Write a personal statement for your portfolio which details what you have done recently to ensure the area in which you work is tidy, safe and organised efficiently. Use the questions below to help you.

1 Take a look at your working area.

   a. Is it neat and clean?

   b. Have you put away everything that you are not using at the moment?

   c. Are there electrical cables running all over the floor that you or your customers might trip over?

   d. Are there tears in the carpet someone might get their foot caught in?

   e. Have you put chairs or other pieces of equipment in places which make it difficult for customers to get access?

   f. What does your organisation expect you to do to ensure your working area is tidy, safe and organised efficiently?

   g. What can you do to improve the safety of your workplace?

   h. What impression do customers get from your workplace?

   i. What about colleagues? Have they made any comments?

2 Find out what your organisation's guidelines are for keeping your work area tidy, safe and organised. Show in your report how you make sure you follow these guidelines.

3 Ask an appropriate person to give you a witness testimony about how you keep your workspace tidy, safe and organised effectively.

4 Make sure your assessor observes you dealing with customers in your workspace.

Give consistent service to customers

What you need to know and learn

- What you need to do to ensure you keep your promises to customers
- What to do if unforeseen circumstances affect promises made to customers
- How to manage situations where your customers' needs or expectations change
- How to help customers you are unable to deal with personally

What you need to do to ensure you keep your promises to customers

We have said that delivering reliable customer service means not just doing so every now and then, but on a consistent basis no matter what is happening around you.

This will include giving excellent service during situations when:

- the unexpected happens
- customers change their minds
- you are personally unable to help
- you are having a quiet time in your job
- you are having a busy time in your job
- people, systems or resources let you down.

Why it is important to keep your promises

In a report commissioned in 2001 by the **Institute of Customer Service** excellence was summed up in one key phrase:

'excellent service organisations are those that are easy to do business with'

This is still the case today. You have your part to play in making it easy for the customer by **keeping your promises**. Take a look at Table 2 which shows some of the comments made by members of the public in the report *Service Excellence = Reputation = Profit*.

Table 2: Comments about service excellence extracted from Service Excellence = Reputation = Profit, Institute of Customer Service, 2001.

Excellent Service	Poor Service
They deliver the promise	**They don't do what they said**
They do what they said	They didn't have it/do it; it was wrong
They don't let you down	You can't get through
If you ask them to do it, it just happens	They let me down
They make it personal	**They are so impersonal**
They give you the time	There was no eye contact
They make eye contact and smile and they mean it	They didn't even acknowledge me
They treat me like an individual	It was plastic service
They go the extra mile	**They don't make any effort**
It's the little touches	They ignored us
They went out of their way	They didn't listen
They explain things	They don't care
They call you back, I didn't have to chase them	The customer is just a problem to them
They deal well with problems	**They don't deal with the problem**
It was quick and easy	They denied responsibility
They took responsibility	They gave me the runaround
They believed me	I ring them every month and each time I have to tell them the whole story

This report was followed up with a further Institute of Customer Service study in 2003 (*Delivering Service Excellence: The View from the Front Line*) which sought the views of front-line employees working in five organisations that had a reputation for delivering excellent customer service. The organisations were First Direct, the RAC, Shangri-La Hotels, Singapore Airlines and Tesco.

To these employees, service excellence meant helping people, customers and colleagues. They felt delivering excellent service was mainly about delivering the organisation's promise and dealing well with complaints. They felt *outstanding* service is delivered by genuinely committed and caring front-line employees.

From reading the table and thinking about the views above you should see that delivering reliable customer service is all about keeping your promises to customers at the same time as living up to the promise made by your organisation.

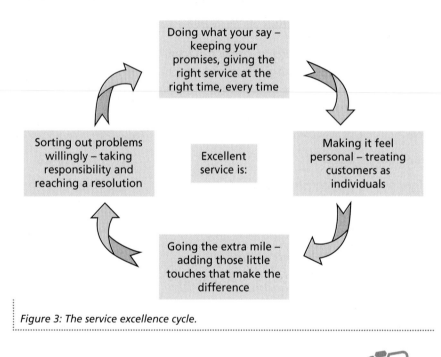

Figure 3: The service excellence cycle.

Portfolio Task   Links to b2b

In the context of your own role, write a personal statement about how you fulfil each of the stages of excellent service.

1 Include specific examples of when you have done this.

2 How does this help you to be reliable?

3 What support does your organisation give you by way of systems and procedures to help you to deliver reliable customer service?

Making realistic promises

One of the biggest customer frustrations is being bounced around an organisation because someone somewhere has not kept a promise to call the customer back. The poor customer has to call the organisation themselves and then ends up getting their call transferred around various departments trying to be connected to the original person who failed to keep a promise.

To ensure you keep your promises you need to be *realistic* about what you are saying you will do. Being realistic means not promising you will do something if you know for sure it will never happen. For example, imagine a customer wants the outside of their house painted. There would be no point in a decorator promising to do it in September, if he or she knows all the jobs already booked will not be finished by then.

One solution would be for the decorator to provisionally book a date which is more realistic but to add that he or she will phone with updates on timescales. Customers prefer to be told the truth even if it is not always what they had hoped for.

Figure 4: Make sure your promises are realistic.

Doing what you say you will

A frequent customer complaint is the one which follows a promise to call a customer back not being met. So make sure you do phone, even if there is no new information to tell a customer. It will let the customer know he or she is not forgotten.

Similarly, if you promise you will send out information to **inform a customer** 'in the post tonight' then do it. Your customer will be watching out for it and will feel disappointed and let down if the information does not arrive.

If you promise to pass information on to someone else, make sure you do. Keep a notepad handy for writing reminders to yourself. It is all too easy to move on to dealing with the next customer and forget all about passing on the message. A written reminder will jog your memory.

Remember – Only make promises you can keep.

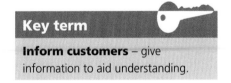

Key term

Inform customers – give information to aid understanding.

Portfolio Task Links to b2.2.1, b2.2.3, b2b

1 If appropriate to your role, check what your organisation's policy is in connection with customer orders:

   a. Are you expected to keep the customer informed?

   b. Are you expected to give the customer information on how he or she might track progress of an order?

   c. Does technology help support a customer who wishes to track an order?

2 Write a personal statement which shows, with specific examples, how you follow your organisation's procedures and systems to help keep promises and keep your customers informed. Ensure you describe why your customer service promises were realistic.

Ask an appropriate person for a witness testimony which supports your personal statement.

Balancing the needs of the customer and your organisation

One way you can balance the needs of your customer and your organisation is to **under-promise** and **over-deliver**.

You under-promise when you advise a customer you will do something in the knowledge you should be able to improve on what you promise. For instance, if you know you can get a customer a product within a week, you might tell him or her it will be delivered in two weeks. That way, if something goes wrong you are covered and the customer is not disappointed. If it turns up within a week, then the customer will be delighted about the early delivery.

By under-promising you are creating an opportunity to over-deliver. For instance, if you promise to arrange to phone a customer within the next three days, he or she may be pleasantly surprised if you are able to get back to them tomorrow.

You should never promise or raise a strong expectation for anything unless you are virtually certain you can meet the expectation. By keeping your promises and your commitments to customers you will be helping to build trust and loyalty between the customer and your organisation. Customer loyalty means customers will come back for more!

Key terms

Under-promise – promising a particular level of service while knowing you will deliver more than that.

Over-deliver – delivering a better service than you have promised.

Portfolio Task Links to b2.2.2

Refer back to your personal statement and the witness testimonies you obtained about keeping promises. Decide which ones involved you balancing the needs of the customer with your organisation.

Now obtain witness testimonies which describe how you did this.

What to do if unforeseen circumstances affect promises made to customers

Sometimes despite all your best intentions and all your planning, things can go wrong. In these situations, it is very important to use your initiative. You will often need to use your initiative to make extra efforts to keep your promises to your customers.

You might have to use your initiative because something unexpected has happened and a commitment you made in good faith can no longer be fulfilled. For example, if you have to cancel an appointment, make changes to a colour or supply a different product to the one that was requested, tell the customer about the unexpected change and offer him or her an alternative solution.

Some typical problems

There may be a combination of reasons (people, systems, resources) for a promise not being met. Figure 5 shows some typical problems that can impact greatly on an organisation's ability to deliver reliable customer service. In general, they are unforeseen situations. However, there is usually a hint of trouble that might occur if you keep your eyes and ears open. So try to be aware of what is happening nationally and locally by listening to the news and to what people around you are saying.

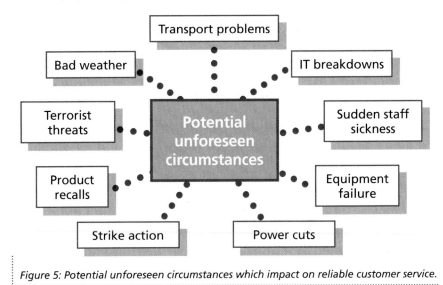

Figure 5: Potential unforeseen circumstances which impact on reliable customer service.

Portfolio Task

Links to b2b

In your own working environment, make a list of the types of unforeseen circumstances which have occurred in the past.

- How does your organisation use its systems and procedures to maintain reliable customer service despite the unexpected happening?

- What is your own role in this?

Write a personal statement for your portfolio.

✓ Checklist – Keeping your promises

- Make realistic customer service promises.

- Offer timescales you know are achievable.

- Only say that someone else (e.g. in another department) will do something if you are sure they will be able to carry out your promise.

- Accept responsibility – do not blame company policy, other people or equipment.

- Return all phone calls when you say you will.

- Be organised.

- Do not over-promise.

- Do what you say you will do.

- Keep your service or product knowledge up to date.

What to do when you cannot keep your promises

Figure 6 shows you what you should be considering when dealing with customers in situations where you are unable to keep your promises. It will depend on the situation you are in as to whether all the steps are relevant at any one time. If you are unable to keep a promise due to something unexpected happening, there is a stronger possibility your customer might be upset and so remaining positive will be crucial.

Going back to the scenarios in the portfolio task, imagine yourself as the customer service practitioner. Here are some suggestions for what you could do to keep the customer informed. Remember that solving problems does not mean laying blame, but it is about finding the best possible solution that ensures the customer is happy. This always involves keeping customers informed by telling the truth.

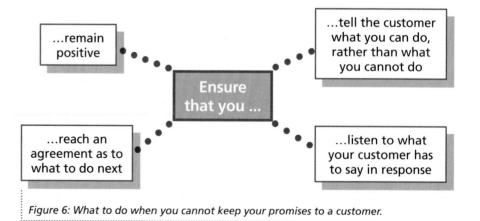

Figure 6: What to do when you cannot keep your promises to a customer.

Portfolio Task

Links to b2.2.4, b2b

1 Put yourself in the shoes of the customers in the following examples. How would you feel in each situation if nobody had bothered to update you on what was happening? Think about the emotions you might feel, for example, angry, sad, disappointed, upset, furious, frustrated. Write a personal statement about this.

   a. It is 10.00 a.m. and you are sitting in the doctor's surgery for a 9.30 a.m. appointment.

   b. You are promised information about a holiday – a coach tour around Scotland. It was meant to be sent to you in the post that same day. A week later it still has not arrived.

   c. The answerphone system tells you *'your call is of value to us....please hold the line. We will get to you shortly.'* You have been holding for 10 minutes.

   d. The dry cleaning is not ready when you go to pick it up.

   e. You have arranged to meet your solicitor Mr X to discuss making a will. You are seen by his assistant, Mr Y.

   f. The supermarket promises there will only ever be one person queuing at each till. There are three people in the queue in front of you.

2 Now think about recent situations you have been involved in at work where the unexpected happened. Write a personal statement for your portfolio.

   a. What happened to your customers?

   b. How did you cope?

   c. How did your customers react?

   d. What organisational systems or procedures did you use to inform your customers about promises you were unable to keep due to unforeseen circumstances?

3 Ask an appropriate person to provide you with a witness testimony about situations where you have needed to inform your customers that a promise you have made cannot be kept due to unforeseen circumstances.

Functional skills

English: Reading and Writing

If you answer the questions in the task in writing, you will have an opportunity to identify a suitable response to the text. This may count as evidence towards Level 1 Functional English: Reading. Your written responses should include sufficient detail to show you have understood the questions and you will need to check them for spelling, grammar and punctuation. Print a copy of your responses as this may count as evidence towards Level 1 Functional English: Writing.

The doctor's surgery – you are the receptionist

Here we have a situation where a customer has arrived expecting to see his or her doctor at a specified time. The appointment time has not been met; perhaps because the doctor has been called out or simply because other people have taken a long time with the doctor.

The appointments system, which states each customer gets ten minutes, has let you down. It is not your fault. However, keeping the customer advised of progress rather than just letting him or her sit there wondering what is happening will show you care.

The travel agency – you are the customer services assistant

In response to a telephone request, you have promised to send out information about a Scottish tour in the post. Later that day you realise this particular tour has been very popular; there are no more brochures and new ones will not arrive until after the weekend. A quick phone call to the customer will keep him or her interested and possibly keep the business within your travel agency.

In this case, resources have let you down. You could tell an appropriate person the Scottish tour is proving very popular so that it does not happen again.

The call centre – you are the customer service agent

There is little you can do here to help customers who have been kept waiting in a telephone queue. If you and your colleagues are answering calls efficiently that is probably the best you can do. The type of answerphone system that keeps customers on hold in a queue is often very annoying to customers, so when they do get to talk to you they might not be in the best of moods.

Here the system has let you down. Empathise with the customer and ensure you sound genuine.

The dry cleaners – you are the shop assistant

There is a delay in getting a customer's dry cleaning ready when promised. You are unable to ring the customer because you only have their name and no contact details.

Here, again, the system has let you down. You could suggest to the shop manager that you take a contact telephone number for each customer when they drop off their cleaning.

The solicitors – you are Mr Y

In this scenario, it would have been best if Mr X had told his customer he could no longer keep the appointment due to unforeseen circumstances. He could then check to see if the customer was happy to see Mr Y or whether an alternative date and time should be arranged.

If Mr Y (you) steps in without the customer being aware of the situation, there is potential for a great deal of dissatisfaction.

Here it is people who have let you down. Mr Y (not to mention the customer) has been let down by Mr X – a clear example of not working well with colleagues. Ask for an informal chat with Mr X to stop the same thing happening again.

The supermarket – you are the check-out assistant

In this scenario, the supermarket has promoted itself as having very short queues. This type of very broad promise is often hard to deliver consistently in practice. For example, if a number of assistants are off sick or, at peak times such as the run-up to Christmas, there may simply not be enough checkouts to cope even if they are fully staffed. As just one of many checkout assistants you need to be aware of the impact of this promise on your customers' expectations and deal with this appropriately.

Here, systems and resources have let you down. What would you do in this situation?

How to manage situations where your customers' needs or expectations change

It is not only you or your organisation that may initiate a change in circumstances. Sometimes a customer's needs or expectations may change for a number of reasons. Figure 7 shows some reasons why this might happen.

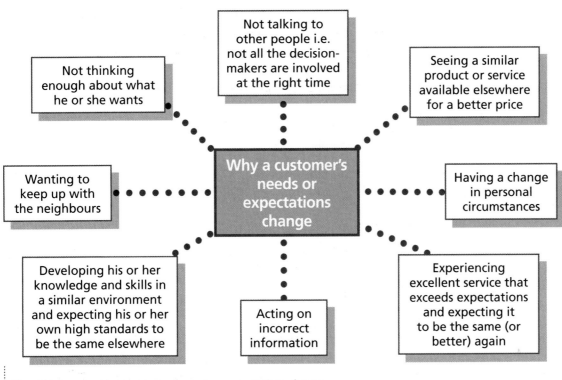

Figure 7: Reasons why a customer's needs or expectations change.

There are so many different reasons why people have a change of mind and so the impact on you will vary with each situation. It is very important that you remain calm when a change of mind occurs. It would be very easy to lose patience having spent some time with a customer who seems to have made a decision and then suddenly starts all over again. Think about shoe shop assistants and the amount of patience needed to help customers get exactly the right pair of shoes in the right colour and size!

You clearly need to be very patient. Take a deep breath and remind yourself that the next customer is unlikely to take so long to make up his or her mind.

In situations where a decision seems to be a long time coming, just tell yourself it's very important your customer makes the right decision. If he or she does not, there is an increased chance of a dissatisfied customer and possibly even a complaint.

Figure 8: Customers sometimes take a long time to make up their mind.

It is easier to adjust your service if a customer tells you of a change of mind. In these situations you would need to check your understanding of what is happening and seek clarification as to what the customer requires.

On other occasions the customer may not tell you directly what is wrong, but you may pick up clues from their body language that all is not well. For example, they may be fidgeting or rubbing their eyebrows. Do not be afraid to ask questions to clarify what a customer wants. For example:

'Is that O.K?'

'You don't seem very sure about that one? Can I get you something else?'

'What about me looking elsewhere for you?'

'Have you changed your mind about that?'

'How else might I help you come to a decision?'

Portfolio Task

Links to b2.2.5

1 Think about a time when you last changed your mind about something that involved customer service.

   a. How did the service provider know your needs or expectations had changed?

   b. How did the service provider react?

   c. What did you do to get what you wanted?

   d. How satisfied were you with the service you received following a change of mind?

2 Using your thoughts about what happened to you, think back to times when you recently dealt with customers whose needs or expectations changed. Write a personal statement and obtain witness testimonies which cover:

   a. How you spotted that the customers' needs or expectations changed – what did the customers do or say?

   b. How you adapted your service to meet their new requirements.

How to help customers you are unable to deal with personally

Luckily, you are not expected to know absolutely everything about your organisation's service or products especially those which are outside your area of responsibility. Customers know that too and they will not expect you to be able to help on every occasion. However, in cases where you are not the right person, customers will expect you to know who can help. They will also expect you to hand them over in a professional way. This may be to another person or perhaps to another organisation.

Reasons you may not be able to help

There are many reasons why you might be unable to help, as you can see in Figure 9.

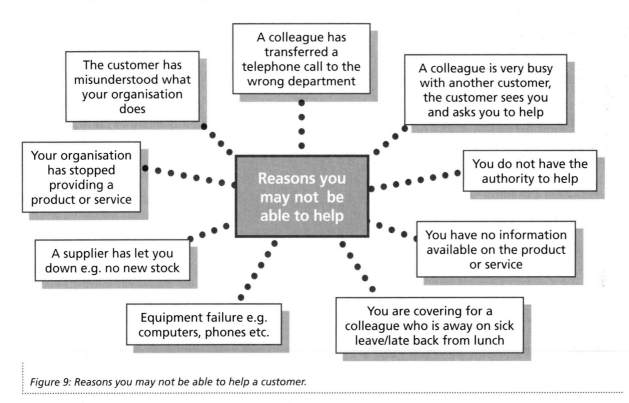

Figure 9: Reasons you may not be able to help a customer.

Portfolio Task

Links to b2.2.6, b2b

Use these questions to write a personal statement and obtain witness testimonies about your behaviour and actions in situations where you have needed to pass customers on to another person or organisation.

1 Think about times when you have been unable to help customers.

- Was this because of something a colleague has done?

- Was this because of something your organisation has done?

- Was it connected with the limits of your own authority?

- Was it because you did not have the necessary information?

2 What did you do?

Steps to take to ensure that you can help

We all know that the unexpected can happen at any time. Just when you thought everything was 'safe' something happens to make you jump. So that you can help the customer in the most effective way possible you need to be prepared for all eventualities.

● Make sure you understand the roles and responsibilities of other people in your organisation. You do not need to know what everyone does — just those who deal with issues, products or services that are associated with your own line of work. This means you can pass customers on to the right person and you will not be bouncing people around your organisation.

● Know where to get easy access to information that may provide you with the right answers in order to help customers.

● Use your listening and questioning skills to find out what it is the customer wants.

● Gather together any information you need to ensure your customers get a better experience than you gave to customers on earlier occasions when you were personally unable to help. This could include, contacts for people in other parts of your organisation, names and addresses of other organisations, local community advice centres etc. This will help you deal with things in a more organised way next time.

● Find out from your manager when you need to seek agreement with or permission from others to help a customer.

✓ Checklist – Helping customers you personally cannot deal with

- Tell the customer what you can do, not what you cannot do.
- Tell the customer what you are doing.
- Keep the customer informed of progress.
- Know who to go to for help.
- Know how to operate the telephone system to transfer a call.
- Keep up-to-date telephone contact lists.
- Remain positive and confident.
- Where necessary, apologise for any delay.
- Record the customer's details/needs/expectations.

Referring customers to other organisations

If your organisation is unable to help a customer, you can often help by pointing the customer in the direction of an organisation that can. This may be a case of saying, 'We don't stock that; however the corner shop will have it', or referring a customer to a more specialist organisation who deal uniquely with what is required.

For example, you may be a landscape gardener specialising in cottage gardens. However, if a customer is expecting a Japanese themed garden you might think you are not the best person for the job. So you might recommend another gardener who you know specialises in this type of garden. In this instance, you would be referring a customer to a competitor.

In both cases, whilst you are not obtaining the business yourself, you are showing that you want to help and, in recommending another organisation, you are maintaining an element of goodwill. In the future, the customer may remember this and come back to you. Likewise, other companies may recommend you to one of their clients.

Portfolio Task   Links to b2b

In some organisations it may not be felt appropriate to recommend other organisations. Find out now what the policy is where you work.

Write a personal statement which shows you know and understand what to do.

Check customer service delivery

What you need to know and learn

- What you can do to check the effectiveness of customer **service delivery**
- How to find out if you have met your customers' needs and expectations
- How to identify if you could improve the way in which you personally deliver customer service
- Ways of sharing customer service information with others

Key terms

Service delivery – the service you have given.

Check delivery – find out if customer satisfaction has been achieved.

Feedback – information you receive about yourself or your organisation.

We have looked at the planning and delivery of reliable customer service. The final stage is to reflect on what you can do to check your service delivery and to identify if it can be improved.

What you can do to check the effectiveness of customer service delivery

In this section, we look at how you can **check delivery** and find out if the service you and your organisation give meets customers' needs and expectations. To do this, you will need to use some of your organisation's methods or systems for measuring the effectiveness of customer service. These methods and systems will vary but they will all involve obtaining **feedback**, analysing and using feedback.

What is feedback?

Feedback is information given about things that you or your organisation do. Sometimes customers will give it without prompting, for example, sending a thank you letter or letter of complaint. On other occasions, customers may give feedback as a result of a request from you or your organisation. You may also receive feedback from colleagues who have observed your work, or from a line manager or supervisor as part of your organisation's performance and appraisal system.

Every organisation will differ as to how it obtains feedback, depending on:

- the size of the organisation

- how sophisticated the organisation's systems and procedures are

- whether funds are available to undertake research

- whether the organisation wants to listen to customers

- the organisation's ability to put any changes necessary (as a result of its research) into effect.

Why obtain feedback?

Whilst more and more people complain or mention they would like something to be different, there is still a huge silent majority that do not give any feedback. When customers do not complain, it is very easy to assume everything is fine and you are doing everything right. Your organisation might believe its products or services are exactly what customers want. But this might not be the case at all.

If your organisation does not actively seek feedback, it runs the risk of making assumptions on behalf of its customers. Instead of giving feedback, customers might be simply walking away and finding what they want elsewhere.

Remember – If you or your organisation do not deliver the right customer service at the right time and at the right price – someone else is waiting to do just that.

Other organisations are waiting to serve your customers.

Ways of obtaining feedback

There are many ways you and your organisation can set about obtaining feedback from customers. Figure 10 illustrates some of the methods organisations can use to capture valuable information from customers.

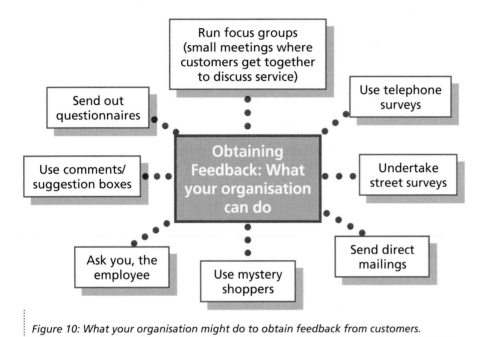

Figure 10: What your organisation might do to obtain feedback from customers.

Questionnaires

A questionnaire about customer service is a series of questions (usually on a form or in a letter) that ask customers about the quality of the service received. The first step in devising a questionnaire is to identify why feedback is required, that is, which specific area(s) of customer service your organisation wants to know about. With this information questions can be devised to create a questionnaire that gives valuable feedback on an organisation's customer service.

Questionnaires may have a single focus or they may cover many issues. For example, an airline might want to know about the helpfulness of crew, quality of in-flight meals, cleanliness of aircraft and the range of products offered during duty-free service (range of issues). Alternatively, the airline might only want to find out about the quality of the in-flight meal (single issue).

Car dealerships often want to find out about the quality of service delivered by their service technicians. Here, they specifically want to know about the customer's experiences before, during and after a car has been serviced. Figure 11 shows a questionnaire (sometimes known as a 'customer satisfaction survey') used by a garage to find out how happy their customers are with the garage when they have their cars serviced.

Moto Quick – top class repairs, top class service

How happy were you with your car service? Tick Excellent, Good, Fair or Poor for each statement

	Excellent	Good	Fair	Poor
The speed with which you were attended to when booking the appointment	☐	☐	☐	☐
The explanation of the work to be done	☐	☐	☐	☐
The availability of parts or accessories	☐	☐	☐	☐
How well you were kept informed of any changes to work agreed	☐	☐	☐	☐
The wait time when collecting your car	☐	☐	☐	☐
Overall value for money for the service or repair	☐	☐	☐	☐
How valued and respected you felt when dealing with our staff	☐	☐	☐	☐

Figure 11: An example questionnaire used by a garage to check customer satisfaction with car services.

This type of questionnaire enables the garage to obtain specific feedback. It can then analyse the information received and use it to improve how it meets customers' needs and expectations.

Questionnaires can be distributed in various ways including:

- handed directly to a customer at the point of service; for example, when the customer collects their car or the airline passenger leaves the plane
- left in shops, hotel rooms, on reception desks, waiting rooms etc.
- put on a web page.

Direct mailings

When a questionnaire is posted direct to a customer, this is called 'direct mailing' (also known by many householders as 'junk mail'!). The number of customers who complete the questionnaires that land on their doormats is very small. This is known as 'a low-response rate'. Some organisations try to tempt customers to fill in questionnaires by offering incentives such as a pen in the envelope, the promise of discount vouchers, inclusion in a prize draw for a holiday, or offering to donate a sum of money to charity for each returned and completed questionnaire.

Telephone surveys

This is the same as the questionnaire approach, except the questions are asked over the telephone. Telephone surveys are not always popular with customers who may feel they do not have the time or inclination to respond. Such telephone calls tend to be made when the caller knows people will be at home, for example, at meal times. These are found to be intrusive and time-consuming and often result in telephones being slammed down on the caller. However, when customers do respond it is possible to gather useful and focused information and many customers feel their opinions are valued due to taking part in a one-to-one conversation.

Focus groups

Focus groups are meetings run by an organisation with a specially selected group of customers, often fairly small in number. Organisations that choose this method usually have specific questions on an important issue that requires feedback.

For example, when an organisation is about to launch a new service or product or to make major changes to existing ones, it may run focus groups to seek reactions and feedback from a selected section of its customers.

The advantage of a focus group is that an organisation has the opportunity to discuss points raised by customers, which is not possible when using a questionnaire type approach. Focus group meetings normally include refreshments and many customers often feel valued or special to be invited to attend a focus group.

Street surveys

When you see someone standing on a street with a clipboard under their arm the chances are they are being employed to obtain feedback from people who might be interested in a range of products or services. This is known as a 'street survey'. They are often used to seek information about customers' buying habits, rather than to seek feedback on the quality of a service provided.

Mystery shoppers

Mystery shoppers are people employed by an organisation to pretend to be a real customer. They may do this face to face or on the telephone. The organisation tells the mystery shopper exactly what areas of service to look at and give feedback on.

The mystery shopper method is very useful for obtaining feedback on service providers. By playing the role of a customer, they will experience first hand your attitude and

Figure 12: Some people will cross to the other side of the street to avoid being approached by someone with a clipboard.

out before the customer leaves you by simply asking 'Is everything OK?' If you get the response 'Well actually no it isn't...' you can then try to get to the bottom of the problem and sort it out quickly.

Use your organisation's systems and procedures

The main system an organisation will have for giving you feedback is an **appraisal** system or a performance-related reward system. These systems are very important as they will measure how well you are doing against set objectives. This may affect your promotion prospects, your career and your pay.

An appraisal usually covers a 12-month period. During those 12 months you should meet with your line manager or supervisor on a regular basis in order to obtain feedback on your work. Your line manager is responsible (with you) for agreeing what you are expected to do and what standards you should reach. For example, achieving this qualification in customer service might be a target to reach by the end of an appraisal year.

Key term

Appraisal – an official review of your performance by your line manager or supervisor.

Portfolio Task   Links to b2.3.1, b2c, b2d

The feedback you seek from customers should fit in with your organisation's systems and procedures. It is important you seek guidance as to what is acceptable in your own organisation. Find this out now and write a personal statement.

Ask an appropriate person(s) for a witness testimony which details how you have worked within your organisation's guidelines and used your organisation's systems and procedures to check you have met your customers' needs and expectations.

How to identify if you could improve the way in which you personally deliver customer service

Key term

Improve service – make changes to enhance customer satisfaction.

The pace of change in business can be very fast, so if you don't keep up to date with changes, you and your organisation will be left behind and your customers will find new places to go. In order for this not to happen, everyone needs to be alert to the need to continuously improve his or her performance.

You can play your part in this by asking yourself 'Is what I do meeting or exceeding the needs of my customers, my organisation and my colleagues? Am I satisfied with my own performance?'

The obvious way of finding out if you need to improve the service you give is to listen to what your customers, colleagues and managers say about your service. You then need to deal with the feedback you receive about your own performance in an appropriate way. This feedback may come to you in a variety of ways either because you asked for it or without a request being made.

To improve the service you give, you must have a clear idea of the skills and knowledge you need in order to do your job effectively. Once you have identified these, you need to decide in which of these areas your strengths lie and what your development needs are, that is, you need to know what you are good at (your strengths) and where you need to improve (your development needs).

Portfolio Task

Links to b2.3.1, b2.3.2, b2d

1 Before you can act on feedback you need to know what your organisation expects from you in your role.

   a. Find out now what skills and knowledge you need to do your job effectively — ask an appropriate person and/or look at your job description.

   b. Copy, or download from the website, the table below, which lists some typical skills required of a customer service practitioner.

   c. Identify the skills that are important for your role and add any other skills you need.

   d. Then decide where your strengths and development needs are.

2 Looking at where your development needs sit, think about the impact of these on your service delivery. Write a personal statement which recalls specific examples of where you feel you could have improved the service you personally give to customers.

Typical skills a customer service practitioner needs.

Skills	Yes	No	Strengths	Development needs
Telephone handling skills				
Communication skills				
Decision-making skills				
Flexibility				
Time management				
IT skills				
Asking for help				
Product knowledge				
Service knowledge				
Systems knowledge				

Sources of feedback

There are many different ways in which you could receive feedback on your performance. Some will be linked into your organisation's systems and procedures. Others will be more informal.

A version of the table used in this task, ready for you to complete, is available to download from www.contentextra.com/customerservice

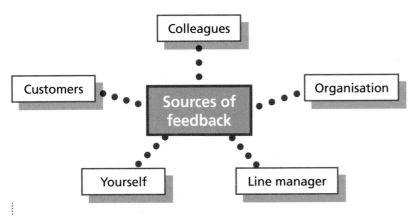

Figure 14: Possible sources of feedback on your own performance.

Informal feedback

Informal feedback occurs when you talk to customers and observe their body language and behaviour. It is unplanned and spontaneous. So, if you notice your customer is reacting to you in a less than positive way, this is a form of feedback. By paying close attention to your customer's behaviour, you can quickly take action, when appropriate, to adjust your own behaviour.

Informal feedback can also be obtained in the following ways:

- from customers or colleagues observing what you do and how you do it
- from colleagues saying things to you in passing (for example, over lunch)
- from having a chat or a gossip with colleagues
- from thinking about and reflecting on your experiences at work.

Formal feedback

This type of feedback is much more structured. Everything is planned in advance by either you, your organisation or your customer. Formal feedback includes comments received in the following ways:

- verbally, that is, over the telephone or face to face
- in writing, for example, thank you letters/emails or letters of complaint
- questionnaires and comment forms completed by customers
- mystery shopper reports
- appraisals/performance reviews.

Remember – You may receive positive and negative feedback. Do not worry if you receive negative feedback – use it as a learning opportunity. Treat it as constructive criticism, giving you a chance to improve what you do.

Feedback from customers

Feedback from customers can come in the form of letters of thanks or complaint or verbally while you deal with customers face to face or on the telephone. Customer feedback will tell you about areas where you might need to improve. After all, your interaction with customers is the most important aspect of your role as a service provider.

Such feedback can be difficult, especially if a customer tells you that you are not doing well enough and you do not understand why. Remember, it is that particular customer's perception of the service you have given but all feedback is valuable and you should use it to improve what you do. Equally, positive feedback will tell you what you are doing well and then you can pat yourself on the back.

Feedback from colleagues

Colleague feedback can be given both informally and formally. You may be given formal feedback from colleagues when you attend a training event, for example, a call-handling skills course. Or, a colleague might be asked to spend some time with you to observe you at work. On these occasions, you could get some valuable feedback on your knowledge, skills and behaviour.

Ask your colleagues questions when receiving the feedback. For example, if you are told you do not have much patience with customers, make sure the person who is giving you feedback tells you about a specific time when this happened. Ask for a description of what you did that showed you were not patient. That way, you will be able to use the feedback more effectively and work on improving what you do.

Informal feedback can take the form of comments made to you over lunch or even overhearing your colleagues gossiping, You might overhear someone talking about you in a negative way to someone else. This may not be very pleasant but it may tell you a lot about your behaviour or that of your colleague.

Feedback from your organisation

This form of feedback will only be relevant to you as an individual if the systems and procedures in use mean that you are named as the person the customer dealt with. Often, this is not the case. Organisational feedback will come from questionnaires completed by customers, comment forms, mystery shoppers etc.

This type of feedback tends to be a general view of an organisation's overall customer service. All the employees have played a part in that overall view, so the feedback relates to the wider team of people of which you are a part. It is up to you to take responsibility as a team member for improving the overall performance of the team in which you work.

However, many organisations recognise the power of rewarding individual employees for a job well done. Some have employee-of-the-month awards, for example, and actively encourage customers to name the member of staff they would like to nominate. Or a customer satisfaction questionnaire might include a statement like this:

> 'We like to recognise people who provide exceptional customer service. If you feel particularly pleased with one or more of our team, please recommend them in the space below.'

Feedback from your line manager or supervisor

Many companies have formal feedback systems in place that will involve you as an individual. The main formal ways of giving you feedback are your performance and appraisal reviews with your line manager or supervisor.

However, your line manager is also likely to give you less formal feedback as part of your daily working life. For example, a line manager might see you calming down an angry customer and praise you for the way in which you dealt with the situation. Or they might ask you to improve your telephone greeting in order to give a better impression to customers.

Treat feedback as a gift: use it to improve your performance.

Portfolio Task

Links to b2.3.1, b2.3.2, b2d

1 Find out now if your organisation has a formal appraisal system.

What do you need to do to ensure you can use it to improve your own performance? Write a personal statement which shows how you have used this feedback to:

a. identify where your service delivery could be improved

b. how you have used it to improve your performance.

Make sure you include some specific examples and also obtain witness testimonies.

Feedback from you

One of the most valuable tools you have for improving what you do is reflecting on the work you have done and how you have carried it out. This involves thinking about the customer service skills you need to do your job effectively and asking yourself if you have shown these skills in your work. For example:

- What went well?
- What didn't go so well?
- Why was this?
- Did I check if the customer was satisfied?
- What could I do better next time?

Portfolio Task

Links to b2.3.2, b2b

1 Make a list of five things which you believe would improve the service you give to customers. Include in your list, something to do with :

a. developing your personal skills

b. improving your product or service knowledge

c. improving your working environment

d. something you have learned from customer feedback

e. something you have learned about your own performance from colleagues.

2 Discuss your list with a colleague who has given you feedback and keep an audio for your portfolio.

Dealing with feedback

If you are alert and aware of what is happening around you, you will pick up feedback constantly. You must then deal with it or it will be a wasted opportunity to improve your performance. So, you have a choice what to do next: you can reject it, accept it, or reflect on it.

Rejecting feedback

Perhaps you strongly disagree with the feedback you receive. For example, you might feel a colleague has given you feedback that did not recognise the situation you were in – maybe you feel that they are focusing on just one aspect of the situation or that they weren't actually experiencing what it was like to be on the receiving end of a customer's unpleasant behaviour.

Even when you reject feedback, you should view it as constructive even if you do not agree with it. Try to see what you can learn from it. When rejecting feedback you do not agree with, never get angry and try not to get too defensive. Stay in control of your emotions.

Accepting feedback

Accepting feedback involves taking the feedback you have been given and using it to identify what you need to improve. You will need to work out ways of developing yourself and improving the service you give. You may need to ask for help or advice with this in order to find out the options for development that are available to you. Figure 15 shows some possible development opportunities.

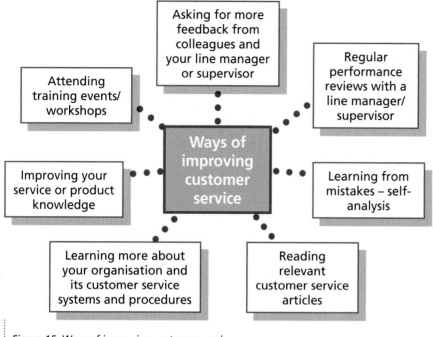

Figure 15: Ways of improving customer service.

You should talk through your plans for improving the service you give with an appropriate person. That way you can both reach agreement as to what you will achieve.

Reflecting on feedback

When you receive feedback it is sometimes wise to not jump to conclusions or make assumptions about what has been said. Try to absorb the comments and think carefully about them later in the day. This is especially important if you have been in a fraught or upsetting situation. Table 3 is a checklist of questions you might ask yourself. At the end of the working day, use these questions to reflect on the day's events.

Table 3: Reflecting on the day's events.

For the good times	For the bad times
What happened today that was great?	What went wrong?
Why was it so good?	What have I learnt?
How do I know that?	What was the impact on my customer?
How can I make it happen again?	What do I need to do to improve?

Unit B2 Deliver reliable customer service

Portfolio Task
Links to b2.3.1, b2.3.2, b2c, b2d

Using the template below as a basis, keep a diary for a month where you write up all the feedback you receive and how you dealt with it. We have given you an example to get you started.

Keep your diary for your portfolio.

My feedback diary.

Date	Feedback	Source	How I dealt with it
13 March	*Email praising my contribution at team meeting on the new product launch*	*My line manager*	*I won't be afraid to speak up during team meetings and will encourage others to do the same. It helped me to research the new product before the meeting so that I knew what I was talking about*

✓ Checklist – Improving your own customer service

- Find out the specific skills needed to do your job.

- Find out what your own strengths and development needs are.

- Find ways of obtaining feedback from customers and colleagues.

- Use the feedback you are given to improve your service.

- Give yourself some feedback by reflecting on your work each day.

- Ask questions on how you could improve your service.

- Learn from your mistakes.

- Seek further feedback on any changes you make to what you do.

Remember – Getting and using feedback to improve your customer service is a continual process.

Ways of sharing customer service information with others

As well as obtaining feedback about your own personal performance, you are also in a position where you will receive all sorts of comments and information about your organisation as a whole. This could come from customers or service partners (for example, suppliers) or colleagues. Anyone who does business with you and your organisation is potentially a source of feedback. In the same way that feedback about yourself can be used to improve your job, feedback about your organisation can be used to maintain its standards for service delivery and is useful **shared information**.

Be alert to issues that need attention

It is very important that you are alert to warning signs that may indicate standards are slipping and report them to the appropriate person. This could be anything from extra long queues developing on a certain day of the week, to equipment breakdowns, to information leaflets being in short supply, to dirty premises. In other words if you spot anything which has the potential to cause standards to slip then you have a responsibility to let an appropriate person know.

Remember to make a note of the issue if you are not able to deal with it on the spot. That way you will not forget. Be as specific as you can so that the person who has responsibility for dealing with the issue is armed with the best information.

How to share the information you have

You could share the feedback you receive using a number of methods including those shown in Figure 16.

Key term

Shared information – feedback, thoughts and ideas that are discussed with colleagues and/or service partners to help improve performance.

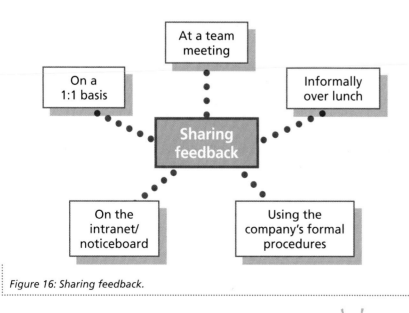

Figure 16: Sharing feedback.

Deliver reliable customer service Unit B2

Always remember to be tactful, especially if what you have to say is sensitive in some way. Perhaps you have frequently had customers tell you a colleague seems reluctant to be of assistance. Before passing on such information, you should be very sure of your facts and be able to back up what you are saying with specific examples. It would not be appropriate to mention this type of matter at a team meeting.

Portfolio Task   Links to b2.3.3

1 In order to share feedback with your colleagues and service partners, make a list of feedback you have received from customers about:

   a. your own performance

   b. your organisation's service delivery or its products or services.

2 Do the same for things you have spotted yourself which you feel should be shared with others. In both lists, include brief details of the feedback you wish to share.

3 Decide how you are going to share this feedback. Write this down against each item on your list.

4 Ensure you are observed sharing this information and/or make an audio of any discussion and/or provide witness testimonies for your portfolio.

Working Life

I'm Martyn and I am a customer service assistant for a private health insurer. I work in a call centre dealing with questions and queries and took a call last Friday afternoon about an insurance claim which hadn't been reimbursed to our customer in full. I took all the details down and could quickly see an error had probably been made by ourselves — the customer's policy was one which should have enabled us to pay the claim in full. Because I needed to refer to our contracts team and because it was late in the day, I advised the customer I would call her back on Monday with an update. She said that was OK. I sent an email to the contracts team and asked them to sort it out and advise me how I should respond to the customer. I also used our 'raise a promise' procedure which sets a marker on my screen advising me of calls I need to make.

On Tuesday, I received a message from my supervisor. Apparently, the customer had phoned first thing Tuesday morning because I hadn't phoned her yesterday. I didn't really see what the problem was as the contracts team had not been in touch with me and so I had no new information to tell her.

Ask the expert

Q If Martyn had followed procedures, why did things go wrong?

A He failed to keep his promise to ring; therefore, the customer's expectations were not met resulting in customer dissatisfaction.

Q Was the promise realistic?

A Yes, if Martyn had kept on top of things and worked closely with his colleagues in the contracts team. He had promised to call with an update, that is, not necessarily with a full answer.

Q Should Martyn have called the customer on Monday?

A Yes, even if there is no new information to hand, a promise had been made to phone on that day. Therefore, the customer has an expectation of contact being made by her insurer.

Q As there was no firm answer to the query, what was the point?

A The promise needed to be kept. You should keep customers informed of progress at all times. Sometimes this means advising them that there is no further information but that the situation is being dealt with. This stops customers thinking they have been forgotten about.

Top tips

Martyn had done the right thing by following procedures — he had made a promise to a customer and had used his organisation's procedures to ensure he was reminded of the need to call her back on Monday. He had also asked the right people — the contracts team — for advice.

Check your knowledge

1 What should you do to ensure you are well placed to deliver reliable customer service?

a. Learn how to be a role model to my colleagues.

b. Take notes during team meetings and briefings.

c. Refer difficult people to someone in authority.

d. Keep my product or service knowledge up to date.

2 How might you seek feedback on your own customer service performance?

a. From customer satisfaction surveys on new products.

b. Through team meetings about changes to service delivery.

c. By asking my line manager, customers and colleagues.

d. By comparing my job description with my colleagues.

3 How can you tell if you have met customers' needs or expectations?

a. By counting the number of responses to customer surveys.

b. By asking colleagues for feedback on my service delivery.

c. By checking the number of customer complaints received.

d. By obtaining and analysing information in customer feedback.

4 How can you ensure you keep your promises to customers?

a. By making realistic promises and keeping customers informed of progress.

b. By ensuring I promise to do everything that customers expect me to do.

c. By seeking support and guidance from more senior colleagues.

d. By never promising to do things quickly during busy times.

5 What do you need to do when you are personally unable to help a customer?

a. Ask the customer to come back later when somebody else might be available to help.

b. Tell the customer that my organisation is unable to meet his or her needs or expectations.

c. Tell the customer what I can do, not what I cannot do, and record expectations accurately.

d. Remain positive and confident and tell the customer I am unable to be of assistance.

6 How might you find ways of improving your service delivery?

a. By asking for permission to not deal with difficult customers.

b. By being flexible and working outside the limits of my authority.

c. By acting on feedback received about my development needs.

d. By assessing how well I perform compared to my colleagues.

7 Why is it important to keep your product or service knowledge up to date?

a. To let my colleagues know I will be able to offer them help.

b. To ensure customers get the cheapest product or service.

c. To ensure I deliver a consistent and reliable service to customers.

d. To create opportunities to further my customer service career.

8 What are the benefits of sharing feedback with colleagues or service partners?

a. It ensures sales targets are met or exceeded.

b. It helps to maintain standards for service delivery.

c. It tells customers I have listened to their comments.

d. It enables health and safety matters to be addressed.

9 What can you do to consider health and safety in your area of work?

a. Follow my organisation's procedures and practices.

b. Ask customers if they require additional help or guidance.

c. Monitor the number of complaints about products or services.

d. Attend a training course about keeping customer information safe.

10 What should you do in situations where customers' needs or expectations change?

a. Follow guidelines on dealing with abusive customers.

b. Make a note on the customer's file to stop it happening again.

c. Be patient and ask questions to check my understanding.

d. Share information with colleagues to see if it has happened before.

Recognise and deal with customer queries, requests and problems

What you will learn:

■ To recognise and deal with customer queries and requests

■ To recognise and deal with customer problems

Introduction

It is a natural part of most service providers' roles to find themselves dealing with questions and queries from customers. This may be as a result of customers wanting more information about services or products, or, customers sometimes expect more from the organisations and the people they do business with. Dealing with queries, requests and problems may form quite a big part of your daily routine.

Because you may be doing this frequently, there is a risk customers will not be treated as individuals. Avoid this by making your customer feel special; the personal touch will add value to their dealings with you and your organisation. You will need to refer some questions and queries to colleagues, so you need to know who to ask for help.

Although you and your colleagues will be trying to get things right first time, sometimes things do go wrong and customers may present you with a problem. Problems may occur as a result of your own actions (or lack of them) or they may be down to factors which are outside your control. These factors include a difference between customer expectations and what is offered by your organisation and a system or procedure failure. Other problems you might deal with include those caused by a shortage of resources (for example, time, money, people, technology) and human error.

Dealing with queries, requests and problems may be a big part of your role.

Some of these problems will be brought to your attention by customers. Others will be spotted by you or your colleagues before the customer realises there is a problem. It is important to try to avoid problems, but if they do occur, the way in which they are solved is as important as making sure they never happen in the first place. Customers who feel they have been badly treated will often end up feeling better about an organisation if the problem is handled well.

When you solve problems you will need to show you have balanced the needs of your customer and your organisation. This will involve you considering the benefits of your solution to both your customer and your organisation as well as the potential risks to your organisation of implementing your solution.

When you recognise and deal with customer queries, requests and problems you must consistently:

● recognise and deal with customer queries and requests

● recognise and deal with customer problems.

You will need to feel confident to be able to deal with customer queries and problems. Improving your confidence will help you greatly in your career because it shows you have the motivation to succeed.

Recognise and deal with customer queries and requests

What you need to know and learn

- How to deal with queries and requests in a positive and professional way
- How to seek help from colleagues if you cannot answer a query or request
- How to keep customers informed of progress

How to deal with queries and requests in a positive and professional way

To deal with queries and requests in a positive and professional way you need to understand it is not only what you say that counts, but also how you say it. There is no point knowing all about your services or products if you cannot then answer queries and requests in a professional way. Being a customer service professional means you know your appearance, your body language and your behaviour all impact on the overall message a customer gets from you.

As a minimum, most customers will expect an accurate and timely answer. This does not necessarily mean an immediate response. It is better to take the time to find out the facts in order to respond accurately than to rush things and end up giving inaccurate information.

Figure 1: Customers need to feel they can trust the answers they are given to their questions.

Portfolio Task

Links to c1.1.1, c1c

1 Think about how your behaviour is affected by the way in which customers ask questions or make requests. Copy and complete the table.

2 Now think about real life situations where anything on the list caused you concern. Write a personal statement which describes how you managed to adapt your behaviour to ensure you

were dealing with your customer in a positive and professional way.

If there are any situations which indicate you may need some help in dealing with your customer's behaviour, we provide hints and tips on dealing with difficult people later in this unit. You might also like to refer to **Unit C4 Deliver customer service to difficult customers**.

How my behaviour is affected by customers' behaviour.

Customer...	Impact on my behaviour
makes a request in a loud voice	
says 'please' and 'thank you'	
smiles	
points their finger at me	
uses inappropriate language	
shakes hands	
frowns	
gives me eye contact	

A version of the table used in this task, ready for you to complete, is available to download from www.contentextra.com/customerservice

Key term

Personal touch – showing that you care by treating customers as individuals and behaving in a friendly way.

The personal touch

Customers also want to feel confident that what they are being told is the truth and that this will be followed through with action if necessary. It is up to you to inspire this confidence in yourself and your organisation. You can start by giving the **personal touch**.

To give the personal touch, all you need to think about is the answer to the question: 'What do I need to do to show my customer I care about their query?'

The personal touch is all about interacting with customers in a friendly way; it does not cost money and it does not take any extra time. Examples include using the customer's name or giving them a smile. Telling the customer your name will create a feeling of trust and will instantly show you are dealing with the query or request in a friendly way. At the end of the conversation say 'Thank you'.

Your organisation may have its own ways of showing that customers' queries and requests are dealt with on an individual basis. It is not just about situations involving face-to-face or telephone contact which can give the personal touch;

service that is delivered online can also make the overall customer experience more pleasant. This might include:

- using web cookies to greet visitors when they return to a website and to auto-fill fields when they order
- posting photos of individual employees to add a face and name to the transaction
- confirming every order and saying 'thank you'
- offering order tracking
- sending electronic confirmation of despatch
- matching and offering additional products or services
- requesting online feedback at the end of a transaction.

Giving the personal touch will help you to deliver service in a positive and professional way.

Portfolio Task
Links to c1.1.1, c1c

1 Make a list of things you do or say to customers which show you give the personal touch.

2 Share your list with colleagues and ask them for a witness testimony which supports your approach to giving the personal touch.

3 Ask your assessor to observe you.

You can give the personal touch by being friendly.

Professional behaviour

Behaviour refers to everything you do and say. People will draw conclusions about you and your organisation based on your behaviour with them. Every customer service professional should have a set of values which drives how each of them behaves with their customers. These values might include:

- trust— keeping promises, being truthful
- openness – taking responsibility
- honesty – saying what you can do, working within the limits of your authority, knowing when to say 'no'
- reliability – being accurate and consistent, knowing where to go to for help
- respect – using courteous and friendly behaviour.

These values will mean different things to different people. When brought to life through your actions and behaviours, you will be showing you are a customer service professional. How do you bring them to life?

Unit C1 Recognise and deal with customer queries, requests and problems

Portfolio Task

Links to c1.1.1, c1c

1 Write down how you bring each of these values to life. We've given you an example to get you started.

2 Discuss this list with your assessor and describe how it demonstrates you are behaving in a professional way when dealing with queries, requests and problems. Ask to be observed.

Functional skills

English: Reading, Writing and Speaking, listening and communication

If you answer the questions in the task in writing, you will have an opportunity to identify a suitable response to the text. This may count as evidence towards Level 1 Functional English: Reading. Your written responses should include sufficient detail to show you have understood each statement and you will need to check them for spelling, grammar and punctuation. Print a copy of your responses as this may count as evidence towards Level 1 Functional English: Writing. If you use your responses as a basis for a discussion with your assessor, you may be able to count this as evidence towards Level 1 Functional English: Speaking, listening and communication.

How I bring professional values to life.

Value	What I do	
Trust	I make sure I make a note of what I've promised to do (e.g. phone back the next day)	_____
Openness	I never blame somebody else and take responsibility for a problem even if it was caused by my colleagues.	_____
Honesty	In situations where I am unable to help I make sure I say what I can do not what I cannot do.	_____
Reliability	I make sure my product knowledge is up to date by attending team briefings.	_____
Respect	When I am talking with an elderly person, I always ask what I should call them because many elderly people prefer to be called 'Mr' or 'Mrs' and not by their first name.	_____

A version of the table used in this task, ready for you to complete, is available to download from www.contentextra.com/customerservice

In **Unit A4 Give customers a positive impression of yourself and your organisation**, we also looked at how your appearance and body language contribute to professional behaviour. Included in the mix are your surroundings. We described how a customer service professional is made up of all these ingredients and how they impact upon your ability to deal with queries and requests. Please refer to pages 109 – 111 for further information.

✓ Checklist – Behaving professionally

- Be aware that your appearance and surroundings have an impact on your service delivery.
- Treating customers as individuals.
- Provide the personal touch.
- Be respectful at all times.
- Be honest and open.
- Accept responsibility.
- Be consistently reliable.

Courtesy and customer service

There should be nothing difficult about showing customers **courteous behaviour** since it is all about having good manners. The opposite of being courteous would be showing rude and offensive behaviour.

If you are following the pointers in the checklist in Table 1 you will be showing good manners and courtesy and will therefore be behaving professionally.

Table 1: How to demonstrate courteous behaviour.

	Courteous behaviour	Insensitive or rude behaviour
Using names	Using the name the customer gives you or asks you to call them by	Using a nickname or title or any other name which you know will be offensive
Doing what you say you will do, when you say you will do it	Following through with actions promised and keeping the customer informed	Breaking your promises. Not bothering to update the customer
Tone of voice	Using an appropriate tone for the situation	Being unaware of the tone of your voice or deliberately using a sarcastic tone
Dealing with rude customers	Remaining calm and professional	Responding with rudeness
Listening	Listening actively, e.g. making appropriate 'noises', giving eye contact, leaning head to one side	Constantly interrupting, avoiding eye contact, looking bored.

Responding to queries and requests

We have said you might be faced with hearing the same query or request many times during the day. It would be very easy to get bored. If this happens, your behaviour might indicate you are not interested in your customer. Your voice might sound flat or you may get easily distracted. If your customer can see you, they may be able to watch you gazing blankly into space. If this happens, your listening skills will suffer.

Answer queries at the appropriate time. If you have to research information or seek help from others, do so. Never guess the answer! If the answer is taking longer to find than anticipated, keep your customer informed of progress.

If a customer has spent time queuing (either on the telephone or face to face) acknowledge this before you answer the query. This shows you care and you will be treating your customer with respect.

Product or service knowledge

Make sure you know where to access information about all the products or services you deal with. Keep this information up to date, as this will help to ensure your responses to queries and requests are accurate.

Know the limits of your authority

Do not make promises which cannot be kept. Know who to ask for help if you are unable to deal with your customer's request.

✓ Checklist – Dealing with queries and requests in a positive and professional way

- Follow your organisation's guidelines for appearance and behaviour.

- Acknowledge any query or request as soon as possible.

- Be friendly & welcoming in the language you use.

- Be respectful – treat your customer with courtesy.

- Give accurate information.

- Say what you can do rather than what you cannot do.

- Know about your organisations products and/or services.

- Know where to seek assistance if you are unable to help.

How to seek help from colleagues if you cannot answer a query or request

Providing great customer service does not mean you have to know *all* the answers to queries and requests. However, you do need to show your customers that you know somebody who does know the answer. Most customers will be quite happy with that, providing you keep them informed about what you are doing to help them and follow through on any promises you make.

A version of the table used in this task, ready for you to complete, is available to download from www.contentextra.com/customerservice

There may also be occasions when you do not have the authority to answer certain queries or agree to certain actions; here too, you will need to know who to go to for help. This might be people you work closely with: your colleagues. Or, it could mean going to someone in another department, building, office or organisation. It very much depends on what it is you need!

Portfolio Task

Links to c1.1.1, c1.1.2, c1a

1 Reflect on all the times you needed help with a customer service issue. Think about what your customer wanted and why you needed to ask for help.

2 Now think about the types of query or request about which you frequently need to seek help or information. Copy and complete this table, adding as many rows as necessary – try to think about five different examples.

3 Now write a personal statement which details specific occasions when this has happened. Ask the people who you have sought help from to provide you with a witness testimony.

Functional skills

English: Writing

If you complete the table in the task in writing you may be able to count it as evidence towards Level 1 Functional English: Writing. Your written responses should include sufficient detail to show you have understood question 2 and you will need to check them for spelling, grammar and punctuation. Print a copy of your responses as this may count as evidence towards Level 1 Functional English: Writing. Do the same for your personal statement.

Queries and requests that I seek help about.

Customers frequently ask me about:	I seek help or information from:

We are sure you would prefer to personally help your customers if you can. Looking at the table your completed for the portfolio task, it's worth your while seeing if there are frequently asked questions which you could deal with in the future by improving your own product or service knowledge.

It's not just about knowing who to go to for help. There are all sorts of things you can do to access information providing you know where to find it. Refer back to Unit F1 Communicate using customer service language, page 9.

Who helps me?

Do you find yourself constantly asking the same person for help? Is this because he or she is the most appropriate person? Or, is it because he or she is always willing to offer help despite his or her own workload?

If your favourite source of help is indeed the most appropriate person, then fine. If not, you would do well to make sure you ask for help from individuals who can best help you and your customer.

Knowing the limits of what you are allowed to do

Sometimes the queries and requests you deal with will be about things which you are not authorised to handle. These might include:

- offering a refund
- a health and safety issue
- going outside the terms of a contract or agreement customers have with your organisation
- queries or requests about products or services which are dealt with by other people in your organisation.

It is especially important to know the limits of what you are allowed to do when dealing with problems. This is because when customers come to you with problems, they look for answers which show you are on their side. You can handle such queries and requests by knowing who best to go to to ask for help or permission to make decisions.

Because you have to refer to somebody else, there are likely to be delays with the customer's query or request being dealt with. Always make sure you tell the customer what is happening.

Portfolio Task

Links to c1.1.1, c1.1.2, c1.1.3, c1.1.4, c1a, c1b

To find out about the times you need to refer to somebody else, copy and complete the grid below. Try to think about five different situations.

Make sure you ask for witness testimonies from the people you refer to, the next time it happens.

When I have to seek help.

When customers ask about:	...I am not allowed to make a final decision without seeking help from:

A version of the table used in this task, ready for you to complete, is available to download from www.contentextra.com/customerservice

How to keep customers informed of progress

It is important to remember that while you are trying to find help or information or seek permission, your customer is waiting. It might not take you long to get help; often a quick phone call may be all that is needed. Sometimes though, it will take a few days, perhaps longer to get the help and information required. Make sure you keep your customer updated. This ensures they do not feel forgotten. Even if you have not quite gathered all the information you need, it is worthwhile updating customers on progress. Your customer will appreciate you are doing your best and will want to know the situation even if the issue is not quite fully resolved.

That includes 'bad news' too! Your customers will prefer this to no news at all. Keeping your customer in the picture also stops unnecessary complaints being made. How many times have you been on the receiving end of customers wanting to know what is happening? This scenario can easily be avoided if you take responsibility for keeping your customer informed.

Figure 2: Always keep your customers informed even with 'bad' news.

Recognise and deal with customer problems

Having dealt with handling customer queries and requests, we will now look specifically at dealing with customer problems.

What you need to know and learn

- What factors might lead to customer service problems occurring
- How to use your organisation's procedures and systems for dealing with problems or complaints
- How to deal with difficult people in a calm and confident way
- When to pass on a problem to a colleague

What factors might lead to customer service problems occurring

When was the last time you experienced superb customer service? How about diabolical customer service? It's probably much easier for you to remember bad service than it is to recall the good times. When a waiter is rude, spills your drink, and brings you cold food, you take note. And, if you are like most people, you will tell your friends. If the service is pleasant or even excellent, you will be aware of it, but you probably will not tell as many people. Service has to be *fantastic* for most people to take the trouble to tell others.

Portfolio Task

Links to c1g

1 In the context of needing answers to a query, request or a problem, think about the worst customer service experience you have encountered as a customer in the last six months. Copy this sentence and write down what happened using the questions below to get you started.

The worst customer service experience I had recently was...

a. What were you trying to do?

b. Was it people that upset you or got things wrong?

c. Or, was it the organisation's processes that let you down?

d. Could you (as the customer) have done things differently to get what you wanted? If so, what?

e. What did you think and feel about the organisation?

f. What did you think and feel about the people who dealt with you?

2 Copy and complete this sentence and keep it for your portfolio.

In order to be satisfied with the service I receive when I have a query, request or problem, I expect this to happen:

3 Now relate your own experiences to what customers normally expect from you when you deal with queries, requests or problems. Complete this statement by writing down your thoughts about this in bullet point format.

When I deal with queries, requests or problems, my customers expect me to:

It does not matter if you are dealing with a query, a request or a problem. Customers will have the same expectations about how they wish to be treated. Broadly speaking, this includes you behaving in a way which conveys trust. Trust is built on foundations of openness and honesty.

Figure 3: What customers expect when they have a problem.

Portfolio Task Links to c1.2.1, c1g

For each of the points listed in Figure 3 decide how you can personally ensure each expectation is met.

Now think about specific occasions when you have dealt with customer problems. Think carefully about the behaviours you used to ensure customer satisfaction. Write a personal statement which describes how your behaviour reflected each of the points listed in Figure 3. Seek the support of your colleagues to endorse this by asking for witness testimonies or ensure you are observed by your assessor.

Why do problems occur?

Let's think of the reasons *why* problems occur in the first place. These reasons might include some of the following factors shown in Figure 4.

We will now look at how each of these might lead to problems and their likely impact on customers.

Equipment

Mechanical breakdowns might leave you unable to work; for example a car that won't start, computer failure, tools that haven't been looked after and then break down – kitchen appliances, garden tools etc.

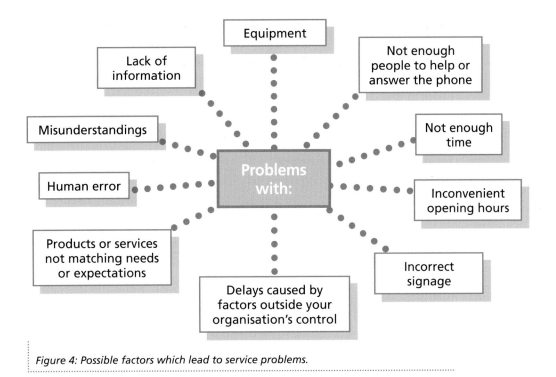

Figure 4: Possible factors which lead to service problems.

Machinery that some customers might find complicated to operate (for example, computers, sat-nav systems, central-heating thermostats, self-service tills) could also cause problems. Remember, the pace of change with technology leaves many people feeling left behind in the race to keep up to date or even get started with new ideas. This could make some customers feel inadequate when faced with situations when they are unable to operate equipment. There will be dissatisfaction with the product or service leading to a lack of trust and confidence. This leads to, at best, questions and queries which you need to deal with and, at worst, complaints.

Lack of information

If customers have insufficient information about products or services, this can cause problems. Lack of information also includes failing to keep customers informed about changes to products or services or about updates on how problems are being resolved. The likely result of keeping customers in the dark is that misunderstandings and a lack of trust develop. Depending on the situation, there might even be health and safety issues.

Not enough people to help or answer the phone

This is a resource issue leading to dissatisfied customers who are not prepared to wait, for example, a customer ringing a call centre may put the phone down rather than be kept in a queue whilst their phone bill is rising. This is one of the most frequent sources of complaint. Customers will also tell friends and family about the frustrations caused by being left hanging on the telephone. Business could be lost, not just from the customers involved but also from people they tell.

Not enough time

Again, this is a resource issue. Do you have to rush serving a customer because there are so many others waiting for you to help? If so, it is unlikely that your customers feel valued. You might also not give sufficient time to explaining things to your customers — they will be more likely to encounter problems as a result of this, which will lead to them returning to your organisation. This could all take more time in the long run.

Inconvenient opening hours

Customers increasingly expect access to products or services when *they* want it. For instance, many hairdressers now offer a service late into the evening. If customers cannot get what they want from your organisation, they will look elsewhere.

Incorrect signage

This could result in customers getting lost within your organisation's premises. If they are unable to find where they want to go because there are not enough (or incorrect) signs (for example, in a hospital or airport) frustration will quickly set in.

Human error

This type of mistake is made because nobody is perfect. Human error might result in questions or queries or more serious problems occurring. Again, health and safety problems could arise.

Misunderstandings

Misunderstandings occur when people say something which is interpreted as being something completely different to what they intended. Or, if someone is not listening properly, it's all too easy to get things wrong. If you are dealing face to face with customers watch out for puzzled looks. On the telephone, listen carefully for signs your customer is following what you say.

Delays caused by factors outside your organisation's control

Industrial action can have a snowball effect on many different organisations. For example, a London Tube driver's strike will affect all the people (including customers) who use the Tube to get to work. The weather can also have a huge impact upon your ability to deliver customer service — strong winds may bring down power lines or rain may force the cancellation of an outdoor event. Although you and your organisation cannot usually be held accountable, your customers will expect you to sort out the problems which may occur as a result.

Products or services not matching needs or expectations

Customers will have expectations about a product or service. These expectations are formed from advertising, from your organisation's reputation and from what you say. If these expectations are not met, problems may occur. For instance, if a customer expects a fridge-freezer to be able to hold large bottles, he or she will then be disappointed to find that the shelves are too small to cope with their favourite drinks bottle. Likewise, if a customer buys flowers with a label that says they will last seven days, he or she will not expect them to die within three days. The result is frustration and more queries for you to deal with or complaints to handle.

Figure 5: Customers want their lives made easier.

Portfolio Task

Links to c1.2.1, c1h

1 Thinking about your own organisation make a list of the types of problems that you feel consistently occur. Include problems:

  • brought to your attention by customers

  • identified first by you and/or by your colleagues

  • resulting from a systems or procedure failure

  • resulting from a difference between customer expectations and what is offered by your organisation.

2 Think about specific occasions when these have occurred. Write a personal statement which shows how you spotted there was a problem from the customer's point if view.

3 Ensure you are observed by your assessor and/or obtain witness testimonies.

How to use your organisation's procedures and systems for dealing with problems or complaints

As you can see, there are many situations which might lead to problems occurring. Some will be brought to your attention by customers. Others you will be able to spot before the customer becomes aware of them. In all cases, you need to know what your organisation's procedures and systems are for dealing with customer service problems.

The organisation's systems and procedures are there to protect you, your customer and your organisation, in order to make sure the needs of everyone are dealt with in an appropriate and successful manner. Try not to think of any system that helps you to sort a problem as 'something else to worry about'. It is there to help you and provide you with a framework for dealing with customer problems.

How many times have you read words similar to these?:

'Buy with confidence – satisfaction guaranteed'

'It works – or your money back!'

'If you don't like what you see – tell us!'

'Our money back guarantee does not affect your statutory rights.'

'Fully insured – references available – tell us if you are not happy'.

Key term

Complaints procedure – the process which a customer should follow in making a complaint.

These statements are all invitations to the customer to return to an organisation if he or she is not fully satisfied with the product or service he or she has bought. So, it is not surprising that things go wrong very quickly if, on them returning, the customer service practitioner does not know how to deal with the customer.

The most common procedure in place is a **complaints procedure.**

Many organisations actively encourage people to contact them with complaints and comments. They go as far as describing in detail what a customer needs to do in order to make a complaint. This shows a willingness to help and to use the information to try to improve customer service in the future. For example, an organisation may describe its complaints procedure in its literature or on a 'How to complain' web page.

There are websites which help people to complain, for example, www.howtocomplain.com and the government website www.consumerdirect.gov.uk

Armed with such advice, it is not surprising more and more people feel ready and able to make a complaint.

Personal details	
Name	
Address	
Town/City	
County	
Postcode	
Would you like us to contact you about this complaint?	Yes ⦿ No ⦿
If yes, how would you like us to contact you?	Please select... ⌄
Details of your complaint	
Type of complaint	Please select... ⌄
Which sector of our company does your complaint relate to?	Please select... ⌄
Please provide us with full details of your complaint.	
Have you contacted us about this issue before?	Yes ⦿ No ⦿
How would you like us to resolve this issue?	

Figure 6: A sample online complaint/feedback form.

Making a complaint – advice to customers

1. Check whether the organisation has a complaints procedure.

2. If there is no complaints procedure, tackle the problem on the spot. Say why you are unhappy and ask what can be done. If necessary, ask for the name of someone you can complain to.

3. Be clear why you are not satisfied. Was it the way you were treated? Was something faulty? Are you unhappy with a decision?

4. It's usually best to complain in writing – by letter or email.

5. Say what you want to happen. Do you want an apology? Do you want a different decision? Do you want the proper service that should have been provided in the first place? Do you want them to change the way things are done in the future?
Keep a record of events. If you speak to someone on the phone, make a note of who you speak to, the date and time of your call and what was said. If you write, keep a copy of your letter/email and any replies you receive.

Figure 7: General advice to customers about making a complaint.

Portfolio Task

Link to c1j

Find out about your organisation's complaints procedures. Write a personal statement covering these questions.

1 What guarantees or offers does your organisation make to its customers for the products or services that you deal with?

2 What promises are made concerning what will happen if a customer has a complaint?

3 What is the customer required to do (if anything) when making a complaint?

4 What are *your* responsibilities to customers who make a complaint?

5 What are *your* responsibilities to your organisation?

How to deal with difficult people in a calm and confident way

Note

Unit C4 Deliver customer service to difficult customers on pages 221 – 233 deals with this area in detail. Please refer to this unit to support your learning.

As a customer service professional, you will sometimes find yourself in a situation where you might feel you are dealing with difficult customers. Of course, very few people set out to be deliberately difficult — that wouldn't make any sense. However, sometimes the situations people find themselves in, cause them to behave in ways which other people find difficult to cope with. It is the *situation* that you need to manage effectively. Do this and any behaviour you find difficult to cope with will undoubtedly improve.

When dealing with customers who have problems, it is important to realise that your own behaviour will directly influence the way they behave with you. Equally, you will be affected by your customers' behaviour.

We all tend to mirror the behaviour of the people we are communicating with. If we copy a customer's bad or awkward behaviour, the situation will certainly escalate. If, on the other hand we behave well with a customer, they are likely to mirror our behaviour and the situation will then improve.

Raise your voice to someone and they are likely to shout back. Lowering your voice and speaking at a slower pace can help to calm an angry customer down until they are speaking in a more controlled and effective way too. This is sometimes referred to as 'behaviour breeds behaviour'.

Difficult behaviour to deal with might include things like frowning, crying, shouting, whispering, pacing up and down, criticising, being passive or aggressive, confident or shy. You will probably be able to add to this list from your own experiences.

Behaviour affects everything you do. Understanding this is crucial to your success when dealing with difficult people. Behaviour is always observable, unlike the *reasons* for your behaviour (that is, your attitudes, beliefs, and emotional feelings).

Clearly, you will not want to do or say anything which makes the situation worse. Always remember that the way you behave has an impact on others.

Portfolio Task

Links to c1d, c1e, c1h, c1j

1 Do you find yourself in situations where you are having to deal with difficult people? Make notes of your thoughts on the following questions:

a. Is it customers' behaviour that causes you concern?

b. Is it the problem itself?

c. How have you helped the customer in this kind of situation?

d. How do you speak to customers who are dissatisfied?

e. How do you adapt your behaviour in these situations?

f. How do you manage to follow your organisation's procedures?

2 Now arrange to discuss with your assessor two or three difficult situations you have been involved with. Make sure you cover:

a. How you spotted there was a problem.

b. What did the customer do that was difficult or awkward? Specifically, what behaviours did he or she demonstrate?

c. How did you react?

d. Were you able to help the customer?

e. Did the customer feel satisfied at the end of your dealings with him or her? How did you know?

Use your notes to help you with the discussion.

Functional skills

English: Speaking, listening and communication

If you clearly discuss your thoughts and opinions with your assessor using appropriate language, you may be able to count this as evidence towards Level 1 Functional English: Speaking, listening and communication.

Figure 8: Behaviour breeds behaviour.

Showing that you care

One key reason why customers behave in a difficult way is disappointment. Perhaps expectations are not met, reputation does not come to life or the whole customer service experience was not up to scratch. When dealing with disappointed customers you must show that you care:

Show you are prepared to listen

Keep quiet and let your customer have his or her say. Do not interrupt.

Empathise

After being given the chance to speak to you, your customer will want to know you have listened and that you understand and care about what they have told you. To show **empathy** you should:

- acknowledge the customer's feelings *'I can see you are disappointed...'*
- acknowledge the facts of the situation e.g. *'I understand the toys did not arrive in time for Christmas.'*

> **Key term**
>
> **Empathy** – understanding and sharing the feelings of others.

Apologise

The customer will certainly want to hear that you are sorry about the problem.

Be careful not to overdo the apologies; this might make the situation worse by building it up into more of a disappointment.

Take ownership

Involve your customer in finding a solution and say what you are going to do next. Seek your customer's agreement to any proposed actions. Carry out your actions.

What kinds of behaviours and actions make situations worse?

You still need to show you care about your customers even when their behaviour is difficult. If dealing face to face with a customer who has a problem, your body language is important.

Here are some examples of body language that could have a negative impact on customers.

- Looking tense, for example, having a wrinkled forehead, puzzled look, hands clasped tightly to your body. This could give the impression you are lacking in confidence and therefore unable to help.

- Looking away when the customer approaches. This might make the customer feel you are not willing to sort out their problem.

- Smiling when a customer is telling you about a problem. This is rude behaviour.

- Fidgeting, for example, moving around unnecessarily, playing with a pen or jewellery. Fidgeting is often interpreted as having something to hide and trying to cover up the fact there is a problem.

- Leaning far back on a chair – this looks sloppy and arrogant. It is almost as if you are saying 'I don't care about your problem. You sort it out yourself!'.

- No eye contact – this shows you lack confidence or that you do not trust your customer or yourself to do the right thing. Dealing with difficult customers always requires you to show confidence.

- Sloppy posture – for example, having a slumped position. It looks far too casual and as if you do not care.

Things you might do or say which are guaranteed to make situations worse include:

- shouting back at customers who shout at you
- using inappropriate language
- forgetting to say 'sorry' when appropriate
- blaming other people or systems
- saying you are 'too busy' to help properly
- not passing information on
- failing to keep your promises
- not knowing where to go for help and support if you are unable to help
- saying there is 'no problem' when the customer says there is.

Often we think that dissatisfied customers will want some kind of monetary compensation for what has gone wrong. This is not always the case; many people just want to be heard. You must listen very carefully to what the customer says. This enables customers to 'get things off their chest' as well as helping you to get to the facts of the problem.

Portfolio Task

Links to c1c, c1d, c1e, c1i, c1k

Think about some times when you have dealt with difficult customers.

1 Looking firstly at successful transactions, what did you do to adapt your behaviour to ensure you remained calm and confident?

2 What about situations which did not go quite so well? Why was that?

3 How did your behaviour help to not make the problem worse?

Discuss these situations with your assessor.

Using assertive behaviour to deal with difficult people

We have seen that when you deal with a difficult situation you will be faced with a variety of different behaviours. Behaving *assertively* and professionally can help you to deal with a difficult situation and to stop it from getting worse. Some people confuse assertiveness with aggression. Behaving assertively is *not* about being forceful, shouting at customers or doing absolutely anything to get your way. It is about behaving in a calm and professional way to defuse a difficult situation.

Remember that behaviour breeds behaviour so if you are dealing with a difficult customer who reacts angrily you may be tempted to react in a similar fashion and become aggressive. What you need to aim for is *assertive behaviour*.

Behaving assertively is about being calm and professional.

Note

Unit A10 Deal with customers face to face dealt with how to manage difficult situations on pages 133 – 140. Please refer to Unit A10's Table 5 How assertive behaviour differs from aggressive or passive behaviour and Table 6 Using voice and body language in an assertive, aggressive or passive manner.

Using assertive behaviour in difficult situations is also covered in **Unit C4 Deliver customer service to difficult customers**.

There is a technique you can use called HEAT to help with calming down dissatisfied customers:

Hear
Empathise
Apologise
Take ownership.

You should also refer to the section Applying HEAT to calm dissatisfied customers on pages 133 – 134 in **Unit A10 Deal with customers face to face**.

✔ Checklist – Behaving in an assertive way

- Remain calm.

- Listen.

- Demonstrate you understand.

- Consider the consequences for all parties of getting what you want/need.

- Ask for what you want/need without offending others.

Check your knowledge

1 What do customers normally expect from an organisation when they have a problem?

a. To obtain a refund for the hassle the problem caused.

b. To discuss the problem with a manager or supervisor.

c. To have the problem solved to their satisfaction.

d. To be given a discount or promotional vouchers.

2 How can you recognise there is a problem from your customers' behaviour and actions?

a. By asking if a product or service meets their expectations.

b. By listening to the tone of voice or observing body language.

c. By discussing sales targets with colleagues and supervisors.

d. By reviewing how many times complaints are received.

3 When is it a good idea to pass a problem on to a colleague?

a. When I would be acting outside the limits of my authority.

b. When I am about to go to lunch or stop work for the day.

c. When my colleagues need me to help them with their work.

d. When I need to attend a meeting with my manager.

4 What should you do when passing a problem to a colleague?

a. Tell my colleague I have not told the customer when it will get sorted.

b. Make a note of the number of times the same customer complains.

c. Make sure all the information I pass on to my colleague is accurate.

d. Avoid apologising and blaming the computer system for any problems.

5 What types of types of behaviour are likely to make a situation worse?

a. Giving plenty of eye contact and taking action on what has gone wrong.

b. Shouting back at a customer and not keeping them informed.

c. Telling a customer what I can do rather than what I cannot do.

d. Asking colleagues for support if I am unable to help.

6 How can you use your voice to calm a difficult customer?

a. By matching the speed, pace and tone of the customer's voice.

b. By taking care not to raise my voice and to speak in a calm manner.

c. By raising my voice to ensure I am heard properly.

d. By asking the customer not to speak whilst I am speaking.

7 Why does assertive behaviour help to deal with difficult customers?

a. It is a procedure which most organisations support.

b. It makes people sit up and listen to what is needed.

c. It shows that equal opportunities legislation is followed.

d. It helps get what is needed without offending others.

8 How can the personal touch help deal with a customer's problem?

a. The organisation does not incur any extra costs.

b. It helps to show a caring and courteous service.

c. Staff do not have to be qualified or trained.

d. It helps colleagues to become involved.

9 Why is it important to follow your organisation's complaints procedures?

a. To comply with external legislation and regulations.

b. To ensure all complaints are dealt with in a consistent way.

c. To show colleagues how to help the complaints handling team.

d. To ensure a complaint is always followed up with an apology.

10 In the eyes of a customer, which of the following would help you to deal with a difficult situation?

a. Acknowledging the problem and showing empathy.

b. Updating my product or service knowledge.

c. Reviewing the complaints procedures.

d. Seeking advice from a team member afterwards.

Unit C4
Deliver customer service to difficult customers

What you will learn:
- To recognise when customers may be difficult to deal with
- To deal with difficult customers

Having to queue

Like most people, Chris is busy and would rather you dealt with him without him having to queue. Having to queue to see you or being kept holding on the phone for ages irritates him. He loses patience and this makes him angry.

Queues are a modern day fact of life whether it be for service given face to face or on the telephone. Most customers appreciate this but some will be less patient than others. What particularly aggravates people is when another customer is dealt with out of turn. It is therefore important for any queuing system to be seen as a fair system. Otherwise, customers' behaviour can quickly turn from showing frustration to anger and even aggression.

Portfolio Task
Links to c4.1.2, c4.1.5, c4b, c4c

1 If appropriate to your role, write a personal statement which shows you understand how your organisation's queuing system(s) has an impact on your customers' behaviour. Include how easy (or how hard) your customers find the queuing system to operate or use.

2 Think too about customers' behaviour with each other. Do they use the system fairly? If not, what is the impact on other customers?

Functional skills

English: Writing

You may be able to count your written personal statement as evidence towards Level 1 Functional English: Writing. Your statement should include sufficient detail to show you have understood the questions and you will need to check it for spelling, grammar and punctuation. Print a copy of your statement as it may count as evidence towards Level 1 Functional English: Writing.

Poor communication

Chris will want any communication (face to face, electronic or by telephone) to be timely and accurate and to result in any queries or questions being answered. If it does not meet his expectations, he will be dissatisfied and could well become annoyed.

Poor communication (or no communication at all, for example, unanswered letters or emails) is a very common cause of difficult customer behaviour. Poor communication could be caused by the service provider's poor attitude or by ineffective organisational systems and procedures.

Portfolio Task
Links to c4.1.2, c4.1.5, c4.1.7, c4b

1 There will have been times when poor communication has resulted in difficult customer behaviour. This could be as a result of:

a. your organisation's services or products (for example, the way it communicates through advertising, the web, product or service information etc.)

b. things you do or say.

2 Write a personal statement (including specific examples) which shows you understand how poor communication affects customer behaviour.

Lack of resources

If a shortage of time, money or staff cause Chris's expectations not to be met, he could well get angry.

Many customers will not understand or accept their expectations not being met because of the organisation's lack of time, money or staff. This is an instant source of aggravation and may quickly lead to a negative change in a customer's behaviour.

Portfolio Task
Links to c4.1.2, c4.1.5, c4b

Think about times when resource issues have had a direct impact on customer behaviour. Write a personal statement (with specific examples) showing you understand how resource issues can provoke difficult customer behaviour.

Making the wrong assumption about a service or product

Chris may have seen all the adverts, been given correct information or discussed a product or service but he might still make the wrong assumptions. This means his expectations are not met and he ends up dissatisfied. Although it was Chris's mistake, he will look to you to offer an explanation.

Customers sometimes hear or see what they want to hear or see. For example, nobody likes bad news so if a service provider has to give this, a customer may simply not hear it that way. Or, a product may have worked in a certain way in the past but alterations to it mean the customer has to use it in a different way. If this is not understood, anger and frustration may occur.

This type of situation means there has been a misunderstanding between the customer and you or your organisation. How the customer reacts will depend on how important the service or product is to him or her. There could be mild irritation or there could be anger and frustration.

I can't understand this.

Figure 3: Poor communication can sometimes be dangerous.

Being given an unpopular decision

If Chris does not get what he wants, he could be provoked into unwanted behaviour.

It is not always possible to say 'yes' to a customer. It is important to balance the needs of the customer with those of the organisation. There may also be legal reasons or health and safety reasons why you have to say 'no' to a customer.

Although a decision may be totally justified and fully explained to a customer, there may still be difficult customer behaviour to be dealt with.

Portfolio Task   Links to c4.1.5, c4.1.7, c4b

If you work in a role where you frequently have to say 'no' to a customer, you may have plenty of examples of having to deal with difficult customer behaviour. Use these to write a personal statement which shows you understand how giving an unpopular decision to a customer can cause difficult behaviour.

Dissatisfaction with an organisation's systems or procedures

Sometimes it is an organisation's systems or procedures which have a direct impact on customer behaviour. For example, a complaints system should be easy to use and many people think expressing their complaint in an email, rather than sending a letter, is the most efficient way of putting a complaint in writing. However, many organisations do not provide this facility, preferring instead to ask customers to write a letter. So, the procedure itself causes added aggravation.

Portfolio Task   Links to c4.1.2, c4.1.5, c4b

Which of your organisation's systems or procedures appear to provoke difficult behaviour in customers? Why is this?

Write a personal statement.

As you can see from Figure 2 (page 222), Chris might be upset by a variety of things; all this is part of normal life and can easily happen to any of your customers and therefore, you will find yourself dealing with difficult behaviour.

How customers handle anger

As you can see, when customers' needs or expectations are not met they may get frustrated and angry. How they deal with this will depend on the individual. Some will hide their anger whilst others may become aggressive.

For example, if a customer experiences the same problem over and over again (say queuing in a shop or being kept waiting on the phone) what started off as a mild irritation gradually becomes a much bigger issue the more it happens. Or, a customer may instantly expect something to happen (perhaps a quick decision on a refund or to talk with a manager). If it does not then he or she may feel an instant surge of emotion and get angry.

Everybody has the potential to get angry, but we deal with it in different ways.

Hiding anger

Some customers hide their anger but take action to show their displeasure. This can be done quietly without disrupting other customers, for example:

- walking out of a shop which has too long a queue without saying anything

- putting the phone down before it is answered.

As a service provider, you may or may not spot this happening. Either way, there is no direct impact on other customers but your organisation will lose business.

In other cases, customers may hide their anger from staff but make it quite clear to other customers they are angry by:

- discussing their dissatisfaction with other customers before walking away

- using body language to express anger.

Customers who hide their anger from you, usually have plenty to say to friends and family about their dissatisfaction.

Alternatively, some customers hide behind sarcasm or humour and make comments which are a more polite way of expressing their true feelings. For example, the following comments may well be expressions of anger.

- 'You look so busy chatting to your friend – I'm really sorry to disturb you.'

- 'Oh, there is someone there! I thought everybody had gone home for the day.'

- 'I've got some spare time. Would you like me to clean this place?'

Being angry but helpful

Customers who can control their emotions may be able to both express feelings and ask for a solution. This involves assertive behaviour and you may hear comments like:

> 'I am very upset by what has happened and I want you to get back to me by the end of the week.'

> 'You have failed to do what you promised and this has made me very angry. Please let me speak to your supervisor.'

> 'This is the third time this has broken and I'm very annoyed. I want a refund now.'

Using assertive behaviour is the best way for a customer to deal with anger and organisations who have customers who react like this should look on it favourably. This is a form of feedback and could usefully be used to improve customer service.

We look at assertive behaviour later in this unit.

Moving from anger to aggression

If a customer is not good at handling his or her emotions, aggressive behaviour may be their only release. They 'blow their top'. This could involve using abusive language or physical threats. Once the anger is out in the open, that is, they have let off steam, the aggression tends to subside and they can then start to calm down.

Customers who use assertive behaviour can often quickly move to being aggressive if the situation they find themselves in is not resolved to their satisfaction.

Unit C4 Deliver customer service to difficult customers

How to recognise the types of customer behaviour you find difficult to deal with

We've looked at the reasons why customers may be difficult to deal with and how they handle anger. We will now turn to thinking about the types of customer behaviour you personally find difficult to deal with. You may think that most people do not like (or find it hard to cope with) customers who are, say, angry. This is not always the case; some customer service practitioners find successfully dealing with challenging behaviour a positive aspect of their job.

Emotion and behaviour

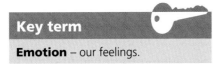

Key term

Emotion – our feelings.

You can spot a customer may be difficult to deal with by watching and listening for signs and signals which may indicate difficult behaviour. Much of this involves understanding how our **emotions** affect the way we behave.

Table 1 shows how our emotions can affect the way we behave and the facial signals you can look out for. Please note, people do vary in how they react so this is a general indicator only.

Table 1: How emotions can affect our behaviour.

Emotion	Facial signals and other actions
Anger	Eyes wide and staring, eyebrows pulled down, wrinkled forehead, flared nostrils, clenched teeth, red face, abusive language
Anxiety	Eyes damp, eyebrows slightly together, trembling lower lip, head slightly lowered down, shaky voice or no voice, loud or quiet tone
Disgust	Eyes and head turned away, flared nostrils, nose screwed up, vocal expressions of dissatisfaction
Fear	Eyes wide, closed or pointing down, mouth open, chin pulled in, head down, white face, raised voice
Sadness/disappointment	Eyes cast down, damp/tearful/crying, head down, lips pinched, shaky or no voice

A version of the table used in this task, ready for you to complete, is available to download from www.contentextra.com/customerservice

You may find some aspects of difficult behaviour easier to handle than others. It all depends on your level of experience in dealing with people and also your own personality type.

Portfolio Task

Links to c4.1.1, c4.1.3, c4a

1   Think of situations you have found yourself in which:

   a. made you feel stressed

   b. you simply found difficult to handle.

2   Copy and complete the table below.

What happened – what my customer did (include the signs and signals of difficult behaviour)	My reaction – what I felt	Outcome for the customer and myself

Unacceptable behaviour

There will be some types of behaviour which your organisation will find unacceptable. Please refer to **Unit F2 Follow rules to deliver customer service** to remind yourself of the legislation designed to protect you, your colleagues, your organisation and other customers from unacceptable behaviour.

Behaviours which your organisation is likely to find unacceptable are:

Discriminatory behaviour

This is where a customer fails to afford you or your colleagues equal respect on the basis of disability, gender, race, religion, age, sexuality and marital status.

Harassment

This is behaviour which is unwanted and offensive and affects your dignity.

Bullying

This is a type of harassment which consists of persistent actions, criticism or personal abuse in public or private which humiliate, intimidate, frighten or demean you or your colleagues.

Unreasonable behaviour

This is when a customer behaves in such a way as to be going outside that which is normally acceptable. For example, a customer who contacts an organisation many times during a short period of time despite being dealt with appropriately, or a customer who asks for complex information without a good reason may be deemed as showing unreasonable behaviour.

Violent and aggressive behaviour

If a customer takes his or her anger to the extreme, you may find yourself dealing with violent or aggressive behaviour. There are warning signs you can look and listen for. These include:

- Facial signals — frowns, pursed lips and snarls. Too much eye contact to the point of staring. Face going red.

- Attack signals — clenching and shaking of fists, moving into your personal space (including sudden movements of the body), banging tables/doors, throwing items, insulting gestures (usually this involves use of the fingers pointed upwards).

- Verbal signals — using abusive language, shouting and screaming.

Violent and aggressive behaviour may be as a result of drink and/or drug misuse.

Unacceptable behaviour policies

Your organisation may have a policy about dealing with unacceptable behaviour. Its purpose will be to help staff deal with customers in a fair and consistent way. It will tell you what actions to take and how.

Typically, an unacceptable behaviour policy will include:

● **Definitions and examples of unacceptable behaviour.**
  For example, the behaviours listed above.

● **The process to be undertaken for each type of behaviour.**
  This is necessary because the impact of each type of behaviour will be different. For example, aggressive behaviour requires swift action whereas unreasonable behaviour may not.

The process may involve these stages:

Stage 1

1 Politely tell the customer the organisation expects its staff to be treated with respect and ask the customer to moderate their behaviour.

2 If the unacceptable behaviour continues, give a warning that the call will be terminated or the customer will be asked to leave the premises. The customer should be given an explanation as to why, for example, 'I am going to stop this conversation as I consider your behaviour to have been inappropriate.'

3 If the behaviour still continues, the threatened action should be taken.

Stage 2

A line manager, senior manager or other appropriate authority will decide what action should be taken. This might involve sanctions. For example, restricting contact to a particular method (such as telephone instead of face to face), limiting contact to a certain time or day, specifying a named member of staff as being the sole point of contact, or asking the customer to enter into an agreement about their future behaviour.

If the behaviour is discriminatory, contact with the customer is usually terminated immediately.

If the behaviour is unreasonable, staff members are usually asked to refer to a line manager or other appropriate authority for advice.

If the behaviour is violent and aggressive, you should:

● stop your dealings with the customer immediately

● take action to ensure your own safety and that of your colleagues

● contact the police if the behaviour is thought to be so threatening that your safety and that of your colleagues is at risk

● complete your organisation's incident report forms.

Portfolio Task

Links to c4.1.6, c4.2.10, c4e c4h, c4j

1 Find out now if your organisation has a policy on dealing with unacceptable and/or difficult behaviour. Discuss with your assessor:

   a. the types of behaviour involved

   b. which situations you need to take action in to protect your own safety or that of your colleagues and customers

   c. who you need to go to for help.

2 Discuss examples of when you have put the policy into action.

Functional skills

English: Speaking, listening and communication

If you clearly discuss the outcome of your findings with your assessor using appropriate language, you may be able to count this as evidence towards Level 1 Functional English: Speaking, listening and communication.

What your responsibilities are when dealing with difficult behaviour

Whilst a situation may be very awkward, you should always try to deliver a high standard of service.

Reporting incidents

Your organisation may have a procedure which tells you what to do about reporting any incidents of extreme difficult behaviour. This would include reporting situations where you have applied sanctions in order to control difficult behaviour. Your organisation will then be able to monitor individual customers and also why their behaviour has been difficult. It can then take action. This will help your organisation to ensure its staff are working in a safe environment. It will also mean other customers are not affected by a particular customer's behaviour in the future.

If you believe a customer may come back for a further discussion (for example, he or she may have asked to speak with a manager but this was not possible), you should let your colleagues know. This is important because an already upset customer will be even more upset if he or she has to repeat everything again. Your colleagues might also need to be aware from a health and safety viewpoint.

Portfolio Task

Links to c4.2.9, c4i

Ask for witness testimonies from colleagues who you have reported incidents to because you believe a customer may return to deal with the matter again.

Health and safety

Nobody goes to work to be abused or attacked and your customers certainly do not want to find themselves involved with unwanted behaviour from another customer.

You should always consider your own health and safety as well as that of other customers and your colleagues. This means being prepared by knowing what your organisation does to support you in difficult situations. If you work in retail, do you know what to do if faced with a shoplifter or you suspect fraud? Do you know what to do if a customer is verbally abusing you? Knowing about your organisation's unacceptable behaviour policy will help you to deal with these situations and to know who to refer to.

Various security measures can help too. Are there any alarm systems, CCTV, protective barriers, or panic buttons which can help?

Do not make things worse

It is especially important not to do or say something which may make things worse. After all, the situation is already red hot; if you say something which aggravates your customer further, you will never be able to take the heat out of the incident and calm the customer down.

Your voice and the words you choose are a very powerful way of generating emotions in someone else. Used effectively, your voice can help you to control a difficult situation.

Do not accuse the customer of being wrong

There are certain phrases which you should avoid. These include sentences which accuse the customer of being wrong. They tend to start with 'YOU....' For example:

'You must be mistaken.'
'You were not told that.'
'Are you sure that was what you were told?'

A physical barrier can help protect you from difficult behaviour.

Avoid saying what you cannot do

It is better to say what you can do, rather than what you cannot do. So avoid phrases like:

'I cannot help you right now.'
'I am unable to sort this out.'
'I will not do that for you.'
'I don't know.'

...without also explaining what you *can* do.

Avoid too much silence

Although you will need to allow an angry customer to let off steam, too much silence can often make a person feel they are being ignored. Clearly, this will only make things worse.

Avoid passing blame and denying responsibility

The last thing any customer will want to hear is a service provider stating what the company rules and procedures are without backing this up with an explanation of why these exist. You should always avoid simply stating rules and procedures as a means of trying to stop a customer behaving in a difficult way.

If you say things like:

'It's not my fault.'
'My colleague did that, not me.'
'That's our policy – there's nothing I can do about it.'
'That's never happened before.'

...your customer may feel you are not prepared to help and this could make the situation worse.

Avoid behaving in an aggravating manner

There are actions you might take which could end up aggravating a difficult situation. These include:

- turning your back on a customer
- using gestures rather than words to direct a customer
- chatting to colleagues whilst a customer is waiting or queuing
- keeping a customer on hold on the phone for a long time
- being sarcastic
- using humour inappropriately.

Please refer to the section on How to manage difficult situations pages 133 – 140 in **Unit A10 Deal with customers face to face** for more information.

Portfolio Task   Links to c4.1.7

1   Make a list of things which you have said or done which have provoked difficult responses from your customers.

2   Discuss your list with your assessor.

Deal with difficult customers

What you need to know and learn

- Why it is important to have empathy for a customer's feelings
- How to use questioning techniques to identify what your customer wants
- How to use a four-step model for handling difficult customers

Note

To achieve this unit, you need to know the difference between assertive, aggressive and passive behaviour. This has been covered in **Unit A10 Deal with customers face to face**. Please refer to the section on pages 133 – 140 'How to manage difficult situations' which deals with this in depth.

Why it is important to have empathy for a customer's feelings

We all need to feel the people we talk to when we are unhappy or angry about something have some degree of understanding about our feelings. We often expect others to know how hurt we feel or how annoyed we are without actually explaining just what is wrong. Customers are no different. They will expect you to almost automatically understand why they are acting in a way which potentially causes a difficult situation to occur. Understanding someone else's feelings is called having **empathy**.

Your customers will want to know you have some empathy for their feelings. This will help them to believe and trust that things will get better, that you will sort out any problem and that their expectations will eventually be met. Showing empathy will also help to calm down any aggressive situations you find yourself in. However, do bear in mind, if somebody is under the influence of drink or drugs no amount of empathy may be enough to do this.

Empathy is about showing you understand and care and can appreciate your customers' feelings. By helping customers to see you do understand you will be starting to build a bridge between the difficult situation and a much healthier one.

Showing empathy is not necessarily about agreeing with everything the customer does or says. Nor does it have to be about being sympathetic. For example, if a customer says, 'I am totally fed up with the way you keep putting your prices up', a sympathetic response would be 'I agree. My company really should do more to keep prices down.' However, responding in this way would not be appropriate. An empathetic response would be 'I understand it must be hard. However, it is necessary for us to do that in order to maintain quality.'

> **Key term**
>
> **Empathy** – identifying and understanding another person's feelings.

How to express empathy to a customer

Firstly, you need to try to switch out of any bad mood or concerns you may have when faced with a difficult customer.

Remember you are a service provider

If you constantly think to yourself 'I'd rather not be dealing with this person', you are not going to do yourself any favours. This is because, your mind will be trying to help you escape or run away from the situation, rather than dealing with the person in front of you or on the telephone. Instead, try thinking to yourself:

'What does this customer need from me and what can I do to help?'

Doing this will mean you have switched from not wanting to help back to being a service provider.

Listen to the customer let off steam

Trying to stop someone expressing their feelings could make matters worse so the next step is to allow your customer a chance to let off steam. Make sure your customer knows you are listening. You can do this by nodding your head or making appropriate sounds.

Having done this, you can now start to show some empathy to your customer.

Use empathetic phrases

These are simple, brief phrases which indicate to your customer that you understand their feelings and situation. These include:

'I see what you mean.'

'I can see you are really upset by this.'

'That must be very frustrating for you.'

'I am sorry about this.'

'I am concerned that you have been treated like that.'

'I can hear you have been deeply disturbed by what's happened.'

This type of phrase shows your customer you have acknowledged how they are feeling and this will continue to help calm the situation. Once a customer knows this, he or she is more likely to trust you and will work with you to seek a solution.

It is no use saying the right words if they sound like you are reading from a script. So, make sure you say the words with an appropriate tone of voice. You need to sound warm and genuine.

Figure 4: Remembering you're a service provider can help you express empathy.

I'm very sorry that you weren't happy with your meal, sir.

Figure 5: Saying 'sorry' can have a calming effect.

Know when to say 'sorry'

Some people find it very difficult to say 'sorry' in their personal life. If you are one of those people, you are likely to have difficulty doing it in your working life too. Saying 'sorry' is sometimes seen as an admission of guilt. As you may well be dealing with an issue you have not previously been involved with, it makes saying 'sorry' even harder. After all, it may have been a colleague who had made a mistake which caused the customer to come in angry – why should you say 'sorry'?

Well, you should because you are part of a team. It's about accepting responsibility for things that go wrong regardless of whether or not you were personally involved. Your customer will feel much better if they hear the word 'sorry'. Do remember though, you should not necessarily be admitting your organisation is at fault. This is important because you will need to get to the facts and you may not know the true story until you start asking questions. If you admit your organisation is at fault before you know if this is the case, the outcome could be costly.

Portfolio Task

Links to c4.2.1, c4.2.4, c4d

Arrange to be observed by your assessor or obtain witness testimonies which concentrate on how you express empathy to your customers. Make sure you get feedback on:

1 your listening techniques

2 the words you use

3 your tone of voice

4 how and when you say 'sorry'

5 the outcome for the customer.

We have looked at the reasons why customers may present with difficult behaviour so you will understand giving an apology is not always needed. For example, when a customer has already been upset by something else. However, in situations where it is appropriate saying 'sorry' can often have an instant calming effect.

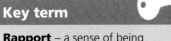

Key term

Rapport – a sense of being comfortable with someone whether or not you know him or her well.

Sustain rapport

If you have been truly empathetic and have started to build the bridge to a more comfortable position you will have gone a long way to establishing rapport with your customer.

You can now start to use your customer's name more. Make sure you are aware of your body language and tone of voice – do not give any signs that you are less than comfortable – keep relaxed.

Please refer to **Unit A4 Give customers a positive impression of yourself and your organisation** for more information on rapport building.

Put yourself in the customer's position

As you start to try to understand the reasons behind a customer's behaviour, you may become aware of how *you* might feel in their situation. This will help you to show empathy as the feelings and emotions will seem real to you too. Do bear in mind though, that what might seem like a minor problem or inconvenience to you, may be very serious to somebody else.

> ✓ **Checklist – Showing empathy to difficult customers**
>
> - Avoid negative thoughts.
> - Let the customer express their feelings.
> - Listen actively.
> - Use brief empathetic phrases.
> - Use a warm and genuine tone of voice.
> - Say 'sorry' when appropriate.

Remember: creating trust, showing empathy and building rapport are all powerful tools when dealing with difficult customers. They are just as powerful when communicating with your colleagues and other customers so the skills you use for this unit will be useful elsewhere.

Assertive, aggressive and passive behaviour

Behaviour can fall into three categories

- assertive
- aggressive
- passive.

A reminder: being assertive involves three steps:

1 **Show you are listening and that you understand:**

'I appreciate what you are saying.'

'I want to help and can understand your frustration.'

'Let me help you here because I can see you are upset.'

2 **Say what you want to happen next:**

'Let's sit down here so we can talk privately.'

'My company does want to help you at this difficult time and will...'

'Please do not shout at me or I will have to terminate the call.'

3 **Seek agreement:**

'OK. So we've agreed that I will deliver a new machine tomorrow?'

'If I've understood correctly, you will repay the outstanding amount by the end of next week.'

'Although I can't agree to that right now, I will talk to my manager and get back to you by the end of the day. How does that sound?'

Unit C4 Deliver customer service to difficult customers

> ☑ **Checklist – Using assertive behaviours to deal with difficult customers**
>
> • Listen actively.
>
> • Discuss things calmly.
>
> • Make brief empathetic statements.
>
> • Stand up for your rights whilst respecting the customers' rights.
>
> • State your views.
>
> • Show you understand the customers' views.
>
> • Avoid blaming others.

A version of the table used in this task, ready for you to complete, is available to download from www.contentextra.com/customerservice

You should now refer to **Unit A10 Deal with customers face to face** for more information on assertive, aggressive and passive behaviours.

Portfolio Task

Links to c4f

Take a look at the following situations and write down on a separate piece of paper or by downloading a copy of the table from the website whether the situation is an example of assertive, aggressive or submissive behaviour.

Functional skills

English: Writing

If you complete the table in the task in writing you may be able to count it as evidence towards Level 1 Functional English: Writing. Your written responses should include sufficient detail to show you have understood each situation and you will need to check them for spelling, grammar and punctuation. Print a copy of your responses as this may count as evidence towards Level 1 Functional English: Writing.

Examples of different behaviours.

Situation	Type of behaviour
A customer discusses things calmly with you	
You blame your company's policy for a problem	
A customer points her fingers at you whilst shouting	
You decide to give in to what the customer wants	
A customer calmly asks to speak to a manager	
You tell a customer who is showing unacceptable behaviour to stop	
A customer keeps quiet even though he or she is irritated	
You give lots of eye contact to a customer who is annoyed	
A customer tells you which course of action they want	

How to use questioning techniques to identify what your customer wants

Keeping calm, showing empathy and using assertive behaviour will help you to deal with a difficult customer. Clearly, you also need to get to understand exactly what the problem is. A solution is needed. You will only achieve this by avoiding making assumptions and by asking questions.

Asking the right questions will help you to get quickly to the root of the problem. There are several types of question you could use:

Open questions

Open questions require your customer to give you a full response rather than a short one-word answer.

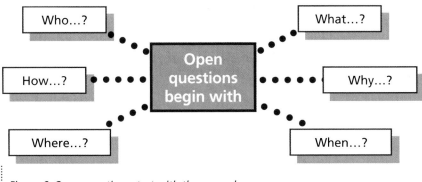

Figure 6: Open questions start with these words.

For example, if you were trying to understand your customer's feelings and what has happened to cause them to be difficult, you could ask:

'Who told you that would happen?'

'Who made you feel so angry?'

'What would you really like me to do next?'

'What has happened to make you feel so sad?'

'Why are you so upset?'

'You seem very annoyed. Why does this letter make you so angry?'

'You seem very disappointed. When can I call you to try to put things right?'

'When will you be able to talk to me about how you are feeling now?'

'Where does it hurt the most?'

'How can I give you what you need?'

Open questions get the ball rolling — you will lead your customer into talking with you.

Sometimes, a question may provoke continued difficult behaviour and you should be prepared for that. After all, your customer is not behaving in a difficult way for no reason. For example, asking 'Why are you so upset?' may spur him or her into

- Use your customer's name from time to time.

- Avoid interrupting (unless the behaviour becomes unacceptable).

- Apologise if appropriate and time this well.

- Watch your voice – keep calm and speak at a steady pace.

- Use your assertive behavioural skills.

Note

In very difficult situations, keep in mind the need to seek help or take action to protect your own safety or that of other customers and your colleagues.

The key stages of our model for handling difficult customers are:

1 Listen actively

2 Ask questions

3 Check understanding

4 Suggest options and agree way forward.

We now bring together the key points you need to remember at each stage.

Step 1 Listen actively

- Be patient.

- Do not interrupt.

- Acknowledge what is said by giving non-verbal cues.

- Watch your body language.

- Do not get defensive.

- Empathise.

Step 2 Ask questions

- Question to understand feelings.

- Question to understand the situation.

- Watch your body language and tone of voice.

- Build rapport.

- Stay calm.

- Be assertive.

- Empathise.

Step 3 Check your understanding

- Ask clarifying questions if necessary.
- Summarise the response to your questions.
- Include both the situation itself and your customer's feelings.
- Ask if your understanding is right.
- Apologise if appropriate.
- Stay calm, be assertive, empathise.
- Sustain rapport.

Step 4 Suggest options and agree the way forward

- Describe your view of the situation.
- Explain your organisation's position.
- Avoid solely stating your company's rules and procedures.
- Balance the needs of your customer and the organisation.
- Keep within the limits of your authority — seek permission or help if needed.
- Give options for actions to be taken.
- Agree on some common ground in order to make progress.
- Be clear as to who is responsible for what.
- Summarise the actions to be taken.
- Remain assertive.

Figure 7: Remember to stay calm, be assertive and empathise.

Unit C4 Deliver customer service to difficult customers

Portfolio Task

Links to All c4.2, c4g, c4i, c4j

Looking at each of the points in the four-step model for handling difficult customers, discuss with your assessor how you have put the model into practice. It is important you also ask to be observed and/or obtain witness testimonies.

Before you discuss, it may help you to make a list of the knowledge, skills and behaviours you use. On a separate piece of paper or a copy downloaded from the website, complete the sentences in the table and keep a copy for your portfolio.

A version of the table used in this task, ready for you to complete, is available to download from www.contentextra.com/customerservice

Functional skills

English: Reading, Writing and Speaking, listening and communication

If you complete the sentences in the table in writing, you will have an opportunity to identify a suitable response to the text. This may count as evidence towards Level 1 Functional English: Reading. Your written responses should include sufficient detail to show you have understood each statement and you will need to check them for spelling, grammar and punctuation. Print a copy of your responses as this may count as evidence towards Level 1 Functional English: Writing. If you use your responses as a basis for a discussion with your assessor, you may be able to count this as evidence towards Level 1 Functional English: Speaking, listening and communication.

Knowledge, skills and behaviours I use.

Step 1 Listen actively
The things I do to show the customer I am listening are:
I give non-verbal cues to show I am listening by:
I take care with my body language because I:
I show empathy by:

Step 2 Ask questions
My questioning technique involves:
I build rapport by:
I keep calm by:
I am assertive because I:
My tone of voice is:
This is important because:

Step 3 Check understanding
I check I have understood correctly by:
I sustain rapport by:
I know when to say 'sorry' because I:

Step 4 Suggest options and agree way forward
I make sure I balance the needs of my customer and my organisation by:
I decide on my options by:
I know when to seek help because:
I make sure I summarise what needs to happen by:
When I am finished with the customer I know I must:

At any stage I know I must...
...keep in mind the safety of myself and others by:
...report back to my manager or appropriate colleague when:
...avoid or restrict some behaviours and actions (body language, voice and words) such as:

Working Life

Hi. I'm Iwan and I work in a call centre dealing with electricity and gas bills. Most people I speak to are reasonable although many are a little frustrated at the amount of time they have had to wait to get through. This means they are already slightly annoyed regardless of the issue they want to talk about. I can tell this by their tone of voice and some make comments like 'at last'.

Last week I dealt with a man who was querying a very large bill on behalf of his aunt. He was unable to give me the information I needed to be able to continue the conversation with him and so I told him that our rules would not permit me to talk to him. He immediately swore at me and was really very rude. He kept telling me he was also a customer and that he knew we were always getting things wrong.

I decided to try to calm things down and made sure my own voice slowed down a bit and remained in a soft tone. However, when I quoted the Data Protection Act to him things got worse. The swearing increased, he was shouting and calling me all sorts of rude names. I had had enough and told him that, in accordance with our unacceptable behaviour policy, I was going to terminate the call. I just about heard him scream something vile and abusive at me before I ended the call. What did I do wrong?

Ask the expert

Q Should Iwan have been more assertive?

A Not really. He had remained calm and used an appropriate tone of voice. The conversation had not really developed enough to try to use an assertive approach. Instead, it had gone from bad to almost impossible — there was no middle ground to try to make things better.

Q Iwan had up-to-date knowledge about relevant policies and legislation and carried through the necessary actions. He also kept calm. Why did the customer's behaviour become more difficult?

A Giving an explanation to a customer involves much more than just quoting back a policy or a rule. If you do this, you run the risk of appearing too 'clever' in the eyes of the customer. As a result, the bad behaviour quickly escalates.

Q What else should Iwan have done?

A He does not appear to have considered an apology — not so much for the bill but more that he could not personally speak to anyone other than the account holder. Similarly, expressing empathy by saying things like:

'I can hear you are very upset by this'

may have calmed the situation down.

Rather than quoting back the policy and the legislation, he should have said what he could do. This needed to happen very early on in the conversation so that matters did not escalate. Saying what you can do (in this case perhaps contacting the aunt directly or asking him to obtain authority to deal with her account) is much better than saying what you cannot do. Explanations need to be full and timely.

Top tips

Know your organisation's policies regarding unacceptable behaviour and carry them out.

Know about any relevant legislation.

Do not expect your customer to appreciate this knowledge being quoted back to them. It will make a difficult situation worse.

Check your knowledge

1 Your manager (or appropriate colleague) should be told about a customer's difficult behaviour because:

a. all members of staff involved need to be disciplined

b. steps might need to be taken to prevent a reoccurrence

c. other customers need to be protected from the individual

d. the customer needs to be charged for any damage done.

2 If a customer is clearly annoyed what should you do first?

a. Take notes on what is said

b. Call for help from a manager

c. Listen actively without interrupting

d. Apologise and be courteous.

3 Customers who are verbally abusive are best dealt with by:

a. speaking clearly and slowly without raising your voice

b. a manager who has undergone special training

c. walking away from them or ending the phone call

d. shouting at them until they calm down and are quiet.

4 How might you show empathy for a customer's feelings?

a. By offering an immediate apology and shaking hands.

b. By getting the most senior person available to apologise.

c. By listening actively and knowing when to say sorry.

d. By offering an apology and giving discount vouchers.

5 What is the main reason why organisations have unacceptable behaviour policies?

a. To protect staff from colleagues who bully or harass others.

b. To ensure colleagues co-operate in difficult situations.

c. To provide the management team with performance feedback.

d. To ensure customers are treated in a fair and consistent way.

6 When customers' behaviour is difficult to deal with you can find out what they want by:

a. not making assumptions and asking questions

b. stating your organisation's complaints procedures

c. taking notes of any discussions and filing them

d. asking them to call when they have calmed down.

7 When a customer becomes difficult to deal with it is important to:

a. tell the customer to stop being difficult in order for help to be given

b. be patient and see the situation from the customer's point of view

c. advise the customer that other people can hear what they are saying

d. remind the customer of your organisation's unacceptable behaviour policy.

8 One of your key responsibilities when dealing with difficult behaviour is:

a. the achievement of any sales or performance targets

b. the ability to talk about other helpful services or products

c. the need to capture feedback on advertising materials

d. the health and safety of yourself, customers and colleagues.

9 When dealing with difficult behaviour it is important to avoid:

a. passing blame and raising your voice

b. saying sorry and admitting fault

c. giving a refund when not requested

d. asking for help from a colleague.

10 Which of the following will help you to deal with difficult behaviour?

a. Being passive, listening patiently and expressing empathy.

b. Seeing things from their point of view and keeping very quiet.

c. Observing how other people react to what is happening.

d. Keeping calm, showing empathy and using assertive behaviour.

Unit D1
Develop customer relationships

What you will learn:

- To build your customer's confidence that the service you give will be excellent
- To meet the expectations of your customers
- To develop the long-term relationship between your customer and your organisation

Introduction

Whilst working through your qualification, you will have become increasingly aware that creating a positive impression is the first vital step in building customer relationships. You want to make sure that every time you deal with a customer, he or she has a good experience.

The same is true if you deal with a customer regularly. Here you will be able to influence what the customer thinks and feels about you and your organisation over a longer period.

Developing your customer relationships ensures your customers want to continue to do business with you and your organisation. You will need to build their confidence, making them aware of the nature of the products or services you deal with and finding out about their expectations of you and your organisation.

Developing customer relationships is also known as building customer loyalty. This means building a lasting business relationship between the customer and your organisation. Customer loyalty means having customers who want to do business with you and your organisation because they trust you to deliver a reliable and appropriate service in a manner which suits individual needs and expectations (see key term on page 251). Having loyal customers is very important, not only for repeat business but also because if things do go wrong a loyal customer is likely to trust you to put it right.

There is also a feel-good factor for you to have loyal customers. It's fantastic for any customer service practitioner to have customers who ask for him or her by name because of the service provided. Sometimes this is not possible; people working in call centres are unlikely to be asked for by name as they are one of many people in a team.

You will need to show that you can build customer relationships on your own as well as with the help of others, for example, people in your team or other colleagues. To do this, you need to:

- build your customer's confidence that the service you give will be excellent

- meet the expectations of your customers

- develop the long-term relationship between your customer and your organisation.

Inspiring customers to remain loyal to your organisation will help you in your career as it will show you have the ability to maintain and sustain a great working relationship with your customers.

It's really good to see you again. I've reserved you your usual table.

Figure 1: Customer loyalty is good for both customers and staff.

Note

Some of the knowledge and understanding you need to achieve this unit is covered elsewhere in this book. Where this is the case, we signpost where you should refer to and, in particular, you should re-visit mandatory **Unit F1 Communicate using customer service language** where we dealt with:

- what services or products your organisation provides

- how you can help to deliver your organisation's service offer

- how the way you behave affects your customer's service experience.

Build your customer's confidence that the service you give will be excellent

Much of what you need to be able to know, understand and demonstrate for this learning outcome, has been covered within other units. We summarise key points and ask you to refer to the relevant sections in this book.

What you need to know or learn

- What helps your customers have confidence in you and your organisation
- How to describe your organisation's services or products
- How your own behaviour affects the behaviour of your customer
- How you can help to deliver your organisation's service offer

---

What helps your customers have confidence in you and your organisation

Here you should be thinking about what customers expect from you and your organisation and the values which you and your organisation need to work to to show customers you really care. This includes things like being:

- trustworthy

- open and honest

- reliable

- accurate.

This applies to both you *and* your organisation. After all, there is nothing to be had from you keeping your promises to customers if your organisation's processes do not back up your good work.

Customers will be confident in **you** when:

- you show you are trustworthy
- you make life easier for them
- you deal with them in an appropriate manner
- you get it right first time.

They will be confident in your **organisation** when:

- products or services meet or exceed needs and expectations
- systems and processes help, not hinder
- your organisation listens.

All this does not happen overnight. Confidence is built by a gradual process of customers seeing that service is consistently given to the level (or greater) that they expect.

One way you can inspire confidence is to ensure you are *reliable*.

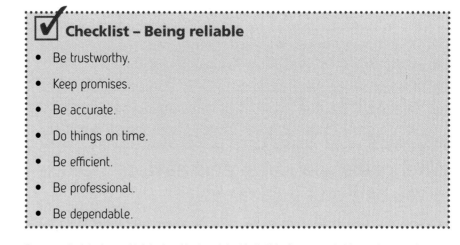

✓ **Checklist – Being reliable**

- Be trustworthy.
- Keep promises.
- Be accurate.
- Do things on time.
- Be efficient.
- Be professional.
- Be dependable.

Recap what being reliable is all about in **Unit F1 Communicate using customer service language**.

Portfolio Task   Links to d1a

1   Make a list of the values you always try to uphold.

2   Now think about times when these have helped you to deliver great service. Make some notes.

3   What about being reliable? Make a list of how you make sure your service is reliable.

4   Using this, explain to your assessor how your values help you to build your customer's confidence that the service you give will be excellent.

How to lose customers

Sadly, losing customers is quite easy since **customer loyalty** develops as a result of a series of good customer experiences. If there are not enough good experiences, customers may look elsewhere.

Look at Figure 2 and see just how easy it is to wave goodbye to a customer. What else can you add to these ways of losing a customer?

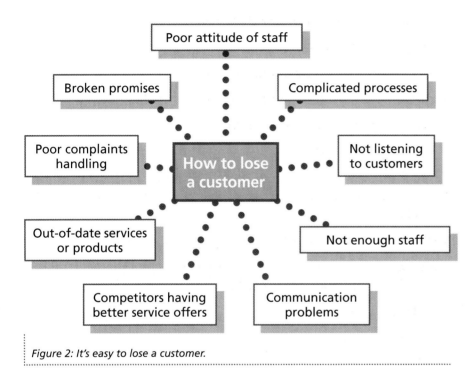

Figure 2: It's easy to lose a customer.

Retention! Retention! Retention!

Customer loyalty is valuable to an organisation because it is usually cheaper and easier to do repeat business with an existing satisfied customer than to find a new one. Also, if something does go wrong, there is a better chance of being able to put things right and keep the customer for the future than there would be with a new customer.

This is called **customer retention** – keep your customers loyal and they will stay with you. It is sometimes a tall order to do this given that customers are very aware that if you fail to impress them, somebody else will want their business.

In **Unit F1 Communicate using customer service language** we looked at the importance of an organisation having a strong reputation. This clearly plays a big part in helping retain customers' business. So, what your customers think of your organisation's services and products will help them to decide whether to stay with you or go elsewhere. If they do wave goodbye, your organisation's financial success may suffer.

Key terms

Customer loyalty – the same customer returning to the same service deliverer or organisation.

Customer retention – the ability to keep a customer loyal to an organisation.

Remember – customers are more sophisticated today than they have ever been. They want value for money and need to be reassured their decision to deal with you and your organisation is the right one. They also know that it is relatively easy to find what they want from another organisation.

Customer retention is also important because you want your loyal customers to recommend you and your organisation to friends and family. Therefore, keeping your customers loyal can help your organisation to win new business.

Providing any loyal customer base is large enough, being successful at customer retention also helps to reduce costs. This is because marketing costs (that is, selling and promoting products and services) can be kept down. An organisation with a large loyal customer base can also look to be in a relatively stable cash flow situation.

Portfolio Task

Links to d1a, d1h

1 Make notes about what your organisation does to keep customers loyal.

2 Now make notes about how you influence the customer experience to ensure customers remain loyal.

3 Use these notes to explain to your assessor the importance of customer retention to you and your organisation. Include the impact of bringing in new customers as opposed to retaining existing customers.

Functional skills

English: Speaking, listening and communication

If you use your notes effectively, they will help you to clearly discuss the outcome of your findings with your assessor. Make sure you use appropriate language. You may be able to count this as evidence towards Level 1 Functional English: Speaking, listening and communication.

How to describe your organisation's services or products

You have already started to look at your organisation's services and products when working through mandatory **Unit F1 Communicate using customer service language**. Please refer to the section entitled *What services or products your organisation provides* on pages 22 – 24 and the associated portfolio tasks.

Refresh your knowledge of the services or products applicable to your role. Think also about describing them in terms of features and benefits.

✔ Checklist – Describing your services and products

- Identify which are relevant to you and your role.
- Know where to find out information.
- Know who to go to to seek additional information.
- Make sure you keep your knowledge up to date.
- Know and understand their features and benefits.
- Tell customers about benefits as well as features.

Portfolio Task   Links to d1.1.1

1   Make a list of the main services and products applicable to your role.

2   List the features and benefits against each one.

3   Using your list, discuss the services and products you handle with your assessor. Make sure you talk about how you feel your knowledge of these services and products helps to build your customers' confidence in you.

How your own behaviour affects the behaviour of your customer

As you work through your qualification you will probably be developing an awareness of how what you do and the way that you do it has an impact on your ability to perform effectively. In other words, your behaviour is directly related to your effectiveness and, therefore, your ability to make your customers feel they can have confidence in you.

Your behaviour

The way you behave with your customers must be in a way which sustains and builds confidence. You may not have realised it but behaviour is a choice. When we wake up in the morning we can choose to be grumpy or we can say 'No matter what, I am going to have a good day!'

Even if something has happened to make you feel sad or angry, you do have the choice to approach customers with a positive frame of mind rather than with a negative attitude. This might mean making an extra special effort on your part to smile and be friendly. It will pay off as smiling is contagious; it will help to instil confidence in your customer (and probably help lighten your mood too). If you choose to be a little down in the mouth, you will get the same back from your customers.

When dealing with your customers your behaviour should be:

● **Professional:** do not allow any negative personal feelings to affect your performance.

● **Understanding:** your customers need you to help them. They will return to you and your organisation if you show them you fully understand their needs and expectations.

● **Patient:** you may have already been asked the same question over and over again. However, it is the *first* time for your customer. Treat him or her as an individual and give the respect he or she deserves.

Assertive behaviour

If you choose to behave assertively, you are likely to be effective in developing a good relationship with your customers. It will also help you to balance the needs of your customer with those of your organisation.

You should now refer to the section in **Unit A10 Deal with customers face to face** entitled How to behave assertively, on pages 135 – 138 for information on how assertive behaviour can help you to be a customer service professional.

Portfolio Task   Links to d1c, d1d

Make notes on:

1   What being a customer service professional means to you.

2   The benefits of using assertive behaviour and how this helps your customers to feel confident about the service you deliver.

Use your notes to describe to your assessor how you behave assertively and professionally.

How you can help to deliver your organisation's service offer

How much do you know about your organisation? Do you know its history and reputation? Do you know the part you and your colleagues play in the wider organisation? Where does your organisation need to be in five years time? Where does it need to be by the end of the year? What are its aims and objectives?

In order to strive to achieve aims and objectives, an organisation's policymakers make commitments to customers based on what they see as their vision for the future success of their organisation. At a high level, these commitments might be about reaching out to a larger section of the community. For instance, a television company might commit to produce more TV programmes for ethnic minorities. Or a hotel might commit to upgrade its leisure facilities.

At an operational level, commitments tend to concentrate more on what the customer can expect by way of standards of service. This type of commitment tends to relate to things such as delivery times, product quality, standards of cleanliness or simply just promises made in the process of delivering customer service.

Key term

Service offer – The extent and limits of the customer service that an organisation is offering.

A **service offer** is a set of promises made by your organisation to its customers. If a promise is broken, customer satisfaction will suffer and expectations will not be met. Potentially, the organisation's reputation will be damaged and there will be little chance of any worthwhile relationship being developed because customer loyalty will not be there.

You will need to know all about your organisation's service offer to help you deliver great customer service and to develop customer relationships. The service offer will help you to know what your organisation is prepared to do and what it is not prepared to do for its customers. If you find out what your organisation aims or commits to do over the short, medium and long term, it will help you to understand where you fit into the wider picture and the part you can play to deliver the service offer.

Signpost

There is a section about service offers in mandatory **Unit F1 Communicate using customer service language** on pages 26 – 29. Please recap this now.

There are many ways in which an organisation creates and distributes information on its commitments as shown in the figure below.

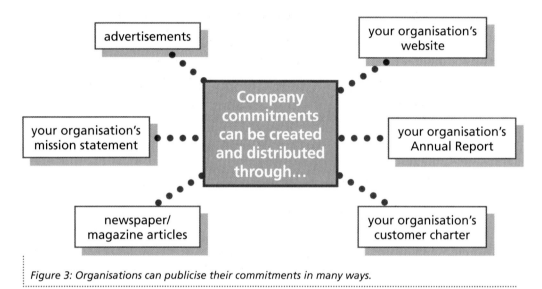

Figure 3: Organisations can publicise their commitments in many ways.

Annual Reports
These describe the progress an organisation has made and the key activities it has undertaken over the past year. Included within an Annual Report will be details of the organisation's financial position and also details of its directors.

Customer charters
These documents set out to explain to customers what an organisation aims to do in order to meet customer expectations, how the organisation will meet or beat targets, how it will provide information to customers, how it will give equal access to services and how customers can complain.

Mission statements
These are statements put together by an organisation to demonstrate what it stands for. A mission statement should set out the importance of quality service and the organisation's basic commitments. You will find mission statements in all sorts of places – from promotional literature to framed notices on the walls of offices and shops.

Typically, a mission statement will include the following:

- the purpose of the organisation
- the mission of the organisation
- a statement outlining its commitment to its customers
- what the organisation's values are (often in relation to both customers and employees).

Not all organisations will have a mission statement. Indeed, many people look on them as hollow words written by individuals far removed from dealing personally with customers, that is, people who do not see what life is like in reality. Whatever your view of them, do remember they are in the public eye and therefore customers will hold *you* accountable for fulfilling them.

Advertisements

A further example of where commitments are made is through the written word on promotional literature or other advertisements. If a leaflet says you will deliver a product within seven days, then your customers will expect just that.

The promises made by your organisation are only going to be met if you and your colleagues play your part in fulfilling them.

So, there are many ways in which your customers can find out about your organisation's service offer. Make sure you are up to date with what has been promised. Knowing about the commitments your organisation makes to customers will mean you know what you need to do to help it maintain them. If you have this understanding, you will be better prepared to carry out your roles and responsibilities more effectively.

Portfolio Task
Links to d1e

Your organisation is likely to make some form of commitment to customers through the media and advertising, by way of a mission statement or simply through posting a notice in a shop window.

1 Research your organisation's service offer and make a list of any promises it includes. Decide what the service offer tells your customer to expect. (For example, free delivery or free delivery if purchase is over £30). If appropriate, include any commitments made which are specific to your team.

2 Make a list of these promises.

3 Now identify what the limits of the service are i.e. what your customers should not expect to happen. Make a list.

4 Discuss your findings with your assessor.

Building confidence about the service offer

Your organisation is unlikely to have made unrealistic promises in its service offer. What would be the point? Customers will constantly be dissatisfied. However, from time to time, things may go wrong and it will then be your job to restore customer confidence that you are doing everything you can to keep your organisation's service promises.

Even when things do not go wrong, some customers need a little extra encouragement to truly believe service promises will be kept. This is usually because of previous bad experiences (not necessarily with you or your organisation) with customer service in general. It takes a long time to create trust and a very short length of time to lose it.

You will need to reassure your customers. So, use positive words and explain what you will do to make things happen.

Do bear in mind the time you need to spend with an individual customer needs to be balanced against the needs of other customers or other responsibilities you may have. Your organisation may well have guidelines about how long you should spend in dealing with an individual customer. This is particularly relevant if you work in a call centre.

> ### ✓ Checklist – Building confidence about the service offer
>
> * Be positive.
>
> * Know what the service offer promises to do for customers.
>
> * Know the limitations of the service offer.
>
> * Say what you can do and be realistic.
>
> * Give full and accurate explanations.
>
> * Keep your promises.
>
> * Keep the customer informed of progress.
>
> * Keep within organisational guidelines relating to time spent with an individual customer.

Portfolio Task

Links to d1.1.2, d1.1.3, d1b, d1c

Write a report which describes how you bring the service offer to life in order to build your customer's confidence that the service you give will be excellent. Write your report by thinking about:

* how you live up to the promises made in your organisation's service offer

* what behaviours you use

* how you ensure the time you give to one customer is in accordance with your organisation's guidelines

* how you reassure customers that service promises will be kept. What do you do?

Obtain witness testimonies which show how you build your customer's confidence that the service you give will be excellent.

Functional skills

English: Writing
You may be able to count your written report as evidence towards Level 1 Functional English: Writing. Your report should include sufficient detail to show you have understood the questions and you will need to check it for spelling, grammar and punctuation. Print a copy of your report as it may count as evidence towards Level 1 Functional English: Writing.

Meet the expectations of your customers

What you need to know or learn

- How to recognise when there may be a conflict between your customers' expectations and what you can provide
- How to defuse potentially stressful situations
- How to work with others to resolve difficulties in balancing the needs of your customers and your organisation

You have looked at building your customer's confidence in the service you deliver and are probably thinking this is simply an extension of what you always try to do when creating a positive impression. You will be thinking about the importance of being respectful and courteous and of ways in which you can develop and sustain rapport.

Your attitude

This will all become much easier to do if you approach each situation with the right attitude. This is especially important where you are dealing with customers whose expectations are not being met.

- Having the right attitude will enable you to choose the right behaviour in the first place. Having the wrong attitude might lead you to pass a customer on to somebody else because you do not want to help.

- Having the right attitude will mean you want to help whatever the situation. Having the wrong attitude will mean you want to help only if you like the customer.

- Having the right attitude will mean you want to help, however close it might be to the end of your working day. Having the wrong attitude will mean you hurry a customer up or avoid them completely.

- Having the right attitude means working co-operatively with your colleagues. Having the wrong attitude will mean you are not an active team player.

- Having the right attitude will mean leaving your personal problems at home (however difficult that might be).

It is your choice whether or not to be a customer service professional. Having the right attitude will help you to meet the expectations of your customers

How to recognise when there may be a conflict between your customers' expectations and what you can provide

Although a customer may have been doing business with you or your organisation for some time, it does not mean that his or her expectations will remain the same. When their expectations change, problems may occur because they will be expecting certain things to happen when, in fact, they might not. Figure 4 shows some reasons why expectations could change.

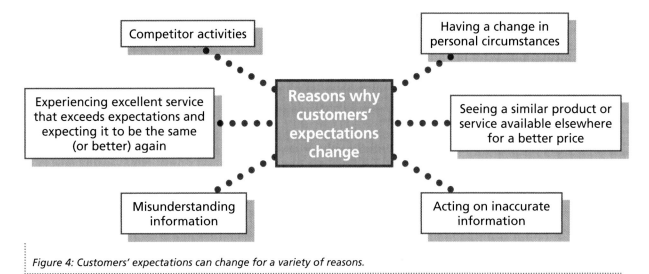

Figure 4: Customers' expectations can change for a variety of reasons.

There is not much you can do about a change in a customer's personal circumstances except to listen carefully to what they say and also to observe any changes in behaviour. That way you can spot any concerns and prevent difficulties arising.

Portfolio Task
Links to d1f

1   Make a list of reasons why your own customers' expectations may change. Do this by thinking about:

● changes to services or products

● changes to your working environment

● staff changes

● competitor activities

● new or amended customer charters or mission statements

● advertising.

2   Think about what your customer's behaviour was like before the changes you have identified came into action. Compare this to what it is like now.

3   Discuss your findings with your assessor.

Unit D1 Develop customer relationships

Always respect the needs of your colleagues. Sometimes picking the right moment to approach someone might make the difference between a successful conclusion or not.

> ## ✔ Checklist – Working with others to help customers
>
> - Develop a basic understanding of the roles and responsibilities of other departments.
>
> - Form positive working relationships with colleagues working elsewhere.
>
> - Keep address/phone/email contact lists up to date.
>
> - Know the limits of your own authority.
>
> - Develop a good working knowledge of key products or services.
>
> - Develop a good working knowledge of alternative products or services.
>
> - Suggest solutions.
>
> - When *you* are asked for help, be co-operative.

Develop the long-term relationship between your customer and your organisation

What you need to know or learn

■ How to give additional help and information to your customers

■ How to discuss with your customers the way in which their expectations compare with your organisation's services or products

■ How to identify new ways of helping customers based on feedback they have given you

■ How to identify ways your organisation could add value for long-term customers

Longer term customer relationships are affected by each transaction a customer has with you and your organisation. Get things right and it will be remembered and a good relationship will continue to develop. Over time, your customer will start to feel loyalty towards you and your organisation. Get things wrong (however small) and there will be a negative impact on the customer/ organisation relationship, making it more and more unlikely for a positive long-term relationship to develop.

Because of this, you can expect the relationship a customer has with you to change over time. Longer term customer relationships are influenced by:

- the personalities of both you and the customer
- changes to your customer's needs and expectations
- changes to products or services
- changes to legislation and regulations.

What we look at now is your role in developing this all important long-term relationship.

How to give additional help and information to your customers

When a customer has a question or makes a comment about a service or product, you will be looking to make sure you respond appropriately. This may mean simply answering the question (or acknowledging a comment) or it may mean doing a little bit more so as to both deal with the issue and create a lasting impression.

Signpost

For more information recap or refer to **Unit A3 Communicate effectively with customers** and **A4 Give customers a positive impression of yourself and your organisation**.

Asking open questions

Asking **open questions** will help you to develop the relationship between your customer and your organisation because this type of question helps you to find out exactly what the customer wants and needs. Using the additional information you get from the responses will mean you are better able to match what the customer wants to your organisation's products or services and helps you think about ways you can give customers added value.

Giving added value is all about going the extra mile. It's about remembering customer names, bringing in the personal touch, surprising the customer and showing you care.

> ### Key term
>
> **Open questions** – questions which start with Who, What, Why, Where, When, How...?

Adding value – the personal touch

We have said that developing a lasting customer relationship builds loyalty and means you have customers who **want** to do business with you and your organisation. They know they will get a reliable and appropriate service in a manner which suits their individual needs and expectations. As you build loyalty you will also be building goodwill. You have a big part to play in this. Often goodwill stems from the personal touch you can bring to your work; the little things that mean so much to people are often the biggest way of building customer loyalty and developing lasting relationships. This is so important for repeat business and also when facing a problem-solving situation with a customer.

Remember:

- A well-handled problem breeds more loyalty than no problem at all.

- It costs five times more to get a new customer than keep an existing one.

- A dissatisfied customer will tell ten others. How many times have you heard friends or family groan about customer service?

Things such as providing comfortable seating, offering to carry baggage or acknowledging customers who are queuing mean the difference between a dissatisfied customer and one who is prepared to stay and will come again. You might think this is no more than being courteous. That may be so; however, it is all too often lacking from the service customers receive.

Here are some examples of how a car dealership might add the personal touch and therefore add value. As you read them, notice how goodwill is built during a series of transactions a customer might have with the same dealership:

- The salesperson notices a family with three dogs looking at estate cars on the forecourt and then invites them into the showroom with the dogs.

- The salesperson arranges for a bouquet of flowers to be on the passenger seat for the purchaser to have when the car is delivered or collected.

Figure 7: Unhappy customers will never feel goodwill or loyalty to an organisation.

- The salesperson phones after a month to check the customer is happy.

- The garage mechanic, after completing a car service, leaves the car's service history manual duly completed and open at the right page on the passenger seat.

There are also lots of things organisations do to try to build loyalty. For instance:

- loyalty cards (for example, Nectar)

- subscriber discounts (especially when a customer first signs up (for example, for satellite TV)

- invitations to previews (for example, a cheese and wine evening event in a department store to see the new season's fashions)

- invitations to special sales days (a sale might start a day early for selected customers)

- special loyal customer promotions (discounts for regular users)

- BOGOFs – buy one get one free (initially an enticement to use a product or service. But, how many people buy something for the first time because of getting something free with it?)

- 'Two for the price of one' or 'buy three from a selected range and get the cheapest free' (again, an enticement, but once using the product or service, a customer might repeat buy).

When you combine what you can do personally to go the extra mile for customers, with the initiatives your organisation takes to build loyalty, you are well on the way to doing all that you can to develop the relationship between your customers and your organisation.

Portfolio Task   Links to d1.3.1, d1a

1 a. List five ways that you can inspire loyalty in your customers.

b. Now think of specific times you have done this.

c. What did you do which meant you were giving additional help or information to your customers?

2 Think about times you have added value by giving the personal touch.

3 Ask for witness testimonies from appropriate colleagues.

4 Discuss your findings with your assessor and describe how this helps to develop the relationship your customers have with your organisation.

How to discuss with your customers the way in which their expectations compare with your organisation's services or products

Remember that your customers will have many and varied expectations for example:

- efficiency of service
- friendliness of the service deliverers
- speed of service
- price/cost
- quality of the product.

You may be in situations where you have to discuss with your customer how their expectations compare with what you and your organisation provides. This may involve you explaining how your organisation's services or products:

- exceed expectations
- do not meet expectations
- match expectations.

You should enter into any discussions with the thought that you are there to foster a long-term relationship. Clearly, where you know you can exceed expectations you can be very positive and almost celebrate the fact that you have 'good news'. This is also the case where expectations match what you are able to provide.

If your customer's expectations are unrealistic or simply wrong, this does not necessarily mean you have lost the customer altogether. If you try to offer an alternative from another source, your customer is likely to be more tolerant of the situation than if you had not made the effort to try. Being helpful in this way is part of developing a good and lasting customer relationship as the customer knows how helpful your organisation is.

How to discuss expectations with a customer

The following points will help reassure the customer that the service you provide is the correct one for them.

- Always remain positive and discuss with the customer what you or your organisation *can* do not what you *cannot* do.

- Get the information you require by listening and asking appropriate questions. This is especially important when dealing with customers over the telephone.

- Discuss the product or service with them in terms of benefits rather than technical features.

- Give the customer a full and clear explanation of how a particular product or service compares with what he or she needs.

- Do not use jargon or confuse the customer with long-winded explanations.

- Repeat back key points you are making and check the customer has understood by seeking his or her agreement.

- Avoid using the word 'but'. Instead, use the word 'however' to explain what you can do, rather than what you are unable to do. For example: instead of saying 'I can get you this in the size you have requested but not in the colour you want' say 'I have it in the size you want. However, the colour I can deliver it in, by tomorrow, is red not blue. Will that be OK?'

- Give a 'can do' plan of action when there are differences between what the customer wants and what you are able to provide. Tell the customer *why* alternatives are being offered.

✓ Checklist – Discussing expectations with a customer

- Create a friendly and courteous environment.

- Listen to the customer's needs.

- Ask open questions to seek information.

- Check back your understanding of the customer's needs.

- Say what you *can* do not what you *cannot* do.

- Avoid jargon and technical terms.

- Offer alternatives where needs or expectations cannot be met.

- Seek agreement to what you are proposing.

Develop customer relationships Unit D1

Portfolio Task   Links to d1.3.2

1 Link your performance when giving explanations to customers, to what you
   know and understand about your organisation's service offer.

2 Ensure you are observed by your assessor or appropriate colleagues when
   you are explaining to customers how their expectations compare with your
   organisation's services or products.

How to identify new ways of helping customers based on feedback they have given you

Asking open questions and finding out about your customers' expectations are all
methods of getting feedback from your customers. However, it is no use listening
and collecting feedback if you do not do something with it.

You need to be responsive to the feedback you receive from customers. If you
work in a very busy environment it is often quite easy to 'forget' the comments
customers make; this means nothing would change or improve in your
organisation. Using customer feedback is a four-step process:

- Identify customer service issues/feedback and record them.
- Discuss feedback with others (when necessary).
- Plan and carry out action to be taken.
- Monitor the results.

Following these steps will enable you to react to comments made by customers so
that you can do something to help improve the service you and your organisation
give to customers. This might mean making significant changes to procedures or
simply doing things which make the customer experience more worthwhile. Think
back to how *you* can add value. Some things you identified need not cost any
money nor take long to put in place, but their impact could be quite dramatic.

Recording feedback

It is easy to forget customer feedback as once you have dealt with one customer,
it is likely you will need to move straight on to helping the next one. Your
organisation may have a system in place for recording feedback. If not, you can
devise your own simple feedback log. Figure 9 shows an example for someone
working in a local advice centre.

DATE	FEEDBACK	ACTION
20 Oct	Help with CV writing is requested more and more frequently	Produce guidance notes. Refer people to online help
29 Oct	Older customers do not seem to like talking to me about redundancy	Ask for feedback from my colleagues as to why this is. What am I doing differently with mature clients? Speak with my Manager about this trend.
1 Nov	Several customers have complained we are not open in the evening.	Spoke to my manager about this trend.
4 Nov	Three customers wanted to be able to use Twitter to communicate with me	We have no facilities for this. Am not sure about privacy. Speak to Sam.

Figure 8: Creating a feedback log can be very simple but effective.

Portfolio Task

Links to d1.3.3

Investigate your organisation's procedures for capturing feedback. Use this or make your own feedback log and start to record customer feedback you receive.

Make sure you regularly share your log with an appropriate person as a means of developing customer relationships.

Keep your log for your portfolio.

Functional skills

English: Writing

If you complete your own feedback log, it may count as evidence towards Level 1 Functional English: Writing. Think carefully about how to structure the log so that the feedback is presented in a logical sequence. Write in enough detail to ensure the feedback is valuable to the reader. Check your log through for spelling, punctuation and grammar.

Advising others of customer feedback

It would be very easy to make assumptions on behalf of customers and set out to take action on feedback received just because the customer wants you to. This is unwise and should not be done unless it's within the scope of your authority.

It would be far better to discuss feedback with the appropriate people in your organisation. That way, you will be doing your part to contribute to a bigger picture of the overall perception of the standard of customer service. Think about sharing feedback with your line manager or supervisor or whoever has the responsibility for dealing with feedback or making change happen.

It is especially important to be alert to comments and feedback which you hear or read time and time again. This is called trend-spotting, in other words many customers think and feel the same thing about a product or service and therefore this adds weight to the feedback. It is quality feedback.

Do not fall into the trap of only remembering poor or negative feedback because positive feedback is equally valuable. For example, if customers frequently tell you they like the way you do something then this would be useful feedback to share with colleagues and the management team. That way, your good practice might be brought in elsewhere in order to add value to the customer experience.

Adding value for long-term customers

If you think about a product or service you have used regularly over the last five years, for example, buying a newspaper, using public transport or filling up the car with petrol you may feel you now expect different things from your service provider. So, however loyal a customer might feel towards your organisation, it is important to be constantly looking to improve service and add value. Otherwise, a customer might suddenly find a competitor has a more attractive proposition. Also, customers can easily become bored by dealing with the same old thing over and over again even if their experiences are good ones.

As well as identifying new ways of helping customers based on their feedback to you personally, your organisation may have a formal process in place to capture customer feedback. For example:

- customer satisfaction questionnaires

- mystery shopper surveys

- monitoring complaints and compliments

- focus groups

- telephone surveys

- comments/suggestion boxes

- street surveys.

You can find more information about these in **Unit B2 Deliver reliable customer service** in the section entitled *Ways of obtaining feedback* on pages 177 – 182.

Becoming involved with looking at this feedback may also provide you with an opportunity to identify added value that your organisation could offer to long-term customers.

Portfolio Task	Links to d1.3.3, d1.3.4, d1.3.5

1 Write down five comments you have received from customers recently. Now think about the action you took and write this down.

2 For those comments received where you took *no* action, identify what you might have done to find new ways of helping customers.

3 Consider who else you involved with your plans.

4 Discuss this with your assessor.

Working Life

My name is Kayleigh and I'm a self-employed personal trainer attached to a health club. I love my job and have successfully built a good business with clients from quite a wide area. I've been working with Meena on a weight-loss programme for some time now and she's recommended her friends to me which is great. Last week she told me her Mum was also keen to start doing something about her fitness levels so I arranged to see her at the weekend.

The meeting didn't go too well. For a start, I wasn't expecting Meena to have a Mum who was quite so old. Had I known that she was nearly 80, I wouldn't have suggested a meeting. When we started to talk it became clear I couldn't possibly help. She was waiting for a knee replacement and wanted to strengthen her leg muscles before this took place. I questioned her about her health in general and it turned out she was diabetic and had high blood pressure. It was really a waste of my time and I felt a bit let down that Kayleigh had not given me the whole story. We said our goodbyes and I wished her good luck with the operation.

I now find that Meena has cancelled the remainder of her appointments with me and there are messages on my mobile from two of her friends who have done the same. Where did I go wrong?

Ask the expert

Q How did making assumptions affect the way in which Kayleigh dealt with Meena's Mum?

A It's likely that Kayleigh's body language gave away her surprise at seeing the age of Meena's Mum. Those all important first impressions were therefore not good if Kayleigh appeared shocked or disappointed. She also appears to think it was a waste of time; this poor attitude would also have been reflected in her tone of voice and body language.

Q Kayleigh could not help, so what should she have done?

A Kayleigh was right to ask questions to establish needs and expectations but made a bad situation (caused by her poor attitude) worse by not offering an alternative solution. For example, as a professional fitness trainer, she should be aware of who could help if she could not. She needed to be a team player.

To correct the poor attitude, she should have shown some courtesy to Meena's Mum. The lack of respect would instantly have been obvious. She needed to adapt her communication style and say what she could do rather than what she could not do.

Top tips

Kayleigh has a successful business and seems to have fallen into the trap of thinking she could do anything for everyone. Never make assumptions. This includes being realistic about your own strengths and weaknesses.

Kayleigh also seems to have a picture in her mind about the type of customers who will want her services. This left her ill-prepared to deal with somebody who didn't fit what she believed to be 'normal'.

There would be other colleagues at the health club who might have helped. Being a team player helps deliver great service and also balances the needs of both customer and organisation.

There was still an opportunity for Kayleigh to continue to develop a long-term relationship with Meena even though she felt unable to help Meena's Mum.

Check your knowledge

1 How should you go about exploring your customer's expectations?

a. By describing the organisation's service offer.

b. By spotting trends in customer feedback.

c. By listening and asking open questions.

d. By seeking help and advice from colleagues.

2 How can keeping a feedback log help to develop the long-term customer relationship?

a. It helps to identify new ways of helping customers.

b. It provides information about buying trends.

c. It enables managers to monitor staff performance.

d. It shows where sales targets need to be adjusted.

3 What can you do to stop a potential conflict occurring when what you can offer differs from what your customer wants?

a. Offer a discount on future business deals.

b. Listen, ask questions and apologise in writing.

c. Listen, empathise and offer an alternative solution.

d. Give information about the complaints procedure.

4 What can you do to ensure the way in which you work with others helps to develop the customer relationship?

a. Avoid asking for help unless in a dangerous situation.

b. Never take sick leave or go on a holiday during August.

c. Be an active team player and share customer feedback.

d. Ask all staff to wear identification such as name badges.

5 What can you do to build your customer's confidence that the service you give will be excellent?

a. Have a deep understanding of my services and products.

b. Attend a training course on handling difficult people.

c. Always follow up customer queries with a written response.

d. Monitor complaints for feedback on my colleagues' performance.

6 Why is customer retention important to an organisation?

a. Because more staff will be needed to cope with an increasing number of customer complaints.

b. Because loyal customers always keep their business in the same place despite what might go wrong.

c. Because it is a legal requirement not to fall below a certain number of customers per each member of staff.

d. Because it is cheaper to do repeat business with an existing satisfied customer than find a new one.

7 What should you always do when making a variation to the service offer which is outside the limits of your authority?

a. Make sure the customer knows I am doing something special.

b. Refer what I want to do to an appropriate colleague.

c. Write down what the customer says in my feedback log.

d. Monitor the actions I take so that I can discuss my performance.

8 What does a long-term relationship between a customer and your organisation rely on?

a. The customer being kept aware in writing of any changes to our services or products.

b. The customer being invited to valued customer promotions and being given discount vouchers.

c. The customer having a realistic view of our service offer and being happy with it.

d. The customer being sent on an annual basis a copy of our mission statement and values.

9 How can you add value to the customer's experience?

a. By giving the personal touch.

b. By saying 'thank you' in writing.

c. By wearing a uniform or name badge.

d. By being fully qualified and competent.

10 Why is it important to be reliable?

a. To ensure I beat my colleagues to a salary rise or promotion.

b. To keep the number of customer complaints to a minimum.

c. To let management know I can work co-operatively with colleagues.

d. To build customer confidence in my ability to give great service.

Glossary

Active listening – paying careful attention to understand more than the words being spoken.

Adding the personal touch – treating the customer as an individual.

Alternating – when both people take turns to exchange remarks, movements and smiles.

Appraisal – an official review of your performance by your line manager or supervisor.

Assertive behaviour – standing up for your rights without violating the rights of your customer.

Benefit – how the product or service can help a customer.

Body language – non-verbal signals that we give out and receive when we are communicating with someone.

Building one-to-one relationships – making a customer feel valued and respected.

Check delivery – find out if customer satisfaction has been achieved.

Closing the sale – the end of the buying process when a customer agrees to purchase.

Cold call – a sales call you make which your customer is not expecting.

Complaints procedure – the process which a customer should follow in making a complaint.

Consumer – an individual who receives or seeks to receive goods or services from a supplier.

Courteous behaviour – being polite and having good manners.

Customer expectations – what customers think should happen and how they think they should be treated when asking for or receiving customer service.

Customer experience – the feelings a customer has about the service received.

Customer satisfaction – the feeling a customer gets when he or she is happy with the product or service provided.

Data controller – the nominated person in a company who applies to the data commissioner for permission to store and use personal data.

Data subject – anyone who has data stored about them which is outside their direct control.

Duty of care – the tradesman or professional must act with reasonable care and skill when dealing with customers.

Emotion – our feelings.

Empathy – identifying and understanding another person's feelings.

External customer – somebody from outside the organisation which is providing him or her with a service.

Feature – what a product or service does.

Feedback – information you receive about yourself or your organisation.

Giving respect – valuing the individual needs of people.

Health and Safety at Work Act 1974 – covers the general duties employers have towards employees and members of the public, and employees have to themselves and to each other.

Improve service – make changes to enhance customer satisfaction.

Inform customers – give information to aid understanding.

Information Commissioner – the person responsible for enforcing the Data Protection Act.

Institute of Customer Service – the professional body which deals with developing customer service people and systems.

Internal customer – a customer who comes from another part of your organisation.

Keeping promises – doing what you say you will do, when you said you would do it.

Mirroring – when both people in a conversation take up the same body posture or copy gestures

Negotiation – a discussion which aims to produce an agreement.

Organisation/company procedure – the detailed guidelines or rules that an organisation uses to deliver customer service.

Over-deliver – delivering a better service than you have promised.

Personal touch – showing that you care by treating customers as individuals and behaving in a friendly way.

Preparation for service – being ready and able to achieve customer satisfaction before dealing with customers.

Product – a physical good providing benefits to customers, for example, food, clothes, furniture, mortgages, savings accounts.

Rapport – a sense of being comfortable with someone, whether or not you know him or her well.

Reputation – the general opinion customers have about an organisation.

Service – an activity carried out providing benefits to customers, for example, rail and bus services, health services, providing information and advice.

Service delivery – the service you have given.

Service offer – the extent and limits of the customer service that an organisation is offering.

Service recovery – when customers feel better about a company after a problem has been resolved than they did before the problem even arose.

Shared information – feedback, thoughts and ideas that are discussed with colleagues and/or service partners to help improve performance.

Under-promise – promising a particular level of service while knowing you will deliver more than that.

Index

PEARSON EDUCATION LIMITED

Edinburgh Gate
Harlow CM20 2JE
Tel: +44 (0)1279 623623
Fax: +44 (0)1279 431059
Website: www.pearsoned.co.uk

First published in Great Britain in 2009

© Greg Holden 2009

The right of Greg Holden to be identified as author of this work has been asserted
by him in accordance with the Copyright, Designs and Patents Act 1988.

ISBN: 978–0–273–72354–7

British Library Cataloguing-in-Publication Data
A catalogue record for this book is available from the British Library

Library of Congress Cataloging-in-Publication Data
A catalog record for this book is available from the Library of Congress

10 9 8 7 6 5 4 3 2 1
13 12 11 10 09

Designed by pentacorbig, High Wycombe

Typeset in 11/14 pt ITC Stone Sans by 30
Printed and bound in Great Britain by Ashford Colour Press Ltd, Gosport, Hants

The publisher's policy is to use paper manufactured from sustainable forests.

Microsoft®
Excel
2007

in Simple
steps

Greg Holden

Use your computer with confidence

Get to grips with practical computing tasks with minimal time, fuss and bother.

In Simple Steps guides guarantee immediate results. They tell you everything you need to know on a specific application; from the most essential tasks to master, to every activity you'll want to accomplish, through to solving the most common problems you'll encounter.

Helpful features

To build your confidence and help you to get the most out of your computer, practical hints, tips and shortcuts feature on every page:

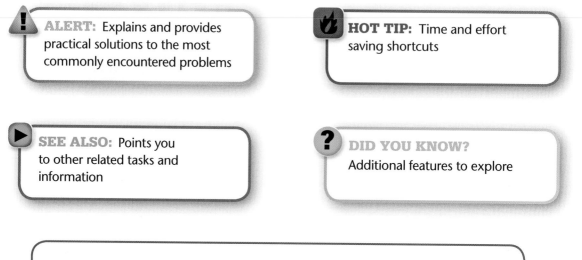

ALERT: Explains and provides practical solutions to the most commonly encountered problems

HOT TIP: Time and effort saving shortcuts

SEE ALSO: Points you to other related tasks and information

DID YOU KNOW? Additional features to explore

WHAT DOES THIS MEAN?
Jargon and technical terms explained in plain English

Practical. Simple. Fast.

in Simple steps

Dedication:

To Zosia and Lucy

Top 10 Excel Tips

Ti

The w
move
But if y
It's no
contig

1 To

2 Dr
th

3 To
pr
of

4 Re

? D
A
a
b
ra
c
le
a
a
ri

? D
W
se
c
th
yo

T

Rig
by
in a

1
2
3
4
5

4

1 Starting to use Excel

Introduction

Maybe you've run across an old-fashioned accountant's ledger in the back of a dusty storeroom. Microsoft® Excel provides you with worksheets that serve somewhat the same purpose. But using the skills you'll learn in this book, you can use Excel to accomplish a variety of personal or business tasks in a fraction of the time it would take if you were using pen and paper.

This chapter introduces you to some of the many basic functions you can perform with Excel, beginning with how to create those worksheets and make them into workbooks. You can use its default setting and download templates, or you can create your own format for your specific project.

You don't need to be either an accountant or a computer whiz to get the most out of Excel. This book will show you step by step how to perform tasks either with a click of your mouse or with shortcut keys on your keyboard. You'll find the tools you need on a tab-based Ribbon and on dialogue boxes. And you can customise the Quick Access Toolbar to get easy access to commands you use all the time. What's not to love?

Launch Excel

Right from the start, Excel lets you do things your way. You can launch the application by selecting it from the Start menu. When the program starts, a blank workbook opens in a program window and you can start working with it right away.

1 Click the Start button on the Windows taskbar.

2 If you started the program recently, choose it from the list of recently used applications.

3 If the program is not on the Start menu, click All Programs.

4 Click Microsoft Office.

5 Click Microsoft Office Excel 2007.

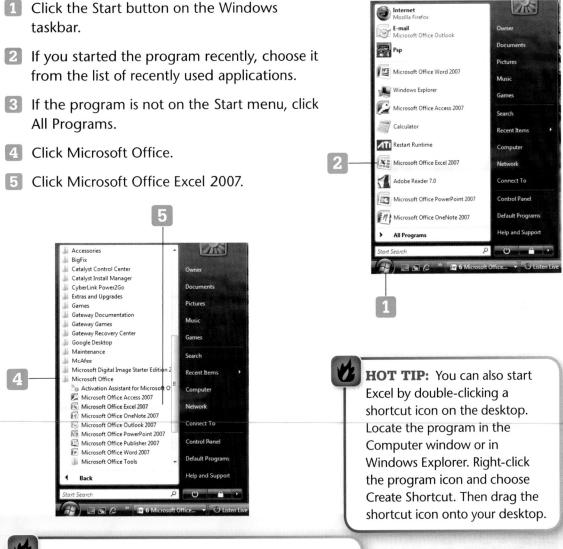

HOT TIP: You can also start Excel by double-clicking a shortcut icon on the desktop. Locate the program in the Computer window or in Windows Explorer. Right-click the program icon and choose Create Shortcut. Then drag the shortcut icon onto your desktop.

HOT TIP: If you work with Excel frequently, you can also 'pin' it to the Start menu so it appears there all the time. Right-click the program's icon (by default, it is located in Program Files\Microsoft Office\Office12) and choose Pin to Start Menu from the context menu.

2 Learning essential workbook techniques

Se

The wh
move it
But if y
It's not
contigu

1 To
ran
tha
in

2 Dra
las
inc
ho
an
rig
ins

3 To
pre
of
the

4 Re
all
ran
sel

?

A
b
t
t
o

3 Managing workbooks and worksheets

Introduction

Excel allows you to modify your workbook by adding and deleting worksheets. You can also move the appearance order of worksheets within the workbook or even rename them if the focus of your workbook changes. Or maybe you're suddenly protective of certain data and want to hide those worksheets. Or perhaps you get a long list of data and need to freeze the column and row headings.

Whenever you modify a worksheet, Excel will recalculate formulas. You never have to worry about your results being out of date. Cell references will automatically be updated in existing formulas. Plus you can insert and delete cells, rows and columns. To suit your preferences you can adjust column width and row height so the worksheet will be correctly structured.

Select a worksheet

When you work with Excel, you store and analyse values on individual sections of workbooks called 'worksheets'. You can just call them 'sheets' for short. Three worksheets appear each time a new workbook opens. The one you work on is the 'active' worksheet. Another name for it is the 'selected' worksheet. You'll be provided with a sheet tab, which is a concept like file folder labels. Selecting a worksheet is important because it enables you to apply formatting and other changes to the entire sheet at once.

1 Display other tabs if you need to by clicking a sheet tab and hitting the scroll button.

2 To make the worksheet active, click a sheet tab.

3 To select several worksheets, press and hold Ctrl as you click other sheet tabs. You'll know that multiple worksheets have been selected when [Group] appears in the title bar.

HOT TIP: You can select all the worksheets by right-clicking any sheet tab. Then click Select all sheets.

Name or rename a worksheet

The names you'll be given are Sheet1, Sheet2 and Sheet3. But you should choose your own name as you create a worksheet so that you can remember what's in it. That way, you'll know which sheet to choose when you're faced with a set of sheets.

1 To name a sheet, double-click the sheet tab. Or you can click the Home tab, click the Format button and click Rename.

2 Type whatever name you've chosen.

3 Press Enter.

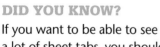

1

Prices remain high for good quality fruit.
Prices remain high for good quality fruit.
Prices falling perhaps due to freezing
weather or half-term.
Prices up on the week with supply and
demand in balance.

2

? DID YOU KNOW?
If you want to be able to see a lot of sheet tabs, you should pick short names. That's because the sheet tab will get bigger to accommodate the size of the name.

HOT TIP: If you need more than three worksheets for your project, add them now so that you'll have all the information you need for your project in one file.

Move a worksheet

When you're ready to reorganise sheets in a workbook, you can arrange them in chronological order or you can make the most important one first. It's easy to move or copy a sheet within a workbook or to a different open workbook.

1 Find the worksheet you want to move and click its sheet tab. Next hold down the mouse button.

2 The mouse pointer changes into an icon that resembles a sheet of paper.

3 Drag it to the right of the sheet tab where you want to move the worksheet, then release the mouse button.

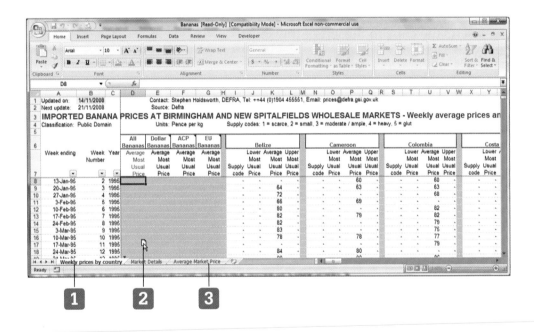

Copy a worksheet

If you need to re-enter data contained on one sheet in another sheet, you can always retype it. But this is time-consuming and brings the possibility of typing errors. It's far easier and more efficient to copy the entire worksheet.

1 Find the worksheet you want to copy and click its sheet tab.

2 Click the Home tab.

3 Click the Format button arrow. Next click Move or Copy Sheet.

4 To copy the sheet to another open workbook, click the To book list arrow. Then select the name of that workbook. The sheets of the workbook you've selected will appear in the Before sheet list. Click a sheet name in the Before sheet list. Excel inserts the copy to the left of this sheet.

5 Select the Create a copy tick box.

6 Click OK.

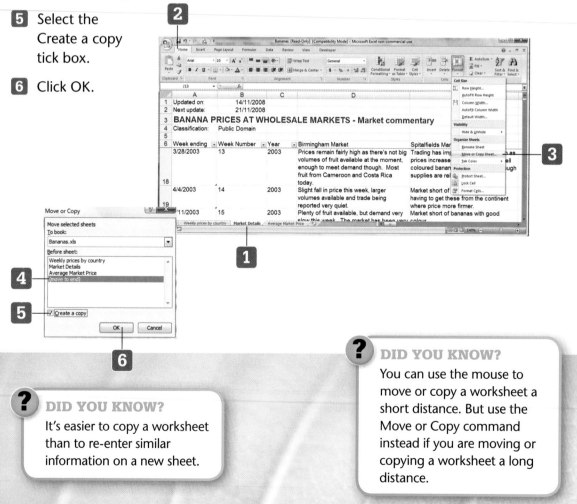

? **DID YOU KNOW?**

It's easier to copy a worksheet than to re-enter similar information on a new sheet.

? **DID YOU KNOW?**

You can use the mouse to move or copy a worksheet a short distance. But use the Move or Copy command instead if you are moving or copying a worksheet a long distance.

Insert a column or row

You don't need to disturb your worksheet to insert blank columns and rows between existing data. To accommodate new columns and rows, Excel repositions existing cells. So that they will refer to the correct cells, Excel also adjusts any existing formulas. Columns are inserted to the left; rows are inserted above the selected row.

1 Select the new column you want to insert and click to the right of its location. Or click the row right below the location of the row you want to insert.

2 Click the Home tab.

3 Click the Insert Cells button and then click Insert Sheet Columns or Insert Sheet Rows. A new column or row appears.

4 To adjust formatting, click the Insert Options button and then click a formatting option.

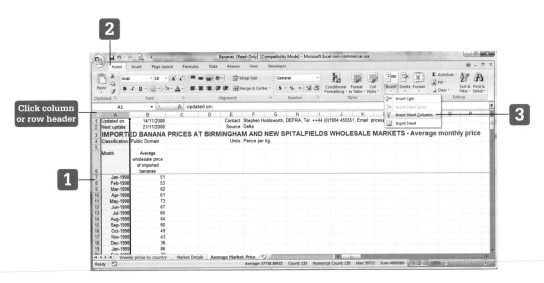

Click column or row header

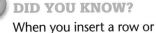

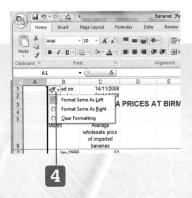

Delete a column or row

Deleting a column or row helps you focus on the data you really need. It also makes an entire worksheet easier to read on screen. When you delete a row or column, adjacent rows or columns move up or to the left to join the remaining data.

1 Select the column header button or row header button that you want to delete.

2 Click the Home tab.

3 Click the Delete Cells button and click Delete Sheet Columns or Delete Sheet Rows.

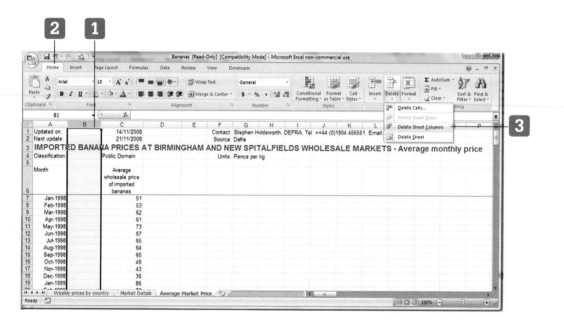

? **DID YOU KNOW?**

Formulas can be rechecked. If you've referred to a column or row in a formula and then deleted it, go back and adjust the formula so it will recalculate.

? **DID YOU KNOW?**

After you delete a column or row, those that are still there will move to the left or up to join the other remaining data.

Hide or display a worksheet

If one of your Excel worksheets contains sensitive information, you might want to hide it so unauthorised users cannot see its contents. You don't have to delete the worksheet, however. Instead, you can hide it.

1 Click the tab of the sheet you want to hide.

2 Click the Home tab.

3 Click Format.

4 Point to Hide & Unhide and choose Hide Sheet or Unhide Sheet, depending on whether or not the sheet has already been hidden.

DID YOU KNOW?

If you hide one or more worksheets in a workbook, that does not affect data or formulas in other worksheets; any cell references remain the same.

ALERT: Hidden worksheets do not appear when you print out a workbook. If you want to print a worksheet that has been hidden, you need to display it first.

Hide or unhide a workbook

You might want to hide an entire workbook if it contains information you don't want others to see. The command is different from that used to hide an individual worksheet.

1 Open the workbook you want to hide.

2 Click the View tab.

3 Click the Hide button.

4 If the workbook has already been hidden, you won't see it. To unhide it, click the View tab in any open Excel window.

5 Click the Unhide button.

6 Select the workbook you want to unhide and click OK.

Hide or display a column or row

Before you delete a column or row, consider hiding it instead. By hiding it, you don't cut the information completely, you just make it invisible while you show the worksheet to others or print it out. It's easy to display the column or row once again when needed.

1 Click the column or row header you want to hide.

2 Click the Home tab.

3 Click Format.

4 Point to Hide & Unhide and choose Hide Columns or Hide Rows. (Or, if the objects are hidden, choose Unhide Columns or Unhide Rows.)

HOT TIP: Drag the mouse pointer to select more than one column or row.

? DID YOU KNOW?

When you hide a column or row, calculations in a worksheet are not affected. All formulas still reference the hidden data if necessary.

Freeze or unfreeze a column or row

Worksheets can quickly become so full of information that when you scroll to the bottom of the sheet, you can no longer see the top of the sheet. Instead of having to scroll up or down, you can temporarily freeze a column or row so that it stays in place on screen no matter where you scroll in the file.

1 Select the column to the right of the column you want to freeze, or the row below the row you want to freeze.

2 Click the View tab.

3 Click Freeze Panes and choose the option you want:

- Freeze Panes keeps rows and columns visible and in place.

- Freeze Top Row freezes the top row.

- Freeze First Column freezes the first column.

DID YOU KNOW?

You can split a screen into up to four panes and freeze two of the panes.

DID YOU KNOW?

You can edit data in a frozen pane as you would another pane, but the cells in the pane remain stationary.

Adjust column width or row height

What happens if you add long strings of data or larger font sizes? If some of your data or labels disappear, you can adjust each column width to fit its contents and you can also adjust your row heights.

1. Choose the first column or row you want to adjust and click its header button. You can select more columns or rows by dragging.

2. Click the Home tab.

3. Click the Format button and click Column Width or Row Height.

4. Type a new column width or row height in points

5. Click OK.

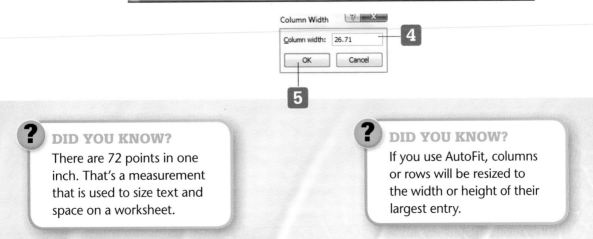

DID YOU KNOW?

There are 72 points in one inch. That's a measurement that is used to size text and space on a worksheet.

DID YOU KNOW?

If you use AutoFit, columns or rows will be resized to the width or height of their largest entry.

Divide a worksheet into panes

If you are working with a worksheet that contains many computer screens' worth of data, you can't see the entire contents at once. Rather than having to scroll up and down between different parts of the file, you can divide it into four panes. That way you can scroll independently through each of the two parts of the worksheet and work with both parts at once.

1 Click a cell, column or row to select the area of the file where you want to create separate panes.

2 Click the View tab.

3 Click Split.

4 If you want to remove the split and return to one pane, click the Split button again.

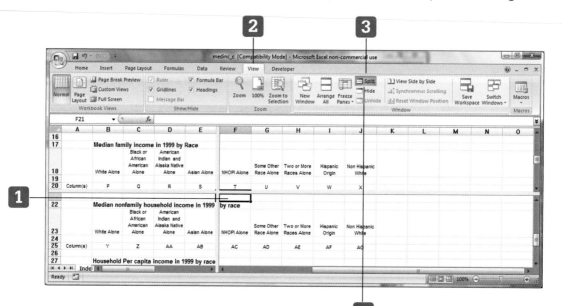

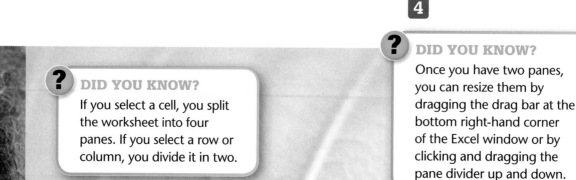

? DID YOU KNOW?

If you select a cell, you split the worksheet into four panes. If you select a row or column, you divide it in two.

? DID YOU KNOW?

Once you have two panes, you can resize them by dragging the drag bar at the bottom right-hand corner of the Excel window or by clicking and dragging the pane divider up and down.

Format numbers

Numeric formats can be applied to numbers to better reflect the type of information they represent. That way the appearance of the data in the cells of a worksheet can be changed without changing the actual value in the cell.

1 Find the number(s) you want to format and select the cell or range they are in.

2 Click the Home tab.

3 Click the Number Format list arrow, then choose a format.

4 To fine tune the format, click a format button.

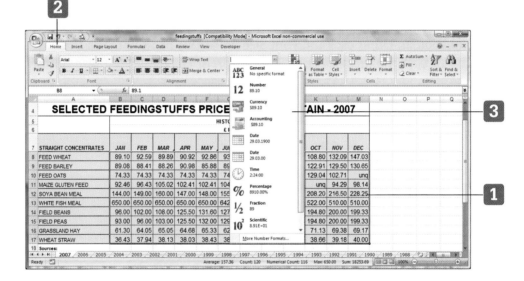

? DID YOU KNOW?

You can apply more than one attribute to the range.

? DID YOU KNOW?

Numbers can be formatted in international currencies: in the Format Cells dialogue box, click the Number tab, click Currency in the Category list, click the Symbol list arrow, then click an international currency symbol.

? DID YOU KNOW?

The buttons on the Home tab Ribbon and Mini-Toolbar can be simply clicked to turn them on and off.

Format text

By default, 10-point Arial is provided on your computer. However, not only can you change the font and its size, you can also choose different attributes. You should also make sure you're using printer fonts (instead of true type fonts) if your worksheet will be created for publication.

1 Select the text you want to work with.

2 Click the Home tab.

3 To change fonts, click the Font list arrow on the Ribbon or Mini-Toolbar.

4 Point to a live preview or click the font you want.

5 To change font size, click one or more of the font size buttons on the Ribbon or Mini-Toolbar. Either click the Font Size list arrow and then click the font size you want or click the Increase Font Size button or Decrease Font Size button.

6 To apply other formatting, click one or more of the formatting buttons on the Ribbon or Mini-Toolbar: Bold, Italic, Underline, Shadow, Strikethrough or Font Color.

HOT TIP: If you don't want Excel to display the Mini-Toolbar, you can turn it off in the Excel Options window.

Apply conditional formatting by comparison

Conditional formatting lets the value of a cell determine its formatting. You can use a formula to determine which cells to format or quickly format only top or bottom ranked values, values above or below average, or unique or duplicate values.

1 Select the cell or range you want to conditionally format.

2 Click the Home tab.

3 Click the Conditional Formatting button and point to Highlight Cell Rules.

4 Click the comparison rule you want to apply to conditionally format the selected data.

5 Specify the criteria you want. Each rule supplies different criteria.

6 Click OK.

Apply conditional formatting based on ranking and average

Another type of conditional formatting is based on top or bottom ranking, or values that are above or below an average you specify.

1 Select the cell or range you want to conditionally format.

2 Click the Home tab.

3 Click the Conditional Formatting button and point to Top/Bottom Rules.

4 Click the comparison rule you want to apply to conditionally format the selected data.

5 Specify the criteria you want. Each rule supplies different criteria.

6 Click OK.

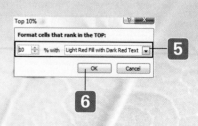

Manage conditional formatting

When you apply conditional formatting to a cell or range of cells, Excel stores the rules associated with the conditional formatting in the Conditional Formatting Rules Manager. You can use the Conditional Formatting Rules Manager to create, edit, delete and view all conditional formatting rules in a workbook. When two or more conditional formatting rules apply to the same cells, the rules are evaluated in order of precedence as they appear in the dialogue box. You can move a rule up or down in the precedence list. Conditional formatting takes precedence over a manual format, which does not appear in the Conditional Formatting Rules Manager.

1 Select the cell or range with the conditional formatting rules you want to edit.

2 Click the Home tab.

3 Click the Conditional Formatting button and click Manage Rules.

4 Click the Show formatting rules for: list arrow and select an option to show the rules you want.

5 Specify the rule you want to change:

- To move the selected rule up or down in precedence, click Move Up or Move Down.

- To stop rule evaluation at a specific rule, select the Stop If True tick box.

- To delete a rule, click Delete Rule.

- To edit a rule, click Edit Rule, make the changes you want and then click OK.

6 Click OK.

Add colour to cells

Fill colours can make your data stand out and can lend consistency to related information on a worksheet. When you no longer need cell formatting, you can remove it.

1 To apply a solid colour to a cell, begin by selecting a cell you want to format.

2 Click the Home tab.

3 Click the Fill Color button arrow and click the colour on the palette you've chosen.

4 To remove the cell shading, click the Fill Color button arrow and click No Fill.

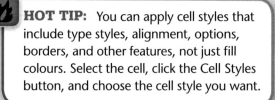

HOT TIP: You can apply cell styles that include type styles, alignment, options, borders, and other features, not just fill colours. Select the cell, click the Cell Styles button, and choose the cell style you want.

Apply a pattern to a cell

Shading gives you another option for calling attention to cells. Shading is especially useful when a worksheet already contains a lot of colours and you want data to stand out even more.

1 Select the cell you want to format.

2 Click the Home tab.

3 Click the Font dialogue box launcher.

4 Click the Fill tab.

5 Click the Pattern Color list arrow and click a pattern colour.

6 Click the Pattern Style list arrow and click a pattern.

7 Click OK.

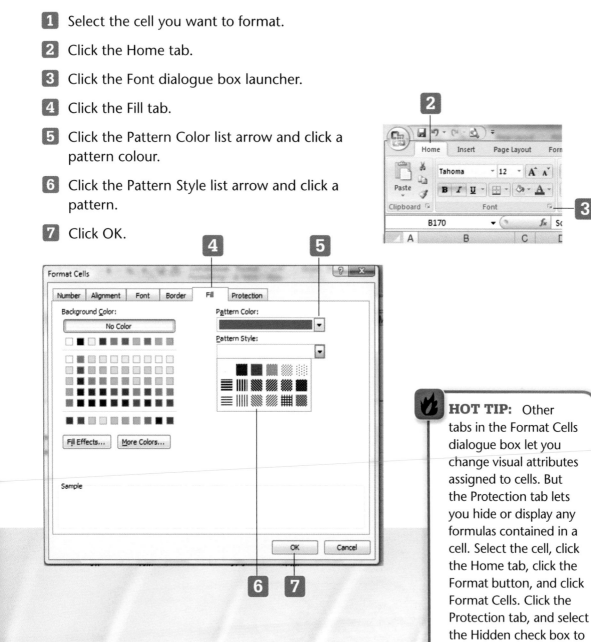

HOT TIP: Other tabs in the Format Cells dialogue box let you change visual attributes assigned to cells. But the Protection tab lets you hide or display any formulas contained in a cell. Select the cell, click the Home tab, click the Format button, and click Format Cells. Click the Protection tab, and select the Hidden check box to hide formulas.

4 Creating formulas and functions

Introduction

A formula is a set of commands and references that calculates values and produces a result. The result can be a sum, an average or a wide variety of more specific options. In order to create formulas, you can use constants (such as the number 101), operators, such as the plus or minus sign, functions that specify what action to perform, and references to cells in your worksheet.

Some Excel features help you do your work more efficiently by avoiding trouble. Formula AutoCorrect is an example: when you press the equals sign (=), Formula AutoCorrect is automatically activated. As you type your formula, valid (and correctly spelled) commands appear in a convenient drop-down list. This chapter describes basic operations you can perform with Excel simply and easily.

Formulas in Excel can be as simple or as complex as you need. Excel automatically recalculates formulas as you continue to work on a file, so your worksheets remain accurate and up to date at all times. You can always make changes to formulas in order to revise the data your worksheet contains.

Create a basic formula

Formulas are powerful features of Excel worksheets. They calculate values you have entered and return results for you. Excel provides you with a set of operators that you can use to perform addition, multiplication, division and other calculations. Each formula starts with an argument: the cell references or values that combine to produce a result. If your formula gets long, you can resize the formula bar to accommodate it.

1 Click the cell that you want to contain the formula.

2 Type the equals sign (=) to begin so Excel will calculate the values you enter. (If you don't, Excel will simply display what you type.)

3 Enter the first argument – a number or a cell reference.

4 Enter an operator such as the asterisk (*) for multiplication.

5 Enter the next argument and repeat values and operators as needed.

6 Press Enter or click the Enter button on the Formula bar. The result appears in the cell.

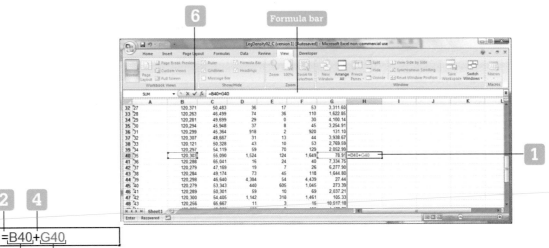

🔥 HOT TIP: Point to a cell rather than typing its address so you reduce the chance of typing errors.

❓ DID YOU KNOW? By default, only formula results are displayed in a cell, but you can adjust the worksheet view to display the formula itself.

Display formulas

By default, formulas aren't displayed in your worksheet cells. When you press Enter or click the Enter button on the formula bar, the calculation you have specified is performed. You may want to display formulas in the cells rather than automatically calculating them, however. Do so by following these steps.

1 Click the Formulas tab.

2 Click Show Formulas.

3 Click the Show Formulas button again to disable formula display.

HOT TIP: Press Ctrl + (Ctrl and the + key) to choose Show Formulas.

Activate Formula AutoComplete

One of Excel 2007's most useful new features is Formula AutoComplete. It provides you with suggestions of valid functions, arguments, defined names and other items that help you accurately complete a formula without typing everything from scratch. In order to use this feature, you first have to activate it.

1 Click the Office button.

2 Click Excel Options.

3 Click Formulas.

4 Tick the box next to Formula AutoComplete.

5 Click OK.

ALERT: You might not see the function you want on the Formula AutoComplete drop-down list. Some defined names, such as the ones used in the SUBTOTAL function, don't appear on the drop-down list – you have to type them manually.

Use Formula AutoComplete

Once you activate Formula AutoComplete, the feature starts working automatically the moment you type the equals sign to begin a formula. After the equals sign, when you type a text string, a drop-down list appears with items that will help you complete your typing.

1 Click the cell where you want to enter the formula.

2 Type = and some beginning letters of a formula to start Formula AutoComplete.

3 Scan the list of valid items, which changes as you type.

4 Make a note of the tool tip that explains what the formula or other item does.

5 Press Tab or double-click an item to select it.

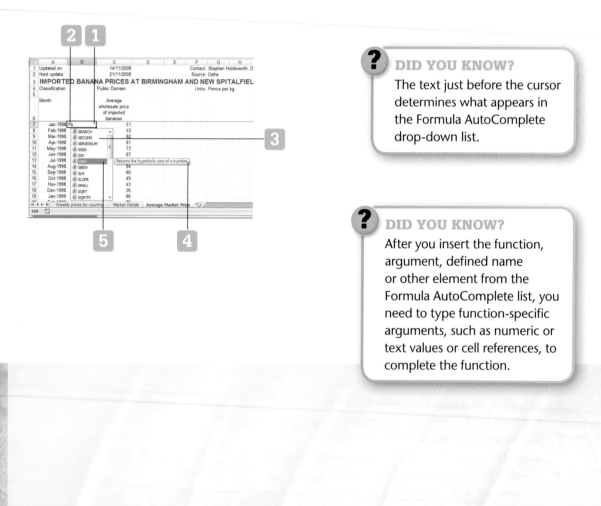

Edit a formula

It's not difficult to edit a formula, especially since the formula bar just above your worksheet data is available for this purpose. But there are a couple of tricks you need to perform in order to enter edit mode and make necessary changes.

1 Select the cell that contains the formula you need to edit.

2 Press F2 to enter Edit mode.

3 Use the Home, End and arrow keys to move through the formula so you can make edits.

4 Press Backspace or Del (Delete) to remove items so you can make corrections.

5 When you have finished, click Enter on the formula bar or press Enter.

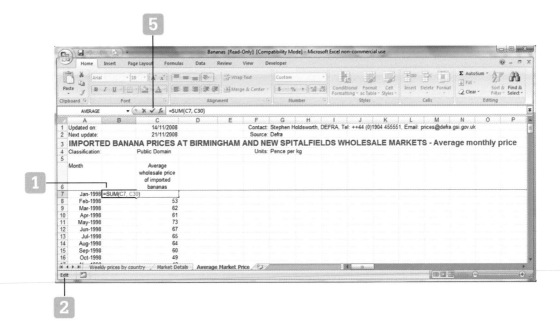

HOT TIP: You can also edit formulas using the copy, cut and paste operations, as you would any other content.

Copy a formula

If you need to copy a formula from one location to another, you have two options: you can use the clipboard or use the AutoFill feature. Since the clipboard option is relatively simple (select the cell, click Copy, click the destination cell and then click Paste), these steps focus on AutoFill.

1 Select the cell that contains the formula you want to copy.

2 Position the mouse pointer over the fill handle at the lower right-hand corner of the cell you have selected.

3 Drag the mouse down until you have selected all of the cells where you want to paste the formula, then release the mouse button.

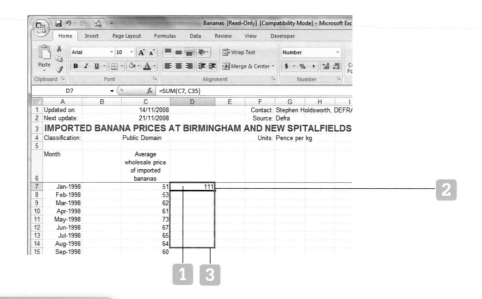

? **DID YOU KNOW?**

You can use the Paste Special command to copy only formulas and not the data contained in cells. Select the cells that contain the formulas you want to copy, click Copy, click where you want to paste, click Paste Special, click Formulas and click OK.

HOT TIP: If you need to recalculate formulas, press the F9 key.

Use absolute cell references

Sometimes, you'll want a formula to perform an action on a specific cell, even if you copy or move the formula to another worksheet. You can do so by making an absolute cell reference.

1 Click the cell where you want to enter the formula.

2 Type the equals sign to begin the formula.

3 Select a cell and type an operator (+, –, * or /).

4 Select another cell and press the F4 key to make the reference to that cell absolute.

5 When you have finished, press Enter or click the Enter button on the Formula toolbar.

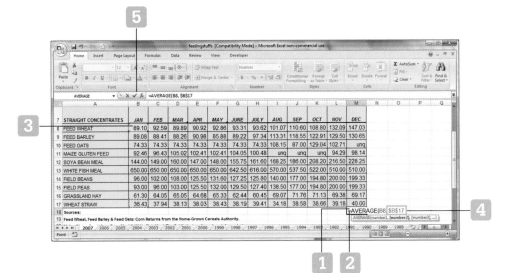

? DID YOU KNOW?

To change an absolute cell reference to a relative one, click in the cell that contains the absolute reference. Then press F4 repeatedly until all dollar signs are removed from the reference.

! ALERT: When you create a formula, Excel assumes it is a relative reference unless you specifically change it to an absolute reference.

Use mixed cell references

You have the option of creating not only formulas that contain absolute or relative cell references but mixed references. A mixed reference is either an absolute column and relative row or absolute row and relative column. When you add the $ symbol before the column letter or the row number you make the reference absolute.

1 Click the cell that you want to contain the formula.

2 Type the equals sign.

3 Select the cell you want to refer to and complete the formula.

4 Click to position the cursor in the formula bar and type $ before the column or row you want to make absolute. For example, A$1 is relative for column A and absolute for row 1, while $A1 is absolute for column A and relative for row 1.

5 Click the Enter button on the formula bar or press Enter.

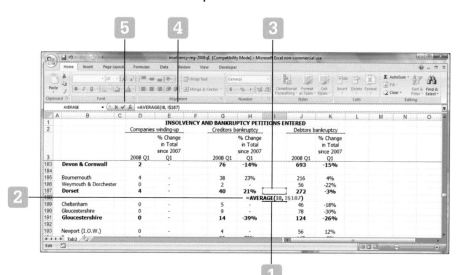

? DID YOU KNOW?

If you copy or fill the formula with a mixed reference across rows or down columns, the relative references adjust accordingly but the absolute references remain constant.

Name a cell or range with the Name box

Rather than making a reference to a range of cells, you can name those cells. Treating them as a single entity with a name makes them easier to remember. It's also easier to type a name such a 'customers' in a formula rather than a range such as B10:B105.

1 Select the cell or range of cells you want to name.

2 Click the Name box at the left edge of the formula bar.

3 Type a name of up to 255 characters for the range.

4 Press Enter.

	A	B	C	D	E	F	G	H	I	J	K	L	M	N	O
1						INSOLVENCY AND BANKRUPTCY PETITIONS ENTERED									
2				Companies winding-up			Creditors bankruptcy			Debtors bankruptcy					
					% Change in Total since 2007			% Change in Total since 2007			% Change in Total since 2007				
3				2008 Q1	Q1		2008 Q1	Q1		2008 Q1	Q1				
223	Bridgend			0	-		9	-		29	-28%				
224	Cardiff			25	-		48	-17%		84	24%				
225	Merthyr Tydfil			0	-		0	-		14	-				
226	Neath & Port Talbot			0	-		8	-		45	36%				
227	Pontypridd			1	-		9	-		43	-9%				
228	Swansea			2	-		20	-		68	-8%				
229	**South Wales**			28	-		94	-5%		297	0%				
230															
231	*Wales*			*30*	-		*167*	*6%*		*664*	*-3%*				
232															
233	Royal Courts of Justice			1,399	5%		1,753	-36%		886	-16%				

? DID YOU KNOW?

A defined name is used to identify a cell, a range of cells, a formula or a constant.

? DID YOU KNOW?

A single name called a 'scope' can be used to identify a worksheet or a workbook.

Identify a cell or range with the New Name dialogue box

You can also designate a name for a cell or range with the New Name dialogue box. This option requires a few more steps than in the preceding task. But you gain more control over the naming process and you can name a workbook or worksheet as well.

1 Select the cell or range you want to name.

2 Click the Formulas tab.

3 Click Define Name.

4 Type a name for the cell or range.

5 Choose a scope for the name – the workbook or a tab, for instance.

6 Click OK.

HOT TIP: Make your selection and then click Create From Selection on the Formulas tab instead of Define Name to create the name more quickly.

DID YOU KNOW?

If you need to widen or narrow the Name box, move your mouse arrow over the space between the Name box and the Formula box until the cursor changes into a double-headed arrow. Then click and drag to the left or right.

Add a named cell or range to a formula

Once you define a name for a cell or range, you can add it to a formula in one of several ways. You can use the Name box, take advantage of Formula AutoComplete, or use the Use in Formula command.

1 Click the Name box down arrow.

2 Choose the name you want from the list of names. The selected name appears in the Name box and all cells referenced by the name are selected.

3 To use Formula AutoComplete, type the equals sign to start a formula.

4 Type the first letter of the name you want to use.

5 Choose the name from the drop-down list and press Tab or double-click the name to add it to the formula.

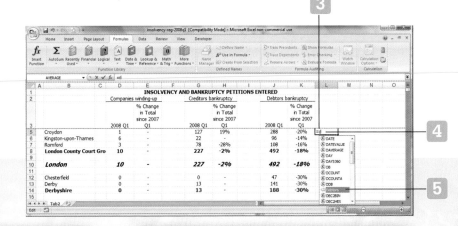

HOT TIP: By default, names use absolute rather than relative cell references.

? DID YOU KNOW?

A name can include uppercase or lowercase letters; names are not case-sensitive.

Enter a name with the Use in Formula command

The Use in Formula command comes in handy when you have a set of names you have already created and you need to choose between them.

1 Click in the cell where you want to add the formula.

2 Type the equals sign (=).

3 Click the Formulas tab.

4 Click the Use in Formula button.

5 Choose one of the available menu options:

- Click the name you want to use in the formula.

- Click Paste Names, select a name and click OK.

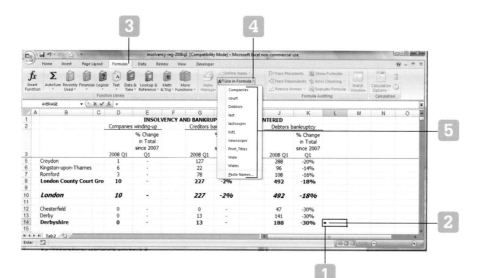

Organise names

Once you have added a group of names to a document, you'll need to delete or work with them. The Name Manager dialogue box lists all of your defined names and table names in one location.

1 Click the Formulas tab.

2 Click Name Manager.

3 Click New to create a new name.

4 Select a name and click Edit to change the name.

5 Select the name and click Delete to remove it from the list. Click **OK** when asked to confirm the delete.

6 Click Close.

ALERT: The Name Manager will not appear while you are editing a cell.

Simplify a formula with ranges

Formulas can become complicated and the more complex they are, the greater the possibility of errors. One way to simplify a formula is to use ranges or names. The preceding several tasks have examined creating and adding names to formulas. When you want to add a range of cells in a formula, follow these quick steps.

1 Click the cell where you would like the formula to be contained.

2 Click the equals sign and a function to begin the formula.

3 Click the first cell of the range.

4 Drag to the last cell in the range. The range address is automatically added to the formula.

5 Type the closed parenthesis to complete the formula.

6 Press Enter or click the Enter button on the formula bar.

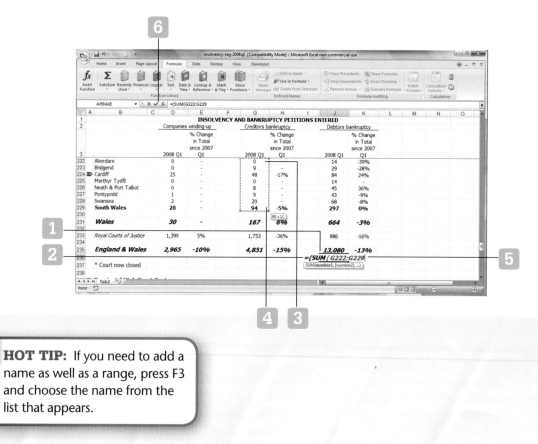

HOT TIP: If you need to add a name as well as a range, press F3 and choose the name from the list that appears.

Display calculations with the status bar

Sometimes, a formula isn't the easiest way to accomplish a task with Excel. For instance, if you need to perform a calculation just to get a preview of a result, you can do so with the status bar. It can display the sum, average, maximum, minimum or count of selected values.

1 Select the cell or range you want to calculate. The sum, average and count of the selected cells appears immediately in the status bar.

2 If you need to see the maximum, minimum or other result, right-click the status bar.

3 Click an option in the context menu to toggle it on or off.

? DID YOU KNOW?

When you use the status bar for a calculation, you don't see the results in the worksheet when they are printed.

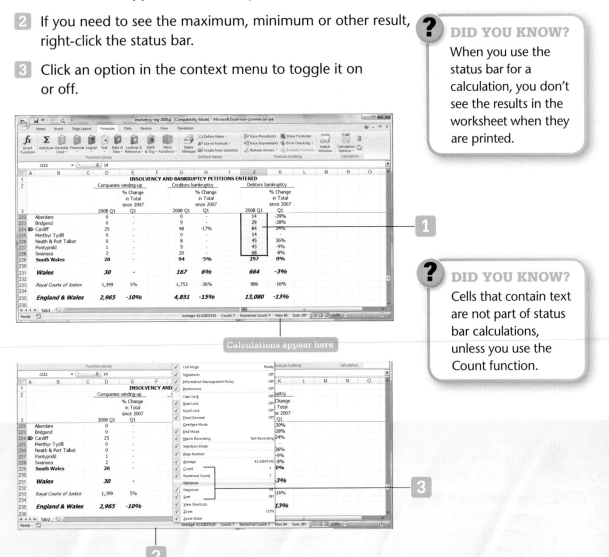

Calculations appear here

? DID YOU KNOW?

Cells that contain text are not part of status bar calculations, unless you use the Count function.

Calculate totals with AutoSum

Another option for quickly adding up a group of cells is the AutoSum button on Excel's Standard toolbar. The advantage of using AutoSum over the status bar is that AutoSum suggests the range to sum. You can change the range if needed.

1 Click the cell where you want the calculation to be displayed.

- To add up a range of numbers, select the range of cells.
- To add up only some of the numbers in a range, select each cell using the Ctrl key.
- To add up a table of numbers, select the cells and leave an additional column to the right and a row at the bottom.

2 Click the Formulas tab.

3 Click the AutoSum button.

4 Press Enter or click the Enter button on the formula bar.

? DID YOU KNOW?
AutoSum isn't just for sums. It can perform other calculations such as Average, Count, Max and Min as well.

🔥 HOT TIP: Press Alt + = to access the AutoSum command.

Convert formulas to values

If you have cells in a worksheet that contain formulas, you can easily convert the cells to values only. You might want to do this if you want the cells to remain constant. One quick option is to use the Paste Special command to paste the contents of the range into the cell to replace the formula.

1 Select the range of cells with formulas that you want to convert to values.

2 Click the Home tab.

3 Click the Copy button.

4 Click the down arrow next to Paste and choose Paste Special.

5 Click the Values option.

6 Click OK, then press Esc to leave Copy mode.

? DID YOU KNOW?

You can delete values and keep formulas in a cell. Click the Find & Select button on the Home tab, click Go To Special, click the Constants option, click the Numbers tick box and clear the other tick boxes under Formula. Then click OK. Press Delete to remove the values.

Create a custom formula calculation

Custom formula calculations let you really get to the heart of your data by analysing it in relation to itself. What this means is that you can do sophisticated analysis to draw out less obvious information from your data. With the new information in hand, you can then present it in a clear and easily understood way with a PivotTable report.

1 Modify your PivotTable in the PivotTable Field List. In this example, the Quarter, Profits and Employee fields have been selected.

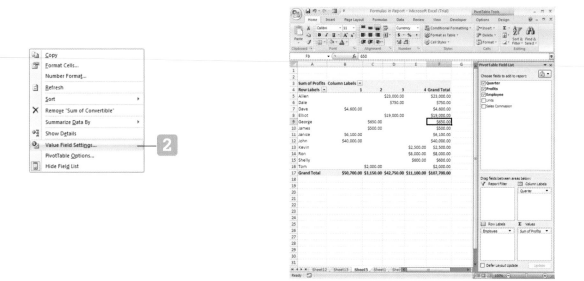

For this example, you're going to format the data using the Running Total in function. As you'll see, this will make your data table clearer and cleaner, and easier to read. The resulting presentation will be ideal for a presentation to someone not as familiar with the data who benefits from a graceful and simple layout.

WHAT DOES THIS MEAN?

PivotTable: Part of a worksheet that summarises a list of data using complex and variable criteria. By charting a PivotTable, you give others an overview of the contents and an easy way to draw conclusions because the information is presented visually.

2 Right-click anywhere within the PivotTable data and select Value Field Settings from the resulting context menu.

3 Click the Show values as tab.

4 Select Running Total in from the Show values as drop-down list.

5 Choose Units as your base field, so that the resulting report will show how many units each employee sold and display only how much revenue was generated.

6 Click OK.

As you can see, profits are now listed only for the Units rows, clearing up the report and making it easier to read.

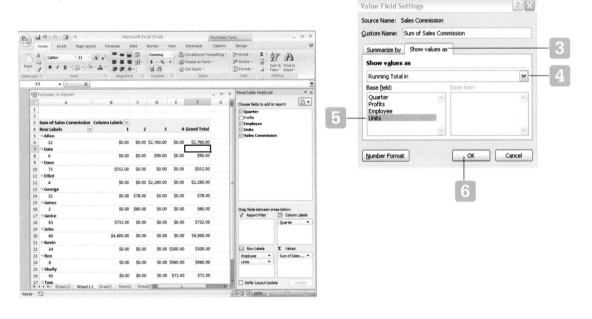

Here is a list of the types of custom calculations you can perform on your PivotTable data.

Calculation	What it does
Normal	Summarises the Values area field
Difference from	Uses the difference between a base and field item to summarise data
% Of	Uses the percentage of a base field item to summarise data
% Difference From	Uses the percentage of difference between a base and field item to summarise data
Running Total in	Shows data as a running total in a base field
% Of row	Uses the percentage of total row value to display data
% Of column	Uses the percentage of total column value to display data
% Total	Uses percentage of the total value from the report to display data
Index	Uses the formula: ((Cell Value)*(Grand Total of Grand Totals))/ ((Grand Row Total)*(Grand Column Total))

5 Working with charts

Introduction

For many people, a page full of numbers arranged in cells is not the easiest way to absorb and understand data. Visual representations are far more effective at presenting an overview than numbers alone, even if the numbers are effectively formatted. A chart gives users a snapshot of trends and patterns that can facilitate decision making.

Excel gives you a variety of presentation formats for charts. The option you choose can be tailored to the type of data you want to present. You can turn your numbers into a bar, line, pie, surface or bubble chart to help your colleagues reach conclusions about the data you have gathered.

This chapter will examine how to create and tailor charts that illustrate trends as well as interconnections between numbers. One set of data can be related to another and a chart can demonstrate this at a glance. You'll also learn how to change a chart type as needed, how to display data in a different style and how to move or resize your chart to optimise the information you need to present.

Choose the type of chart you need

Excel gives you plenty of options when it comes to creating the right type of chart for your needs. Your job is to choose the chart that presents data in just the right way. If you want to compare parts of a whole, select a pie chart. To compare different figures across geographic regions, choose a column chart. When you need to track data as it changes through time, choose an area chart.

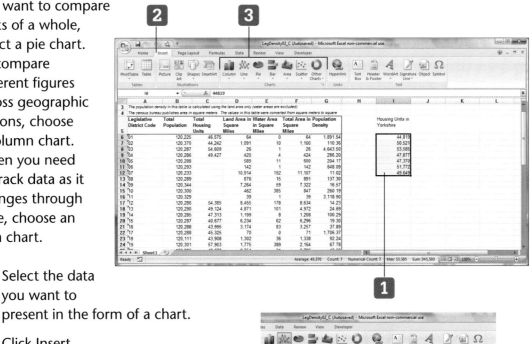

1 Select the data you want to present in the form of a chart.

2 Click Insert.

3 Click one of the common chart types in the Chart tool group.

4 Select a sub-type from the type of chart you have selected.

? DID YOU KNOW?

Charts in Excel have a set of essential elements:

- Title: text that identifies the purpose of a chart.
- Data marker: a bar, circle, dot or other object that illustrates a data point.
- Y-axis: the vertical axis of a chart.
- X-axis: the horizontal axis of a chart.
- Data series: a set of related data points in a chart.
- Legend: instructions that explain the colours or symbols in a chart.

Choose from all chart types

The previous task outlined the general steps involved in creating a chart with Excel. As you can see, it's a quick process. You can either create an embedded chart – a chart that is embedded in an existing worksheet – or one that is displayed on its own worksheet. If you open the Charts dialogue box launcher, you can choose from among all available chart types.

1 Select the data you want to present in the chart.

2 Click the Insert tab.

3 Click the Charts dialogue box launcher.

4 Click a chart category.

5 Select an option.

6 Click OK.

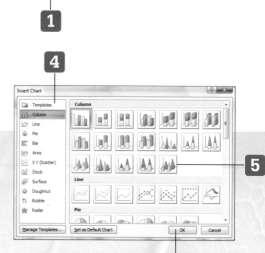

HOT TIP: To create a default chart, select the data you want to present, then press F11 to create the chart on a new sheet, or Alt+F1 to create an embedded chart on the current worksheet.

DID YOU KNOW?

Embedding a chart in an existing worksheet is a good option when you want to view chart data separately from worksheet data.

Select parts of a chart

In order to edit or work with a chart once you have created it, you need to select its elements. A chart element is an object that makes up the chart – an axis, the legend or the data series.

1 Click anywhere in the chart to select it. The Chart Tools tabs appear above the Ribbon.

2 Click either the Format or the Layout tab.

3 Click the down arrow next to Chart Area.

4 Click the chart element you want to select. When you have selected a chart element, selection handles appear around it.

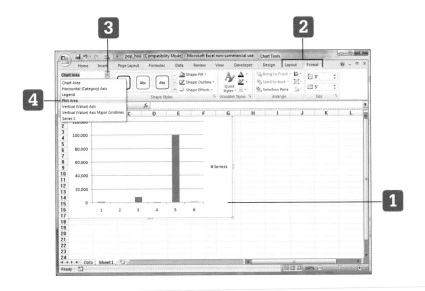

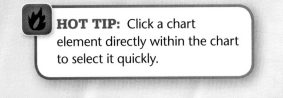

HOT TIP: Click a chart element directly within the chart to select it quickly.

SEE ALSO: The parts of a chart are listed in the first task in this chapter, Choose the type of chart you need.

Edit a chart

You can edit a chart by changing any of its features at any time. You might want to change the colours associated with a bar, line or other element, for instance. When you edit a chart, you do not change the data used to create it, you only change the presentation.

1 Select the part of the chart you want to edit.

2 Choose Design to change colours or other visual elements.

3 Click the Layout tab to change the legend or other parts of the chart.

4 Choose an option from the drop-down list.

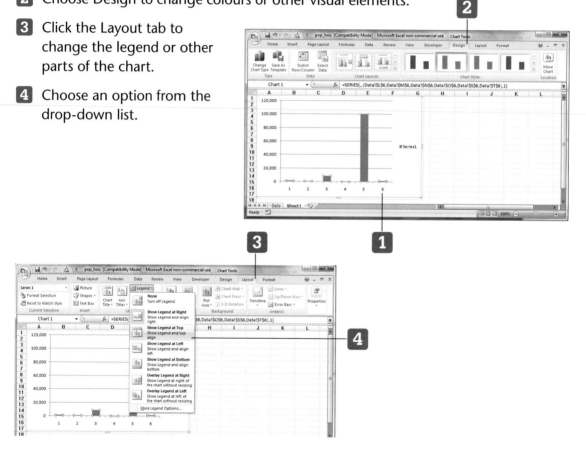

HOT TIP: Point to any object in a chart to see what it's called.

Format chart elements

The Format tab, which appears under Chart Tools when you select a chart, contains options that control the way data is presented. The formatting options differ depending on the element you have selected.

1 Click anywhere in the chart to select it.

2 Click the Format tab.

3 Click the Format Selection button.

4 Choose the options you want. Those for Border Styles include:

- Width: this adjusts border thickness, in points.

- Compound type: if the border style is compound (i.e. it contains two styles), the combination appears here.

- Dash type: if the border is a dash, the type appears here.

- Cap type: if the border includes a cap, choose whether it should be square, round or flat.

- Join type: determines whether the join between top and side is bevelled, round or flat.

- Arrow settings: determines the style of an arrow's two ends.

5 Click Close.

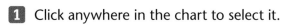

Move a chart

If you are working with a chart that has been embedded in a worksheet, you can move it easily. That way it won't interfere with the other data on the sheet.

1 Click anywhere in the chart you want to move to select it.

2 Position the mouse pointer over a blank area of the chart, then click and drag the pointer. The outline of the chart moves to indicate that it is being moved to a new location.

3 Release the mouse button.

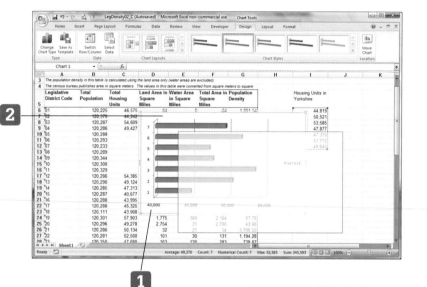

Resize a chart

When you click on a chart element such as its legend, selection handles appear around that element. When you click in an empty part of a chart, selection handles appear at the corners and the sides of the chart. Click and drag any of the chart selection handles to resize the chart.

1 Click an empty area of the chart you want to resize to select it.

2 Position the mouse pointer over one of the selection handles.

3 Drag the handle to resize it.

4 Release the mouse button.

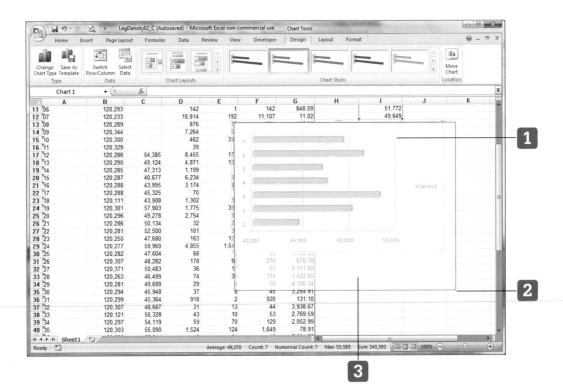

ALERT: If you resize a chart by dragging it downwards, make sure you don't interfere with legends or axis titles.

HOT TIP: If you want to restore the chart to its previous size, press Ctrl+Z to undo the resizing.

Edit a chart's title

When you create a chart, it typically includes a title, axis titles and a legend. You can adjust the position and contents of the title in case the data changes or if you want to emphasise part of the contents.

1 Click anywhere in the chart you want to edit. The Chart Tools tabs appear.

2 Click the Layout tab.

3 Click Chart Title and choose one of the options that appear:

- None will make the title invisible.

- Centered Overlay Title adds a title without resizing the chart to accommodate it.

- Above Chart moves the chart title to the top and resizes the chart.

- More Title Options lets you specify custom chart title settings.

4 Double-click the title text box to position the cursor and change the title if needed.

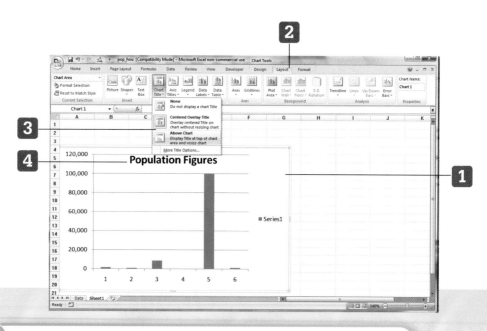

? DID YOU KNOW?

A title that is formatted as an overlay does not overlap other chart contents; the chart is resized so the title does not interfere with it. A title that is formatted as an overlap has its text on top of the chart, so the text might appear to be on top of bars, axes or other contents.

Change chart labels

You can change the legend and data labels in your chart at any time. The legend is text that helps viewers understand colours and symbols used in the chart with the data they represent. Data labels are values next to the bars, lines, dots or other objects that make data easier to interpret.

1 Select the chart you want to edit.

2 Click the Layout tab under Chart Tools.

3 Click the Legend button, then select one of the available options.

4 Click the Data Labels button, then choose one of the Data Labels options to either show or hide the labels.

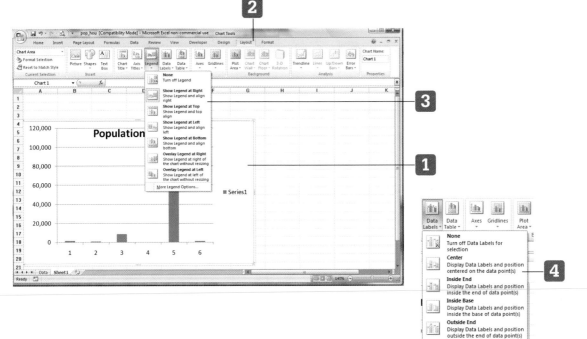

? DID YOU KNOW?

The first four table legend options control where the legend appears in relation to the chart. The next two overlay options position the legend either on the right or the left. The last option, More Legend Options, lets you specify custom options for your legend.

? DID YOU KNOW?

The first two data label options let you show or hide the labels. The third lets you specify custom options: you can choose what text they contain, decide on their position and choose a separator to go between them.

Change a chart's type

If one of your colleagues doesn't understand what your chart is intended to portray, you can try another option for presenting your data. Excel gives you plenty of chart options from which to choose, including both 2-D and 3-D layouts.

1 Click anywhere in the chart you want to change to select it.

2 Click the Design tab under Chart Tools.

3 Click the Change Chart Type button. The Choose Chart Type dialogue box appears.

4 Choose the type of chart you want.

5 Choose the specific sub-type of chart.

6 Click OK.

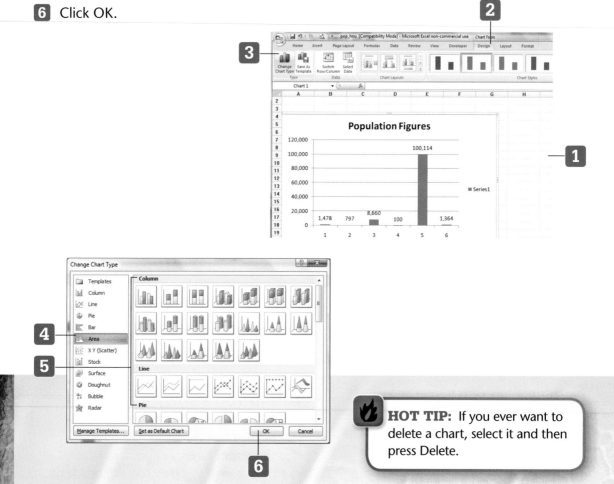

HOT TIP: If you ever want to delete a chart, select it and then press Delete.

Adjust layout and style

Once you choose the type of chart you want, you can refine its appearance by adjusting its layout and style. The layout of a chart is the arrangement of elements within its type. For instance, if you choose the bar chart type, you can choose a 2-D or 3-D layout, or you can decide to have the bars run horizontally rather than vertically. The style of a chart refers to its colour choices as well as its background.

1 Select the chart you want to edit.

2 Click the Design tab under Chart Tools.

3 Scroll through the sets of layouts and choose the layout you want.

4 Click the scroll up or down arrows in the Chart Styles section of the Design tab and choose the style you want.

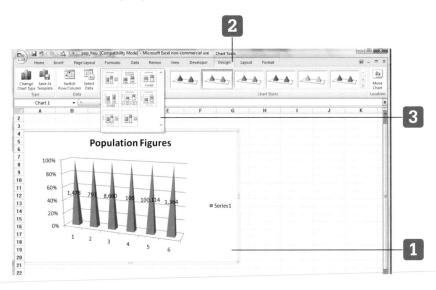

? DID YOU KNOW?

You can customise your chart by choosing different colours or line thicknesses. You can then save your customised settings by clicking Save As Template in the Design tab so you can apply the settings to other charts you create.

Change a chart's axis

An axis is a reference line that borders an edge of a chart, either along one side or along the top or bottom. Axes are typically named y (for vertical), x (for horizontal) or z (for 3-D charts). You might want to change the axes of a chart if the axis labels (the labels next to bars or other objects) become too difficult to read because they are too long.

1 Click the chart to select it.

2 Click the Layout tab under Chart Tools.

3 Click the Axes button, point to Primary Horizontal Axis or Primary Vertical Axis and choose one of the available options.

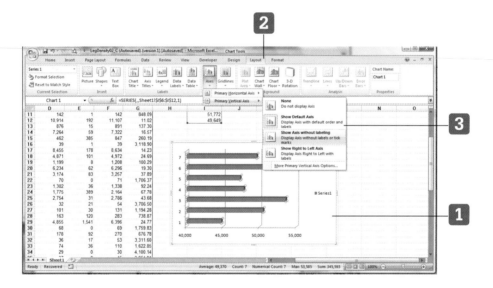

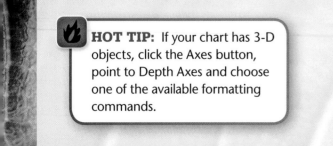

HOT TIP: If your chart has 3-D objects, click the Axes button, point to Depth Axes and choose one of the available formatting commands.

? DID YOU KNOW?

You can also change the gridlines, the lines that run horizontally or vertically behind the chart that help the viewer determine the values of its data points. Click the chart to select it, click the Layout tab, click the Gridlines button and choose one of the formatting options.

Work with pie charts

Pie charts are striking and effective tools for presenting parts that make up a whole. You might use a pie chart to illustrate the ethnic groups within a particular population, or the proportions of expenditures within a budget. Excel lets you choose predesigned variations on the pie chart theme in order to call attention to individual slices by pulling them out from the adjacent pieces.

1 Select the data you want to format as a pie chart.

2 Click the Insert tab.

3 Click the Pie button and choose a simple design from those shown in the drop-down list.

4 Double-click a pie slice to select it.

5 Drag the pie slice out and away from the centre to 'explode' it from the pie so that it stands out.

6 Release the mouse button.

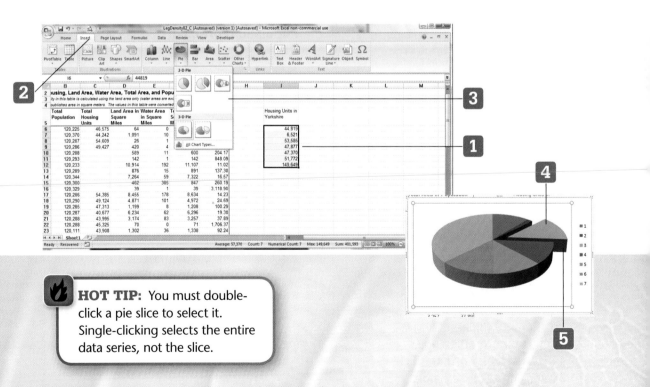

HOT TIP: You must double-click a pie slice to select it. Single-clicking selects the entire data series, not the slice.

Format chart text

The text that accompanies a chart is formatted in a generic font and style. You may want to format the text to correspond to other documents or to match your organisation's style. The text formatting controls on the Home or Format tabs allow you to change the text's appearance.

1 Click the chart to select it.

2 Highlight the text you want to format.

3 Click the Home tab.

4 Use the text controls to choose a font, font size and styles (bold, italic or underline).

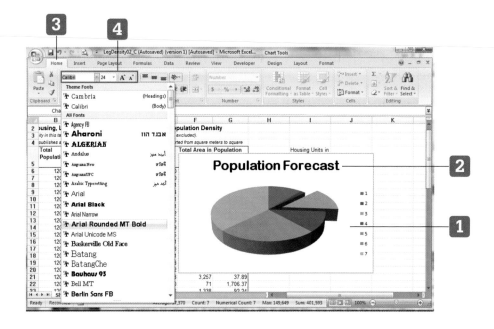

Change a chart's background

A chart's readability can be affected by its background. If the background is too bright or too similar in colour to the colours in the chart, it can make the chart hard to read. If the background contrasts strongly, it can make the chart easier to view and give it a more dramatic effect.

1 Select the chart you want to edit.

2 Click Layout and then click Chart Wall, Chart Floor or Plot Area, depending on which part of the layout you want to change.

3 Choose More [Element] Options.

4 Click Solid fill.

5 Click Color.

6 Choose a colour from the palette.

7 Click Close.

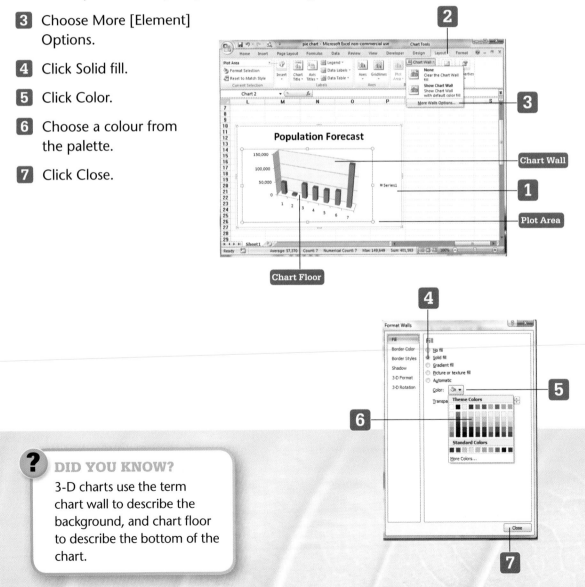

? DID YOU KNOW?

3-D charts use the term chart wall to describe the background, and chart floor to describe the bottom of the chart.

Create a PivotChart from a PivotTable

When you create a PivotChart, a new tab called Analyze appears. It contains controls for collapsing or expanding fields, refreshing or clearing data, and showing or hiding features such as the Field List.

1 Click anywhere in the PivotTable.

2 Click the Options tab.

3 Click PivotChart.

4 Choose the layout option you want.

5 Click OK.

? **DID YOU KNOW?**

The PivotChart Filter pane lets you filter out data that appears in the chart. Tick a box next to a criterion to add it to the chart; untick it to remove it.

Customise a PivotChart

Even if you create a PivotChart from data presented in a PivotTable, the results aren't 'written in stone'. You can always adjust them to clarify your report. If you ever want to rename a report, just click the Options tab, type the new name in the PivotTable Name box and press Enter.

1 Click the Layout tab to adjust the PivotChart.

2 Click the Format tab to fill shapes, change type designs or alter other visual aspects of the chart.

3 Click the Analyze tab to refresh data, clear filters or add filters, or change the active tab.

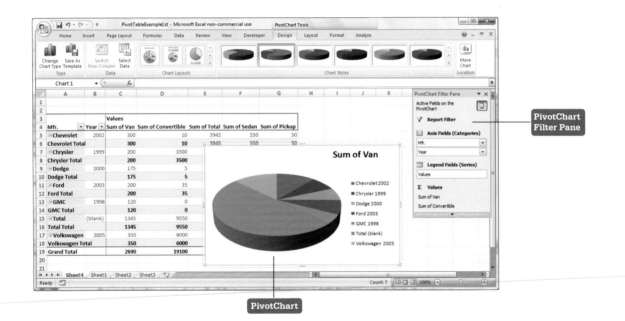

PivotChart Filter Pane

PivotChart

Modify a PivotChart

In Excel 2007, all of the tools available for modifying charts are also available for PivotCharts. In fact, the PivotChart Tools that appear when you create a PivotChart differ from the regular Chart Tools only in that they also include an Analyze tab. Of course, when you create a PivotChart, you have all the flexibility that it provides.

1 Select a substantial amount of data to create your sample PivotChart, but not so much that it's hard to create a coherent image.

2 Make sure that you've selected only the aforementioned cells to be represented in your PivotChart by clicking in the provided range field.

3 Select PivotChart from the Table group in the Insert tab and choose New Worksheet.

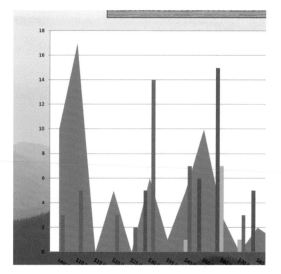

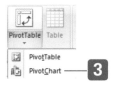

4 Tick all of the boxes in the PivotTable Field List.

5 Click Change Chart Type on the Design tab. Choose Stacked Column in 3-D and click OK.

6 Now you can take advantage of all the same customisation options you had with regular charts, but with the added flexibility of a PivotChart.

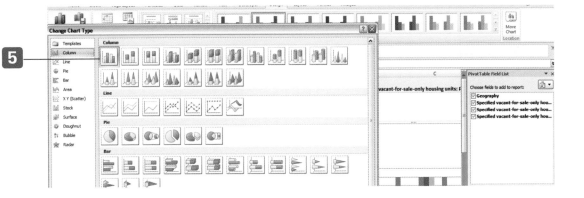

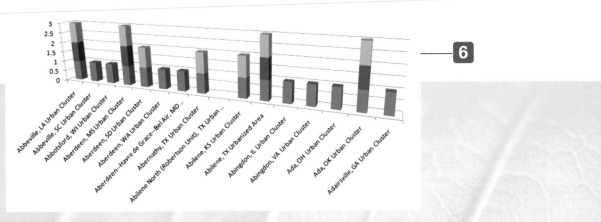

6 Interpreting worksheet data with tables

Introduction

Any tools you can provide that make it easier for your readers to analyse and interpret the data you present with Excel are advantageous for you. Tables (which were known as lists in previous versions) are among one of the most powerful and flexible tools Excel gives you. You can quickly convert a group of cells into a table and use Quick Styles to make its contents easy to interpret.

In order to enter data into tables, you can make use of pick lists, which use rules to restrict what is entered in specified fields. Drop-down lists of entries also enable you to provide consistent data entry for you and your colleagues.

Once your table contains the data you want, you can sort it using buttons on the Ribbon, or by making use of the AutoFilter feature. You can also create PivotTables, which highlight data for easier viewing and make it simple for you to add or delete criteria you want to present. Once you learn to work with tables, you'll find they make it simple to present reports or select exactly the information you want your colleagues to analyse so they can make informed decisions.

Create a table

In order to create a table, you first select the data you want to present, as you would any other feature. However, you need to make sure that the field names are positioned in a single row in the first line of the list. In addition, each record in the table should be on a single row. Once you create the table, you can enter data directly into it, in any order; you'll learn to sort the data later in this chapter.

1 Open a blank worksheet.

2 Enter field labels on the first row of the table.

3 Type information for each record in a separate row.

4 Select all the cells in the table, including labels.

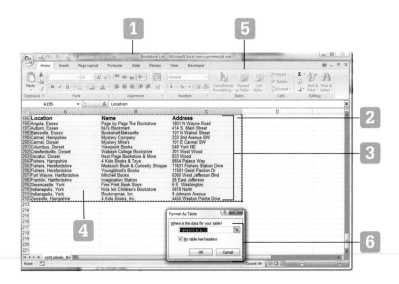

HOT TIP: To delete a data table, select it and then press Delete to delete the entire table. If you want to keep the cells and just delete the data, click Clear and choose Clear Contents.

ALERT: Make sure your table records do not contain any blank rows.

5 Do one of the following:

- Click the Table button on the Insert tab.

- Click the Format as Table button on the Home tab and choose a table style.

6 Adjust the table size, tick the My table has headers box and click OK.

Table headers

Table data

Apply a style to a table

When you click the Format as Table button on the Home tab to create a table, you have the option of formatting the table. However, you can assign colours to the headers and data in a table at any time. You choose from a gallery of table styles that is based on the current theme.

1 Select a cell, a range of cells or the entire table.

2 Do one of the following:

2 **More button**

- Click one of the designs shown in the Table Styles tool group on the Design tab.

1

- Click the Design tab under Table Tools and click the More button, then select a table style from the gallery.

- Click the Home tab, click Format as Table and choose a table style from the gallery.

Table Styles gallery

? **DID YOU KNOW?**

If you want to copy a table style from one table to another, use the Format Painter. Select a cell that has the formatting you want to copy, click the Format Painter button on the Home tab, drag to scroll across the cells you want to format and release the mouse button.

? **DID YOU KNOW?**

To clear a table style, click any cell in the table, click the Design tab under Table Tools, click the More arrow under Table Styles and click Clear.

Modify a table style

If you have a design you want to emulate or a set of colours you need to match exactly, you can choose a table style and then modify it to suit the needs of the project. You can also create your own custom table style.

1 Click the Home tab.

2 Click the Format as Table button.

3 Do one of the following:

- Click New Table Style to create a new style.
- Click Modify to change the table's current style.

4 Type a name for your style.

5 Select the element you want to change.

6 Click Format.

7 Click the Font tab to change the font and the Border tab to select a cell border style.

8 Click the Fill tab to select a colour for the table element you have chosen.

9 Choose a colour and then click OK.

10 Clear or tick the Set as default table quick style for this document box.

11 Click OK.

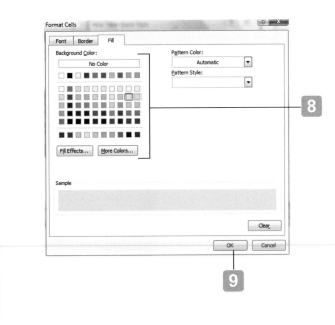

? DID YOU KNOW?

You can delete a custom style by clicking the Home tab, clicking the Format as Table button, right-clicking the style you created and choosing Delete.

Show or hide parts of a table

By default, Excel displays a standard set of elements with a table, including headings, columns and rows. You can format the table all at once or any one of these elements individually. You also have the option of hiding formatting elements you no longer need.

1 Select the cell or cell range in the table you want to edit.

2 Click the Design tab under Table Tools.

3 Clear or tick the box next to the element you want to show or hide:

- Header Row hides or displays the top row of the table.

- Total Row hides or displays a total row at the bottom of the table.

- Banded Rows hides or displays the colour of rows that have been banded.

- First Column highlights the first column so you can format it.

- Last Column highlights the last column so you can format it

- Banded Columns hides or displays the colour of columns that have been banded.

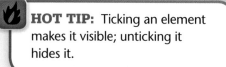

HOT TIP: Ticking an element makes it visible; unticking it hides it.

Total data in a table

One of the best things about data in worksheets is the ability to find totals or perform other calculations quickly. Tables provide you with a Total Row option that instantly finds the total of data in a row.

1 Click a cell in a table.

2 Click the Design tab under Table Tools.

3 Click the Total Row box. A total row is added at the bottom of the table.

4 Click the cell in the column for which you want to calculate a total and click the drop-down list arrow.

5 Choose the calculation you want to perform by selecting it from the drop-down list.

? **DID YOU KNOW?**

You can calculate data in a column as well by clicking a cell in a blank column and then typing a formula.

? **DID YOU KNOW?**

When you add a total row at the end of a table, a drop-down list appears for each total cell along with the word Total in the cell at the extreme left. The drop-down list lets you perform a calculation using a function you choose.

Insert a row or column

Once you create a table, you can add or delete rows or columns as needed, but the process differs slightly from that for conventional worksheet data. To select column data, click the top edge of the column header. To select an entire column, double-click the top edge of the header. To click a row, click its left border. To select an entire table, double-click the upper left-hand corner.

1 Click a cell in the table or select a row or column.

2 Click the Home tab.

3 Click the down arrow next to Insert and choose one of the following:

- To add a column, choose Insert Table Columns to the Left or Insert Table Columns to the Right.

- To add a row, choose Insert Table Rows Above or Insert Table Rows Below.

HOT TIP: To select only the data in a table rather than the entire table, single-click the upper left-hand corner and then press Ctrl+A.

Resize a table

Often, you need to resize a table, to make it either easier to read or more compact so it fits better next to other contents.

1 Click anywhere in the table.

2 Click the Design tab.

3 Click Resize Table.

4 Type the range of cells you want the table to fill.

5 Click OK.

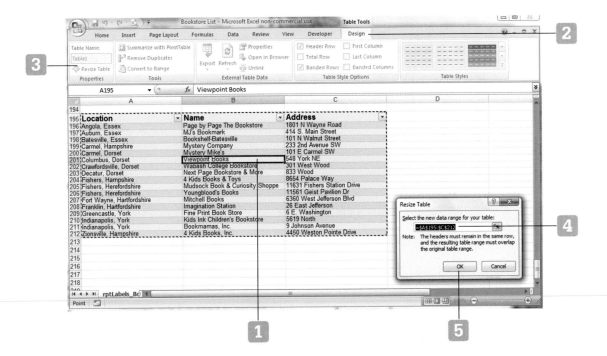

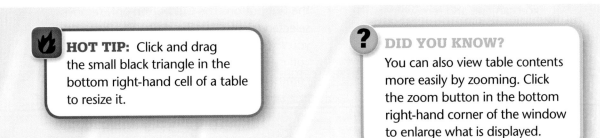

HOT TIP: Click and drag the small black triangle in the bottom right-hand cell of a table to resize it.

? DID YOU KNOW?

You can also view table contents more easily by zooming. Click the zoom button in the bottom right-hand corner of the window to enlarge what is displayed.

Delete rows or columns

It's a good idea to keep tables compact and to delete rows or columns if you no longer need them. You can do so by using a range of Delete options on the Home tab.

1 Click any cell in the row or column you want to remove.

2 Click the Home tab.

3 Click the down arrow next to Delete and then choose Delete Table Rows or Delete Table Columns.

Enter data with a drop-down list

Typing data item by item can be time-consuming. A faster way is to enter data from a drop-down list, also called a PickList. The PickList feature becomes available once you have entered at least one record in a list. It makes suggestions based on your previous entries; if you are entering a series of records that includes the same city or postal code, for instance, you can choose it from a list rather than typing the characters repetitively.

1 Right-click the cell in which you want to enter data chosen from a list.

2 Choose Pick From Drop-down List from the context menu.

3 Make a selection from the list.

4 Press Enter or Tab to accept the choice and add it to the cell.

HOT TIP: You can press Esc to cancel the entry if you want to make another choice.

Create a drop-down list

If you don't see the data entry options you want in the drop-down list Excel gives you, you can create your own custom drop-down list. A custom list is useful because it gives you and your colleagues a way to enter data consistently.

1 Type a set of entries in the order you want.

2 Select the range of cells.

3 Click the Name box, type a name and press Enter.

4 Select the cell where you want the drop-down list to appear.

5 Click the Data tab.

6 Click the Data Validation button.

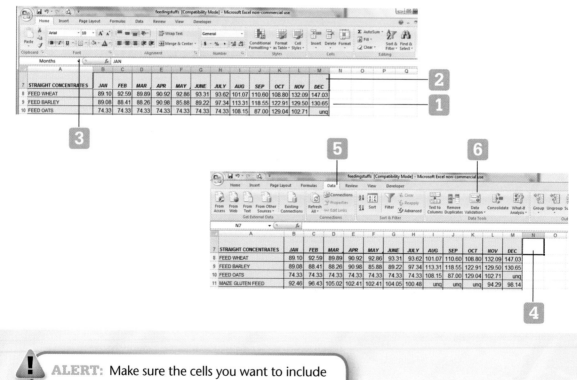

ALERT: Make sure the cells you want to include in the drop-down list don't include any blank cells.

7 Click the Settings tab.

8 Click the down arrow next to Allow and click List.

9 Enter the values you want.

10 Click the Input Message tab and type a message to be displayed when someone makes an invalid entry.

11 Click the Error Alert tab and select an alert style.

12 Click OK.

Sort table data

Sorting is one of the most effective tools Excel gives you to help interpret data. Sorting allows you to reorganise the information you have recorded so you can view it according to a pattern. Ascending order sorts records from A to Z, earliest to latest or lowest to highest. Descending order does the reverse – Z to A and so on.

1 Click the table cell that has the field name by which you want to sort.

2 Click the Data tab.

3 Click one of the sort buttons, Sort Ascending or Sort Descending.

4 If you need to reapply the sort to other cells in the table, click the Reapply button.

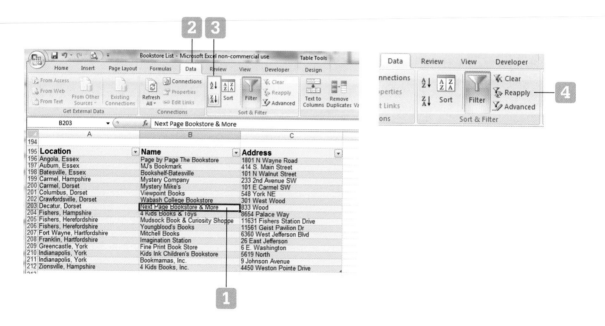

? DID YOU KNOW?

You can also sort a list using one or more sort fields – fields you select to help arrange list data. Suppose you have arranged one record, or one set of cells, using the sort criteria you want to use. You can select the cell and then click the Sort button to sort by those attributes.

Analyse data with a PivotTable or PivotChart

A PivotTable is an ideal tool for summarising data using complex criteria. A PivotTable lets you quickly choose the fields and criteria you want to use to present in the table. You can also format the table as a table, or make the data easier to read by formatting it as a PivotChart.

1️⃣ Click anywhere in the table or select a range of cells.

2️⃣ Click Insert.

3️⃣ Click the PivotTable down arrow and choose PivotTable or PivotChart.

4️⃣ Click the Select a table or range option, or click Use an external data source, click Choose Connection and select a connection to a remote file.

5️⃣ Choose the New Worksheet or Existing Worksheet option.

6️⃣ Click OK.

7️⃣ Tick the boxes next to the fields you want to include in the PivotTable.

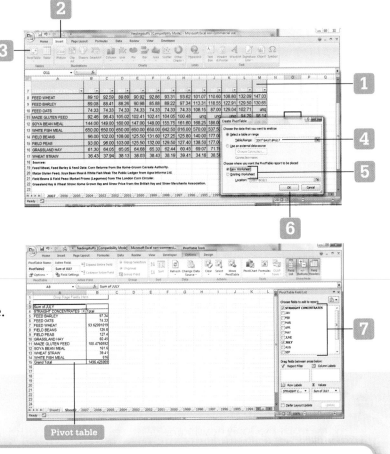

Pivot table

Update a PivotTable

Once you create a PivotTable, it's particularly easy to modify its contents. You can use the PivotTable Field List or the Options tab under PivotTable Tools. By using these options, you don't have to recreate the title whenever you want to add new data to it.

1 Click any cell in the PivotTable.

2 Tick or untick the boxes in the PivotTable Field List.

3 To reorder the position of a field, drag its name in the Field List to one of the other boxes.

4 Click Update to manually update the report layout.

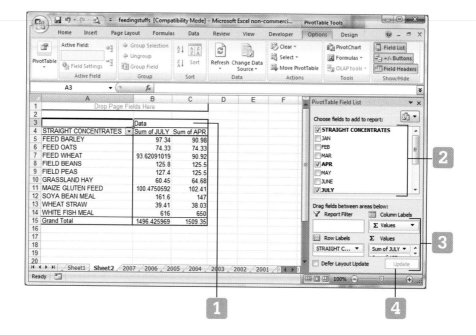

? DID YOU KNOW?

The PivotTable Tools heading appears only when you have clicked inside a PivotTable.

Convert text to columns

Excel provides you with an easy-to-use wizard that leads you through the process of separating the contents of cells into individual columns. For instance, if a cell contains a series of numbers, you can use the wizard to separate each number into its own column.

1. Select the range of cells you want to convert into columns.

2. Click the Data tab.

3. Click Text to Columns.

4. When the first screen of the wizard appears, click Delimited.

5. Click Next.

6. On the second screen, select the type of delimiter you want to use and clear other tick boxes.

7. Follow the rest of the steps in the wizard; when you've finished, click Finish.

DID YOU KNOW?

The options shown in the wizard differ depending on the type of delimiter being used to separate the cells' contents into separate columns.

Create an outline

Excel data can be formatted as an outline, which presents a hierarchical set of information that is easy to interpret. A set of data in outline form consists of items that can have multiple topics or levels of information within them.

1 Organise a set of data in hierarchical fashion. Select the data you want to convert into an outline.

2 Click Data.

3 Click the down arrow next to Group and choose Auto Outline.

	Total	0-14	15-17	18-64	65 and over	0-14	15-17	18-64	65 and over	White alone
		Male					Female			Race:
6	120,021	13,604	2,961	39,454	3,793	12,857	2,694	39,232	5,426	102,352
7	120,225	15,678	3,205	37,367	4,310	14,337	3,033	37,556	4,739	101,563
8	120,450	12,626	2,441	38,006	5,518	12,289	2,285	37,878	9,407	104,806
9	120,300	13,639	3,113	36,379	6,072	12,934	2,835	37,032	8,295	112,883
10	120,199	15,602	2,935	38,237	3,624	14,253	2,715	38,122	4,711	107,488
11	120,195	12,486	2,865	34,729	7,445	12,118	2,644	37,209	10,699	111,752

HOT TIP: When creating data for an outline, place summary rows below detail rows and summary columns to the right of detail columns.

7 Creating and modifying graphics and shapes

Introduction

Anything you can do to make the data in your Excel spreadsheets easier to interpret will make your work more valuable to your colleagues. Previous chapters have discussed formatting, tables and colour themes. In this chapter, you'll explore the many options Excel gives you for working with graphics that can make your presentations look professional and visually appealing.

Because Excel is part of Microsoft Office, you gain access to the extensive library of clip art that comes with the application suite. You can also browse through clip art that Microsoft makes available to Office users online. Once you add a graphic image, you can resize, recolour and crop it as you would in any other Office application.

Simple graphic images will enhance your worksheets, but Excel also includes the ability to add specialised objects. WordArt is a feature that can enhance labels and titles and that comes with many style choices. You can also insert SmartArt graphics to illustrate a sequence of steps in a process or the relationships between points of information.

Locate and insert clip art

When you need an image for a worksheet, the quickest option is to add clip art. Clip art is artwork that has been made available by its creators for use by others. An extensive library is available to users of Excel and other Office applications. You search for it through the Clip Art task pane and browse for the image you want in a library called the Clip Organizer.

1 Click the Insert tab.

2 Click the Clip Art button. The Clip Art task pane opens.

3 Type a keyword or phrase that describes the image you want.

4 Click the Search in arrow to limit the search to a particular collection.

5 Click Go.

6 Double-click the image you want to add it to the current Excel document.

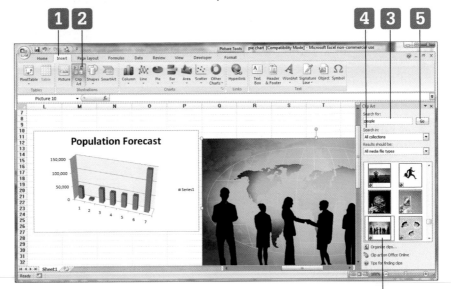

? DID YOU KNOW?

Once you locate an image in the Clip Organizer, you can click the down arrow next to it. (The arrow appears when you pass your mouse pointer over the image.) Choose an available option, such as Insert, or choose Find Similar Style to locate images that are similar to the one you have chosen.

! ALERT: There are plenty of clip art resources on the web, such as Barry's Clip Art (www.barrysclipart.com). But read the fine print: sometimes the artists require you to give them credit or restrict the use to personal or nonprofit purposes.

Resize and move an image

Most of the images in the Clip Organizer are initially far too big in width and depth to be accommodated in their entirety in a worksheet. You need to resize them to make them fit alongside any charts or tables you have created.

1 Click one of the resize handles around the image you have inserted.

2 Drag the image toward its centre to make it smaller; drag it outwards to enlarge it.

3 When you've finished, release the mouse button.

4 Single-click the image and drag it to move it anywhere in the current worksheet.

5 When the image is positioned correctly, release the mouse button.

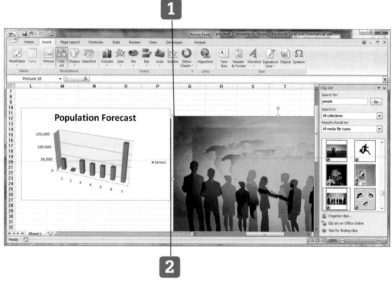

ALERT: If you don't want to distort the image by changing the ratio of width to height, press and hold down the Shift key as you resize.

Find clip art online

The Clip Organizer is extensive, but it might not have the image you are looking for. To search a wider range of possibilities, you can go to Microsoft Office Online. This is a website that Microsoft makes available to its customers so they can browse and insert clip art.

1 Click the Insert tab.

2 Click the Clip Art button. The Clip Art task pane opens.

3 Click Clip art on Office Online. Your web browser opens (if it isn't open already). It connects to the Microsoft Office Online Clip Art home page.

4 Click the Search list arrow and choose the media type you want to find.

5 Click Search.

6 When you find an image, tick the box beneath it, click Download and then click Open.

> **⚠ ALERT:** You have to be connected to the Internet in order to access Microsoft Office Online.

Divide clip art into categories

The images that come with the Clip Organizer are organised in their own categories. But you might want to set aside some images for your own use, particularly if they apply to ongoing projects. In this way, you can assemble your personal collection of clip art images.

1 Click the Insert tab.

2 Click the Clip Art button.

3 Click Organize clips at the bottom of the Clip Art task pane.

4 Click the File menu in the Clip Organizer, point to Add Clips to Organizer and choose On My Own.

5 Locate the clip you want to add and click the image to select it.

6 Click Add To.

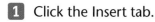

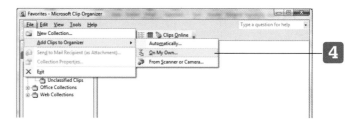

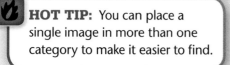

HOT TIP: You can place a single image in more than one category to make it easier to find.

7 Click the collection to which you want to add the clip.

8 Click New to create a new folder that describes the artwork you are gathering.

9 If you clicked New, type a short name that clearly identifies your artwork.

10 Click OK.

11 Click OK.

12 Click Add.

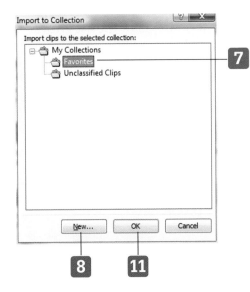

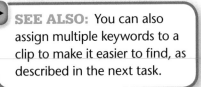

> ▶ **SEE ALSO:** You can also assign multiple keywords to a clip to make it easier to find, as described in the next task.

> **?** **DID YOU KNOW?** You can create a new clip art collection by clicking the File menu in the Clip Organizer, clicking New Collection, typing a new collection name and clicking OK.

Change clip art properties

You don't have to use clip art 'as is'. You can move it, change its name or add keywords to it that make it easier to find when you're doing a search.

1 Click the Insert tab.

2 Click the Clip Art button.

3 Click Organize clips.

4 In the Clip Organizer, point to the clip you want to categorise, click the list arrow and choose one of the available options:

- Copy to Collection lets you place a copy of the image to another category.

- Move to Collection lets you move the clip to a different category.

- Edit Keywords lets you add descriptive keywords to the image.

5 Choose Preview/Properties to view current information about the image and change keywords.

6 Review the file size, physical size, file format and other properties.

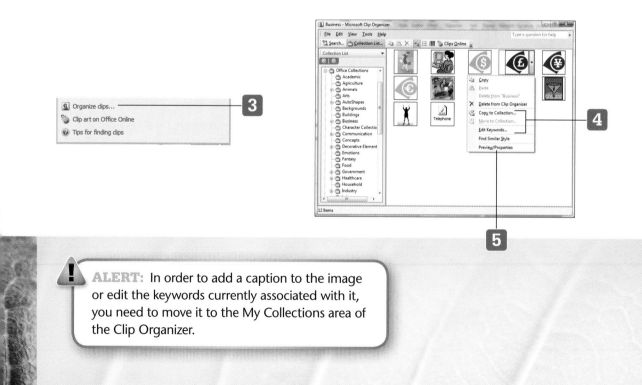

ALERT: In order to add a caption to the image or edit the keywords currently associated with it, you need to move it to the My Collections area of the Clip Organizer.

7 Click Edit Keywords to change the keywords associated with the file.

8 Type a caption for the image here.

9 Type a keyword here.

10 Click Add.

11 Click Apply if you want to save the current changes without closing the dialogue box.

12 When you've finished, click OK.

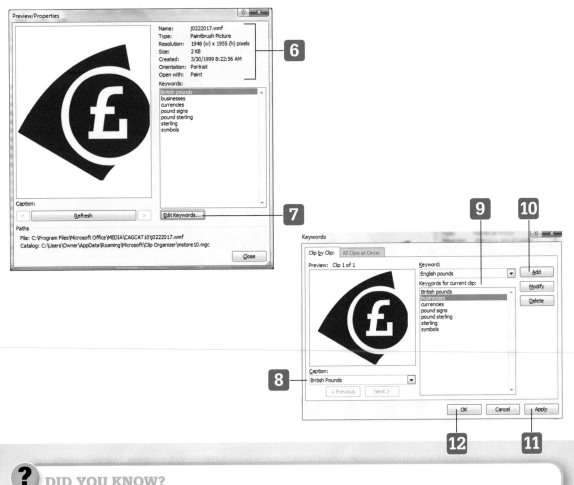

? DID YOU KNOW?

You can also change image properties in the Clip Art task pane. Pass your mouse pointer over an image, click the down arrow next to the clip and click one of the options shown (Copy to Collection, Move to Collection, Edit Keywords and Delete from Clip Organizer).

Add artwork to the Clip Organizer

The Clip Organizer isn't just a repository for clip art provided by Microsoft. You can make use of the Organizer as a tool for collecting and arranging your own artwork – your photos, drawings and artwork you have either generated yourself or had created for your office (such as your company's logo).

1 Click the Insert tab.

2 Click the Clip Art button.

3 Click Organize Clips at the bottom of the Clip Art task pane.

4 Click the File menu, point to Add Clips to Organizer and click On My Own.

5 Click the Look in down arrow and select the folder on your file system that contains the image you want to add.

6 Click the File as type down arrow and choose the type of file you want to view.

7 Click the image(s) you want to import and click Add.

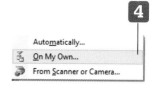

? DID YOU KNOW?

You can use the Clip Organizer as an online photo and media album. Import photos, sounds and videos and arrange them in folders within My Collections so you can find them more quickly.

Remove artwork from the Clip Organizer

The Clip Organizer can quickly become crowded with files. If you no longer need an image stored in the Organizer, you can remove it, which will make the application less crowded and save disk space.

1 Follow Steps 1–3 in the preceding task to open the Clip Organizer.

2 Pass your mouse pointer over the image you want to remove and click the down arrow next to it.

3 Choose Delete from Clip Organizer to remove the clip from all categories in the Organizer.

4 Choose Delete from [category] to remove the image only from the currently open category.

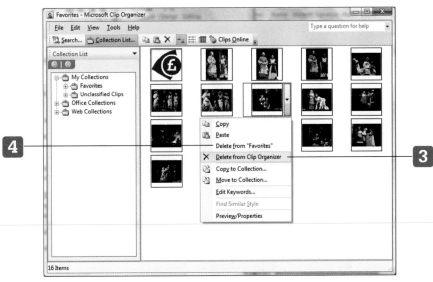

? **DID YOU KNOW?**

Most of the clip art contained in the Clip Organizer is created and stored in the Windows Media Format, which has the .wmf file extension. This format, like other graphic formats, compresses image files to conserve disk space. You might still encounter a file (particularly a photographic image) that consumes lots of space and that should be removed.

Scale an image

Page layouts can quickly become complex and crowded. At the same time, it's important to use white space effectively in order to maintain a professional-looking design. It can be helpful to scale an image: to change its size with precision to fit a predefined space instead of dragging it, which is quicker but less precise.

1 Click the image you want to resize.

2 Click the Format tab under Picture Tools.

3 Click the Size dialogue box launcher.

4 Tick the Lock aspect ratio box to maintain the image's height and width so it doesn't get distorted.

5 Click the up and down arrows to enter a size or type numbers in the Height and Width boxes.

6 Click Close.

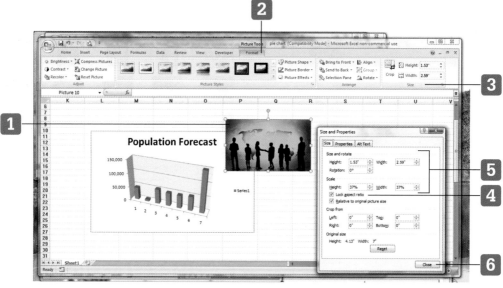

? **DID YOU KNOW?**

You can enter a numeric size in the Size boxes or a percentage size in the Scale boxes in the Size and Properties dialogue box.

▶ **SEE ALSO:** See Resize and move an image earlier in this chapter for instructions on how to drag an image's handles to change its size.

Change brightness and contrast

Brightness and contrast are two of the most common and effective adjustments you can make to any image. These controls appear under Picture Tools, which appears only when you select an image.

1 Click the image you want to adjust.

2 Click the Format tab under Picture Tools.

3 Click the Brightness button and do one of the following:

- Choose a positive brightness value to lighten the image or a negative value to darken it.

- Choose Picture Corrections Options to adjust brightness interactively using a slider tool.

4 Click the Contrast button and do one of the following:

- Choose a positive contrast value to increase colour intensity or a negative value to decrease it.

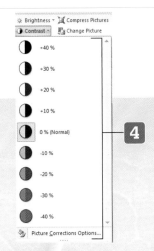

- Choose Picture Corrections Options to adjust contrast interactively using a slider tool.

HOT TIP: If you are unhappy with the changes you make, click Reset Picture to return the image to its starting point.

Draw a shape

You don't want to make your worksheets look unprofessional by drawing a clumsy or amateurish image atop your nicely arranged data. Excel helps by supplying ready-made shapes you can insert with a few mouse clicks and then edit as needed.

1 Click the Insert tab.

2 Click the Shapes button.

3 Click the shape you want from the Shapes gallery.

4 Drag the cursor (which appears as a plus sign) down and to the right to draw the image.

5 Release the mouse button when you have finished.

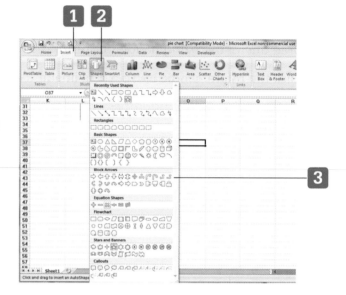

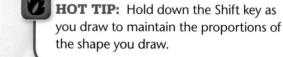

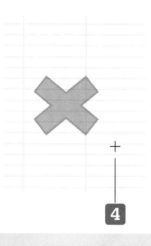

Resize a shape

Once you insert a shape, you are free to resize it as you would any other image. You can drag the image using one of the resize handles. You can also change the size to a precise measurement using the Size dialogue box launcher.

1 Select the shape you want to resize.

2 Drag one of the sizing handles to resize the image.

3 Click the rotate handle to 'spin' the image.

4 Click the Size dialogue box launcher to scale the image with precision.

5 Use the controls to change the image size.

6 Click Close.

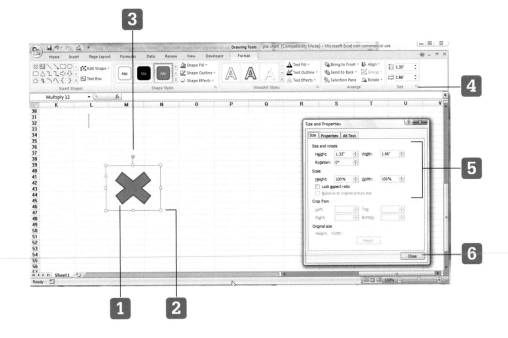

HOT TIP: To delete a shape, select it and then press the Delete (Del) key.

Add text to a shape

Captions and labels make data in a worksheet easier to interpret and they help with shapes as well. You can add text to a shape just as you would any text box. Select the shape object and start typing.

1 Select the shape that you want to contain the text.

2 Type the text you want.

3 To make text corrections, click anywhere in the text to position the cursor and then edit the characters.

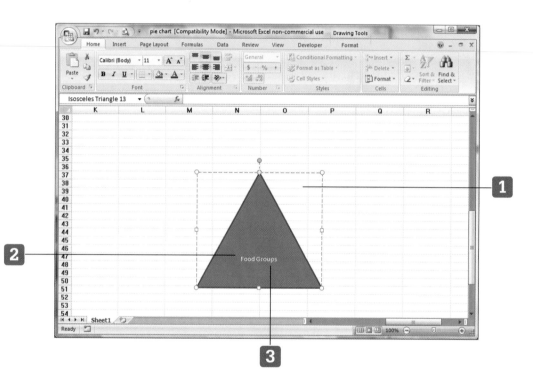

Draw a line or arrow

Lines and arrows are popular shapes you can add to spreadsheets. They are perfect for illustrating trends or for directing the viewer's attention to important contents. Both can be found on the Shapes gallery.

1 Click the Insert tab.

2 Click Shapes and choose one of the line or arrow shapes in the Shapes gallery.

3 Drag the pointer to draw a line or arrow. The locations of the end points depend on where you start and stop dragging.

4 Release the mouse button when you've finished and use the resize handles to move or resize the line or arrow as needed.

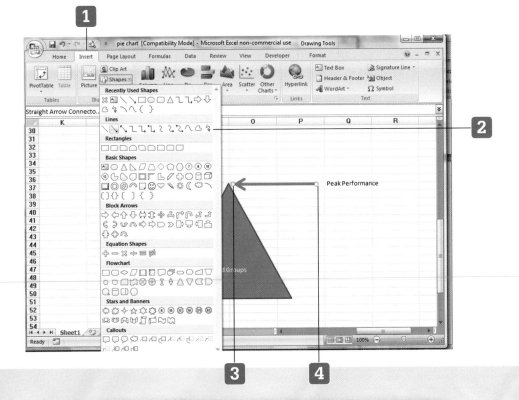

? DID YOU KNOW?

If you need to change the formatting of an individual line or arrow (or another shape), you can use the Shape Outline button on the Format tab, which lets you change line thickness or specify a dashed instead of a solid line.

Apply a Quick Style to a line

You can always format a line, arrow or other shape by using the formatting tools on the Home tab or on the Format tab under Picture Tools. But you'll save time adding multiple formatting attributes to a line or arrow by applying Shape Quick Styles.

1 Click the shape you want to format.

2 Click the Format tab.

3 Scan the Shape Styles tool group for colours and styles. Click the scroll up or down arrows or the More down arrow to view additional options.

4 Pass your mouse pointer over a style to view a live preview in the current shape.

5 Click the style you want from the gallery to select it.

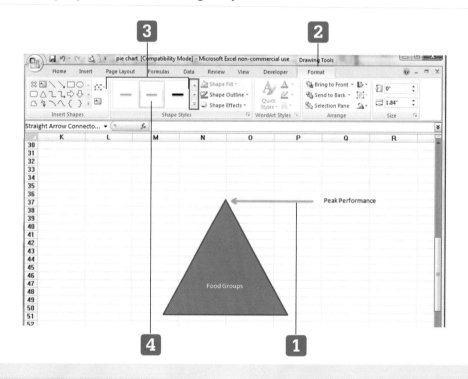

? DID YOU KNOW?

You can also modify a shape by using other options on the Format tab, such as the Shape Outline or Shape Fill buttons.

? DID YOU KNOW?

Each style in the gallery has a name (such as Accent 1), which appears as a tool tip when your mouse hovers over the style.

Copy or move an object

Once you create, edit, scale and style a shape or other object, you'll probably need to move or copy it to a new location at some point. You have two options: you can drag the object with your mouse or use the Size and Position dialogue box to precisely position it.

1 To use your mouse, drag the object to move it, or press and hold down the Ctrl key while dragging the object to copy it.

2 To use Excel's menus, select the objects you want to copy or move.

3 Click the Home tab.

4 Click the Copy or Cut button.

5 Click in the location where you want the object to be moved, whether it is in the same worksheet or in a different one.

6 Click the Paste button.

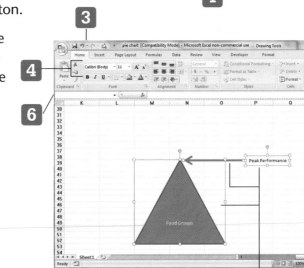

? DID YOU KNOW?
You can copy objects to the Office clipboard and then paste them to other parts of the same workbook or different workbooks, or even other Office documents.

HOT TIP: Press Shift+Click to select multiple objects so you can move or copy them together.

Fill an object with colour

The Format tab under Picture Tools gives you a variety of ways to quickly add formatting to shapes that complements the data in the rest of your worksheet. Two controls you should take advantage of are the Shape Fill button and the Fill section of the Format Shape dialogue box.

1 Select the shape you want to format.

2 Click the Format tab.

3 Click Shape Fill.

4 Select the fill colour option you want.

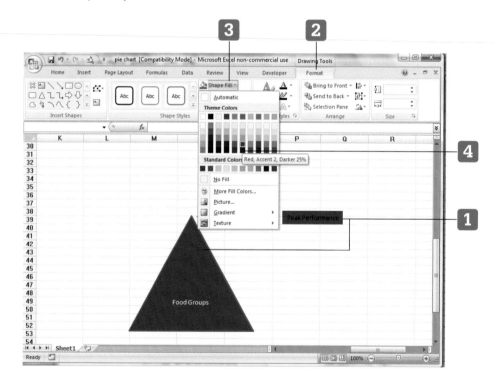

🔥 HOT TIP: To remove a colour fill, click the Shape Fill button and then click No Fill.

? DID YOU KNOW?
You can specify a colour and line style as a default. Right-click the object and choose Set as Default Shape from the context menu.

Distribute objects

Excel gives you grids and guides to align objects to a specific position. The Align commands under the Format tab enable you to position the objects in relation to one another or to other contents in your worksheet.

1 Select the objects you want to position.

2 Click the Format tab under Drawing Tools.

3 Click the Align button and choose one of the following:

- Click Snap to Grid to align the objects relative to the worksheet's grid.

- Click Snap to Shape if you want to align the objects relative to each other.

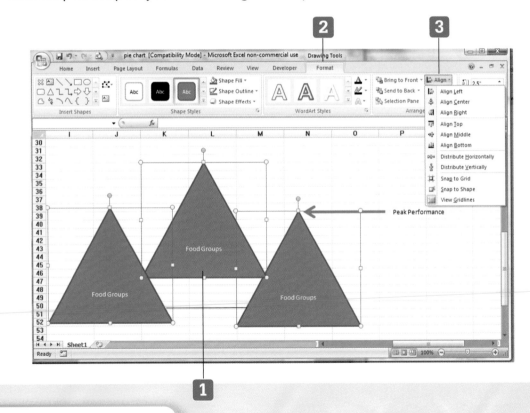

? DID YOU KNOW?

Click Distribute Vertically or Distribute Horizontally to evenly distribute the objects you have selected.

8 Publishing workbooks and worksheets

Specify the print area

When you are ready to print a worksheet, you can choose exactly how much of the document you want to print. Doing so can save you a lot of wasted toner and paper. The print area is the part of your worksheet that Excel will send to the printer.

1 Select the range of cells you want to print.

2 Click the Page Layout tab.

3 Click the Print Area button and choose Set Print Area.

? DID YOU KNOW?

You can expand a print area by clicking the cell where you want to extend the print area. Click Page Layout, click the Print Area button and choose Add to Print Area.

🔥 HOT TIP: To clear a print area, click the Print Area button and choose Clear Print Area.

Preview a worksheet before printing

Even after you have set margins, specified page size and chosen the area of the worksheet you want to print, you have one more chance to check the document before output. It's a good idea to verify that the page looks the way you want to save time, toner and paper. Print Preview shows you how your document will look when it prints.

1 Click the Office button, point to Print and choose Print Preview.

2 Tick the Show Margins box to adjust margins visually.

3 Click Close Print Preview to return to the worksheet without printing.

4 Click the Print button if you want to print directly from Print Preview.

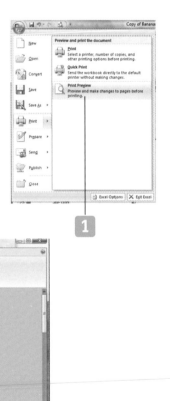

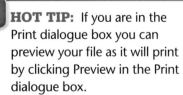

? DID YOU KNOW?
You can zoom in and out to view data more easily on the Print Preview tab.

🔥 HOT TIP: If you are in the Print dialogue box you can preview your file as it will print by clicking Preview in the Print dialogue box.

Print a worksheet

When you have set your margins and page setup and previewed your worksheet, you're ready to print it. You have the option to print all or part of the worksheet or choose secondary features that you want printed such as gridlines, column letters or row numbers.

1 Click the Office button, point to Print and choose Print.

2 Click the Name down arrow and choose a printer if needed.

3 Click Properties to change printer properties if needed.

4 Choose whether you want to print the entire document or just a page range.

5 Choose the number of copies you want.

6 Click OK to print.

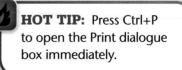

HOT TIP: Press Ctrl+P to open the Print dialogue box immediately.

Create a PDF file

PDF is a commonly used abbreviation for Portable Document Format, a file format Adobe Systems Incorporated created for its PageMaker and other files. It compresses files, preserves complex layouts, embeds nonstandard fonts and includes images, all in compact packages that can be quickly transmitted over the Internet or another network.

1 Click the Office button, point to Save As and point to Other Formats.

2 When the Save As dialogue box opens, choose the location where you want to save the file.

3 Type a file name for the PDF file.

4 Tick this box if you want to open the file after saving it.

5 Click Options, choose publishing options for the PDF file and click OK.

6 Click Publish.

1

? **DID YOU KNOW?**

If you don't see the PDF option when you point to Save As, you need to download an add-in. Choose the Add-Ins for other formats option and read the instructions in the Help window that opens.

2

3

4

5

6

? **DID YOU KNOW?**

To view a PDF file, you need to have Adobe Reader which you can download from the Adobe website (www.adobe. com).

Create an XPS document

XPS stands for XML Paper Specification. It is a secure fixed-layout format created by Microsoft that lets you retain the form you intended when a file is sent to a printer or a monitor. XPS is a good option if you are preparing a file to be printed on paper and not modified.

1 Click the Office button, point to Save As and choose PDF or XPS.

2 Make sure XPS Document is listed in the Save as type list.

3 Choose a location for your file.

4 Type a name for your file.

5 Click Options to set publishing options for the file.

6 Click Publish.

? DID YOU KNOW?

XPS format preserves live links with documents. It is also compatible with a technology for protecting content called Windows Rights Management.

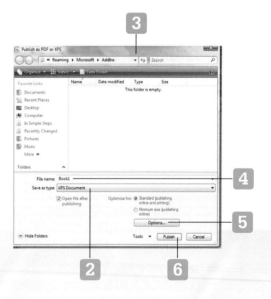

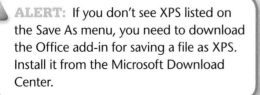

ALERT: If you don't see XPS listed on the Save As menu, you need to download the Office add-in for saving a file as XPS. Install it from the Microsoft Download Center.

Save a workbook as a webpage

One of the most popular ways to publish a file is to save it as a webpage. That way anyone can view it on the Internet or your local network with a web browser. When you save an Excel document as a webpage you convert it to HTML format.

1 Click the Office button, point to Save As and choose Other Formats.

2 Click the Save as type down arrow and choose Web Page.

3 Click the Look in down arrow and locate the folder where you want to save the file.

4 Type a name for the file.

5 Type a title for the webpage.

6 Click Save.

? DID YOU KNOW?

A title is different to a file name: it appears in the dark bar at the top of a web browser when you open a webpage.

Open a workbook in webpage format

Excel isn't a web browser, but it has the ability to open a worksheet that you have previously saved as a webpage. Opening it as a webpage allows you to quickly switch from HTML to standard Excel format without losing any functionality.

1 Click Office and choose Open.

2 Click the Files of type down arrow and choose All Web Pages.

3 Click the Look in down arrow and locate the webpage file you want to open.

4 Click the file to select it.

5 Click Open.

HOT TIP: If you want to open the file in your web browser rather than Excel, click the Open button and choose Open in Browser.

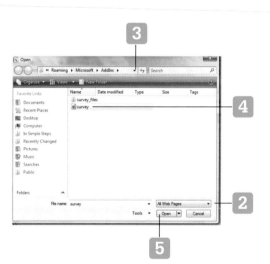

Preview a webpage

Before you open a worksheet as a webpage, and before you even save it as a webpage, you can get a preview of how it would look on the web. By previewing the file you can see if there are any errors that needed to be corrected before they appear online.

1 Open the workbook you want to preview.

2 Click the Web Page Preview button on the Quick Access Toolbar. Your default web browser opens and displays the document as a web page.

3 Click the Close button to quit your browser and return to Excel.

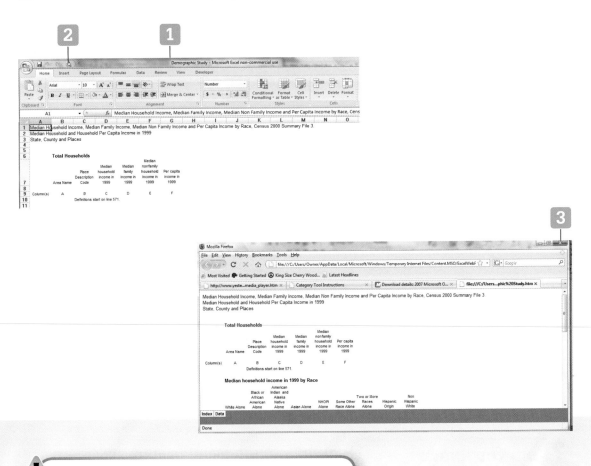

ALERT: If you don't see the Web Page Preview button on the Quick Access Toolbar, you'll need to add it. Click Office, choose Excel Options and click Customize to add the button.

Create a hyperlink

An Excel worksheet can contain links to specific sites on the Internet. Such links enable you and your colleagues to jump to resources that are related to the data you are presenting.

1 Select the cell, object or text that you want to convert to a hyperlink.

2 Click the Insert tab.

3 Click Hyperlink.

4 Click one of the icons in the Link to: bar that denotes the type of link you want to create.

5 Type or select the name and location of the webpage you want to link to.

6 Click OK.

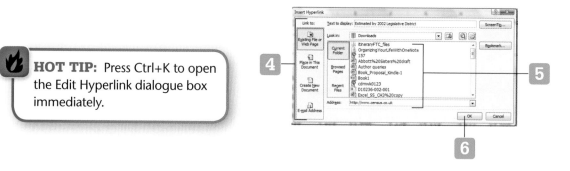

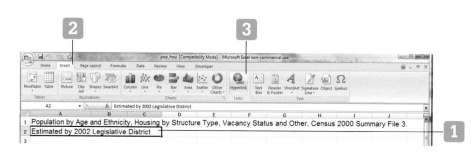

HOT TIP: Press Ctrl+K to open the Edit Hyperlink dialogue box immediately.

? DID YOU KNOW?

When your worksheet contains a hyperlink, it is formatted in a cell as blue text.

Format a hyperlink

Excel provides you with extensive options for formatting many kinds of data types, including hyperlinks. It pays to format hyperlinks clearly so viewers know they are clicking on a link and aren't surprised when a web browser opens.

1. Click the Home tab.

2. Click Cell Styles.

3. Right-click the Linked Cell option and choose Modify.

4. Click Format.

5. Choose the formatting options you want.

6. Click OK.

? DID YOU KNOW?

You can copy or move a hyperlink. Right-click the hyperlink you want to copy or move and choose Copy or Cut from the context menu. Right-click the cell you want to contain the link and choose Paste from the context menu.

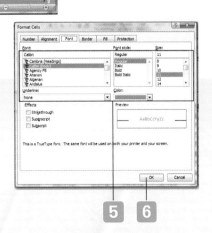

9 Protecting and securing your data

Introduction

Much of the information you will gather and present with Microsoft Excel 2007 is financial – budgets, expenses, projections, salaries and other records. No matter whether you're working in an office or keeping records for your household, it's a good idea to protect your worksheet data so that unauthorised individuals cannot gain access to it.

It's also important to be able to choose and control which content is displayed and which is protected, and Excel gives you many layers of control over what you restrict. You can lock individual cells so they cannot be changed; you can password-protect a worksheet or an entire workbook. You can also encrypt workbooks – or all of the above. You have the option to implement many layers of control or just one, depending on your needs.

This chapter examines common security options available to Excel 2007 users. You can set security options at the Trust Center. That's also where you'll find technology information that relates to document privacy, safety and security from Microsoft. In this chapter you'll find out how to make the most of the Trust Center. Other features such as digital signatures and encryption are particularly powerful additions to this version of Excel; they ensure that your data won't be accessed even if you send it to someone else over the Internet.

Protect a worksheet

Passwords can be used to protect a worksheet. That way you won't have to worry about losing your hard work if others have access to your files. You're probably already familiar with the drill. You supply your password and then you enter it again when you want to work on the file.

1 Click the Review tab.

2 Click the Protect Sheet button.

3 Select the tick boxes for the options you want protected in the sheet.

4 Type a password.

5 Click OK.

6 Retype the password.

7 Click OK.

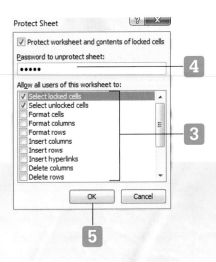

> 🔥 **HOT TIP:** Be sure to remember or write down your password(s), because you won't be able to open your files if you forget. They are case sensitive, so you have to supply them exactly as they were first entered.

Lock and unlock worksheet cells

If you don't want to bother with a password but you do want to make sure changes to your data won't be made accidently, you can lock your worksheet cells.

1 Select the cell or range you want to lock or unlock.

2 Click the Home tab.

3 Click the Format button and then click Lock Cell to lock or unlock the current selection.

? DID YOU KNOW?

This toggle command turns on or off the Locked tick box on the Protection tab in the Format Cells dialogue box.

? DID YOU KNOW?

Unless you add password protection to the worksheet, your users can also unlock the data and make revisions.

Lock other worksheet elements

Sometimes, you want others in your organisation to be able to view or edit workbooks, while protecting data in parts of the current worksheet. You might have some dates and figures that must remain constant, for instance. If that's the case, you can use the Protect Sheet control to establish element-level protection for the worksheet.

1 Click Review.

2 Click Protect Sheet.

3 Tick the boxes next to any elements in the worksheet that you want to protect.

4 Untick the boxes next to any elements in the worksheet that you want to be able to edit.

5 Enter a password to prevent users from undoing your protection.

6 Click OK.

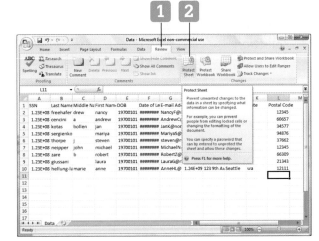

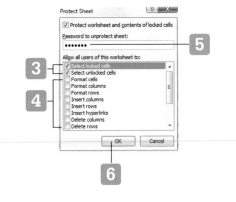

? DID YOU KNOW?

The Password to unprotect sheet: box prevents individuals from being able to unprotect any elements you have protected. If you don't enter a password, anyone can click Review, click Protect Sheet and untick an element so they can edit it. If you do enter a password, if someone attempts to make changes to the protection of any element, they are prompted to enter a password first.

Encrypt a workbook

If you want to take your security up a notch, consider scrambling your password. Actually you can let Excel do the deed through the process of encryption. All you have to do is remember your password.

1 Click the Office button, point to Prepare and click Encrypt Document.

2 Type a password.

3 Click OK.

4 Retype the password.

5 Click OK.

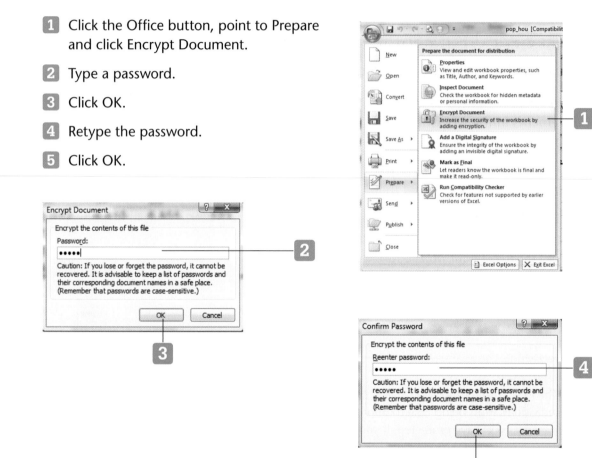

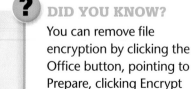

Password-protect a workbook

If your workbook is going to move from person to person, a password will make sure that only those who know the password can open it.

1 Select the workbook you want protected.

2 Click the Office button and then click Save As.

3 Click Tools and click General Options.

4 Type a password in the Password to open: box or the Password to modify: box.

5 Select or clear the Always create backup tick box.

6 Select or clear the Read-only recommended tick box.

7 Click OK.

8 Retype the password.

9 Click OK.

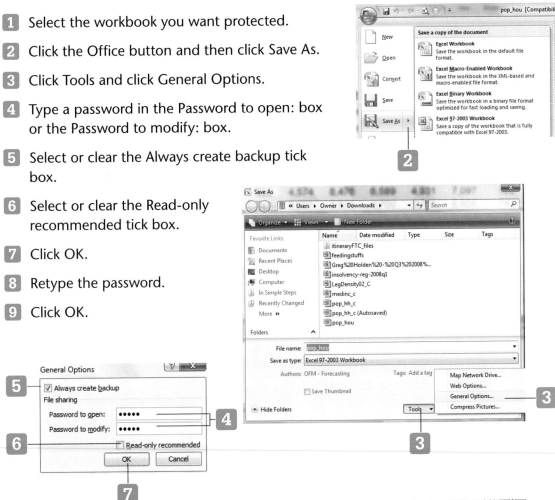

? DID YOU KNOW?

If you want a memo to be distributed to a work group but not be changed, setting it as read-only is useful. Password protection will be in place the next time you open the workbook.

Set add-in security options

An add-in is a great way to customise your Ribbon. However, hackers can use this added software code to do bad things such as spreading a virus. By setting security options, you can make sure your add-ins are safe.

1 Click the Office button and click Excel Options.

2 In the left pane, click Trust Center.

3 Click Trust Center Settings.

4 In the left pane, click Add-ins.

5 Select or clear the tick boxes you do or do not want.

6 Click OK twice.

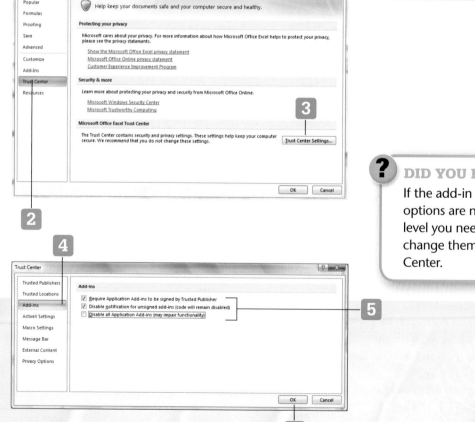

? DID YOU KNOW?

If the add-in security options are not set to the level you need, you can change them in the Trust Center.

Add a digital signature

An artist signs a painting, so you might want to add an invisible digital signature to your workbook. It's a way to prove your identity by providing a stamp of authentication.

1 Click the Office button, point to Prepare and click Add a Digital Signature.

2 Click OK.

3 Click the type of digital signature you want.

4 Click OK.

5 Follow the steps shown on the Microsoft Office Online site to obtain your digital ID.

HOT TIP: If you're not sure whether or not a workbook is digitally signed, you can use the Signatures task pane to view or remove valid signatures.

DID YOU KNOW?

Before you can add a digital signature, you need to get a digital ID or digital certificate. Find out how to obtain one on Microsoft's website: http://office.microsoft.com/en-gb/outlook/HP012305371033.aspx). That will provide an electronic way to prove your identity.

View a digital signature

Whether you create a signature or you open a workbook that includes someone else's signature, it's a good idea to take a look at the digital file and understand what you are looking at. That way, you can be sure the signature is genuine and the workbook is reliable.

1 Look for the red ribbon icon in the status bar that indicates a file has been digitally signed.

2 Single-click the icon.

3 Pass your mouse over the signer's name.

4 Click the down arrow and choose Signature Details from the drop-down list.

5 Notice whether the signature is considered valid or not.

6 Click View.

7 Click Details to view when the signature was created as well as the algorithm used to create it.

8 When you've finished, click OK.

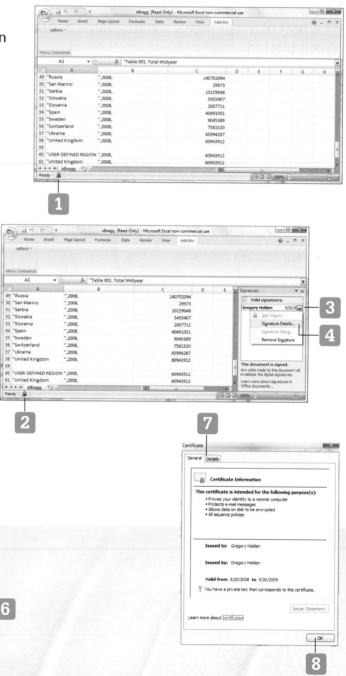

Adjust Message Bar security options

You now have the option of having a Message Bar appear below your Ribbon when a potential problem arises. When potentially unsafe content is detected in an open document, it will provide a security warning and options to enable external content or leave it blocked.

1 Click the Office button and click Excel Options.

2 In the left pane, click Trust Center.

3 Click Trust Center Settings.

4 In the left pane, click Message Bar.

5 Click the option you want for showing the Message Bar.

6 Click OK twice.

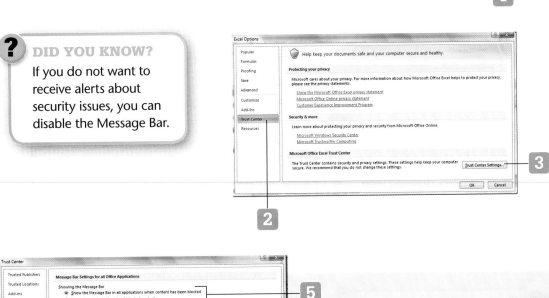

? DID YOU KNOW?

If you do not want to receive alerts about security issues, you can disable the Message Bar.

10 Sharing your data with your colleagues

Introduction

Sometimes you're in a work group with colleagues on the other side of the continent. Sometimes you're setting up a budget with your spouse. Sometimes you're exchanging soccer statistics with parents of the other players on your child's team. Instead of dealing with sticky notes on hard-copy outputs, Excel lets you insert electronic comments within worksheet cells. Changes can be tracked. And then they can be sent to another person for review using email or an Internet fax service.

By using a variety of techniques, you can link, embed, hyperlink, export or convert data to create one seamless workbook that is a group effort. You can also use Excel to create and edit connections to external data sources, such as Microsoft Access, to create more permanent links to data.

Share a worksheet

Collaboration takes on a new meaning when a group of people have equal responsibility for data within a single workbook. Sharing the Excel way means users can add columns and rows, enter data and change formatting.

1 Open the workbook you want to share.

2 Click the Review tab.

3 Click the Share Workbook button.

4 Click the Editing tab.

5 Select the Allow changes by more than one user at the same time tick box.

6 Click OK.

7 Click OK again to save your workbook.

Microsoft Office Excel

This action will now save the workbook. Do you want to continue?

OK   Cancel

Share Workbook

Editing | Advanced

☑ Allow changes by more than one user at the same time. This also allows workbook merging.

Who has this workbook open now:

Greg Holden (Exclusive) - 12/7/2008 3:05 PM

Remove User

OK   Cancel

HOT TIP: Maybe all team members are not created equal. Maybe one has veto control. Excel can keep track of changes and the team leader can accept them or reject them at a later date.

Configure sharing options

Simply sharing a file isn't always enough. You may also need to control how long to maintain changes other users make and to specify how long their changes should be saved. You can do so by configuring sharing options.

1 Open the workbook you want to share.

2 Click the Review tab.

3 Click Share Workbook.

4 Click the Advanced tab.

5 Choose one of these options to specify how long to keep changes, in days.

6 Choose one of these options to choose when changes should be changed.

7 Click OK.

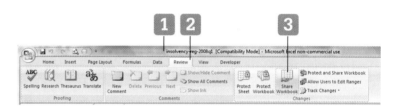

DID YOU KNOW?

You can also choose one of the Conflicting changes between users to resolve conflicts between changes made by shared users.

Create a cell comment

A comment in Excel is the equivalent of leaving a message to yourself on your answering machine. Or it could be like the to-do list your spouse helpfully tapes to the refrigerator door. To create a comment:

1 Click the cell to which you want to add a comment.

2 Click the Review tab.

3 Click the Edit Comment button.

4 Type the comment in the comment box.

5 Click outside the comment box when you have finished or press Esc twice to close the comment box.

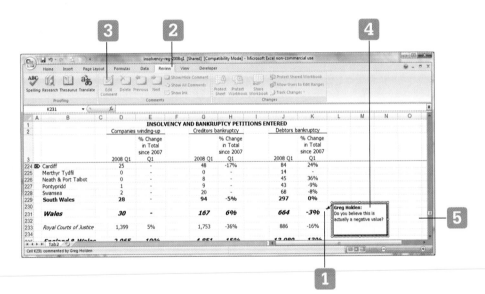

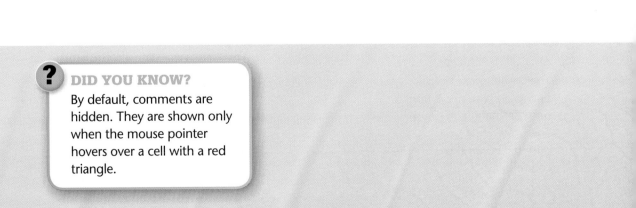

DID YOU KNOW?

By default, comments are hidden. They are shown only when the mouse pointer hovers over a cell with a red triangle.

Read a comment

A comment is like a sticky note attached to a file. But you have to know how to find comments and how to read them in order to take advantage of them.

1 Position the mouse pointer over a cell with a red triangle to read its comment.

2 Move the mouse pointer off the cell to hide the comment.

3 Click the Review tab.

4 Choose the navigation option you prefer.

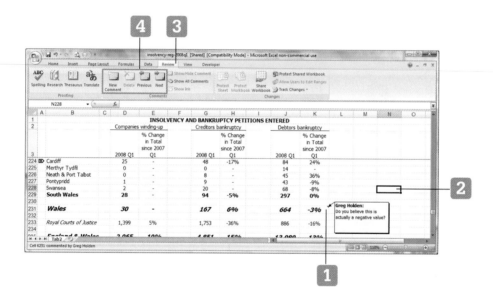

Edit a cell comment

Comments are just like any other text on a worksheet. You can edit or even format them so they stand out from the surrounding comments.

1 Click the cell with the comment you want to edit.

2 Click the Review tab.

3 Click the Edit Comment button.

4 Click the Home tab.

5 Use the formatting controls to format the comment if needed.

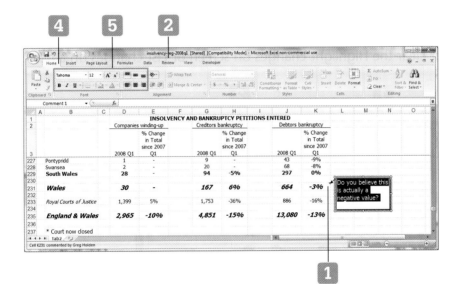

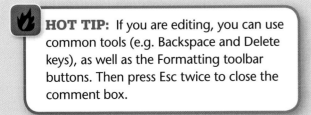

HOT TIP: If you are editing, you can use common tools (e.g. Backspace and Delete keys), as well as the Formatting toolbar buttons. Then press Esc twice to close the comment box.

Review tracked changes

Once you activate Track Changes for a document, you and your colleagues can take full advantage of it by moving from one change to another and accepting it or rejecting it.

1 Click the Review tab.

2 Click Track Changes and then click Accept/Reject Changes.

3 Change tracking, if needed, and click OK to start reviewing changes.

4 Choose Accept, Reject, Accept All or Reject All.

5 Click Close.

Protect Shared Workbook
Allow Users to Edit Ranges
Track Changes
  Highlight Changes...
  Accept/Reject Changes

2

Select Changes to Accept or Reject

Which changes

☑ When: Not yet reviewed ▾
☐ Who: Everyone ▾
☐ Where: [   ] 🔢

OK   Cancel

3

Accept or Reject Changes

Change 1 of 1 made to this document:

Greg Holden, 12/7/2008 3:54 PM:

Changed cell B239 from 'Provincial High Court Centre' to 'Provincial Court Centre'.

Accept   Reject   Accept All   Reject All   Close

4   **5**

? DID YOU KNOW?

When you or anyone else applies the Track Changes command to a workbook, the message '[Shared]' appears in the title bar of the workbook. That way you know that this feature is active.

Email a workbook for review

When your workbook is ready to show, you don't have to take it on the road. You don't even have to open your regular email program. Excel has its own email program that allows you to send your workbook to others for review as an attachment, as either a workbook, PDF or XPS document. Your reviewer can use the same procedure to send your workbook back to you when they have completed their comments.

1 Click the Office button, point to Send and click Email, Email as PDF Attachment or Email as XPS Attachment.

2 Enter email addresses or select users from your address book.

3 Enter a message for your reviewer, with instructions if necessary.

4 Click the Send button.

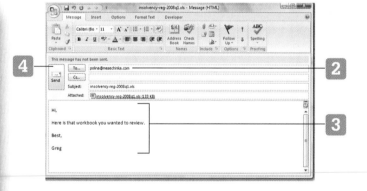

? DID YOU KNOW?
An e-mail program, such as Microsoft Outlook, needs to be installed on your computer and your e-mail account needs to be set up. A Compatibility Checker will appear and you'll need to click Continue or Cancel to stop the operation.

? DID YOU KNOW?
By default, the subject line that appears contains the file name of the workbook you're sending.

🔥 HOT TIP: To add recipients from your address book or contacts list, click To, click the recipients' names, click To, Cc or Bcc until you're done and then click OK.

Work with XML

Excel is a great program, but in some cases it might be helpful to store data independently of its format. That way you can use the data more seamlessly in other forms. XML is short for Extensible Markup Language and it's now your best friend.

1 Click the Developer tab.

2 Click the Source button.

3 In the task pane, click XML Maps.

4 Click Add.

5 Locate and select the XML schema file you want to attach and then click Open.

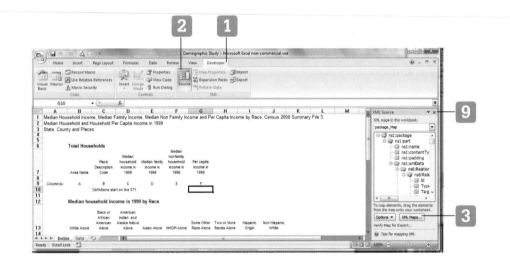

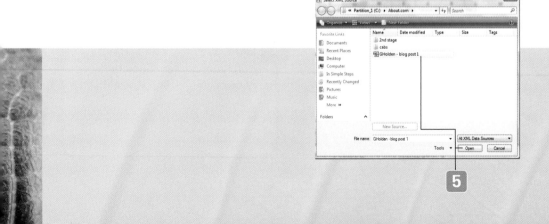

6 If necessary, click OK to create a schema based on the XML source data.

7 To delete or rename an XML schema, select the schema and then click Delete or Rename.

8 Click OK.

9 When you're done, click the Close button on the task pane.

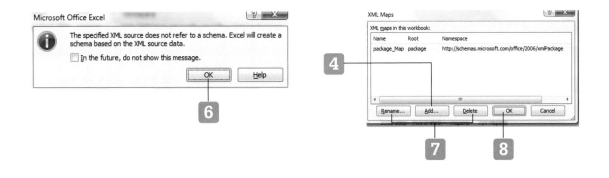

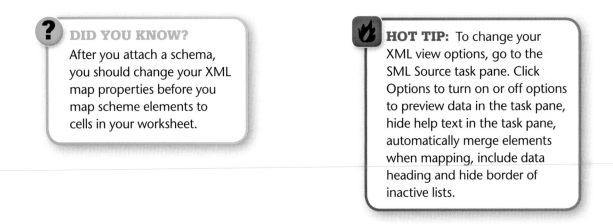

? DID YOU KNOW?

After you attach a schema, you should change your XML map properties before you map scheme elements to cells in your worksheet.

🔥 HOT TIP: To change your XML view options, go to the SML Source task pane. Click Options to turn on or off options to preview data in the task pane, hide help text in the task pane, automatically merge elements when mapping, include data heading and hide border of inactive lists.

Change XML properties

You won't need to know the XML language to attach an XML schema. Just remember that an XML schema is a set of rules that defines the elements and content used in an XML document. And you can change the XML properties of any file before you attach or export it.

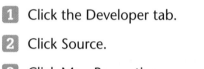

1 Click the Developer tab.

2 Click Source.

3 Click Map Properties.

4 Rename the map if you wish.

5 Change the map options.

6 Specify the refreshing or importing data option you want.

7 Click OK.

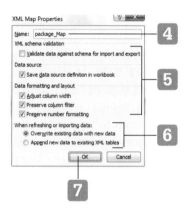

Export data in XML

Once you finish formatting your XML file, you can export or save the data for use in other XML-compatible applications.

1 Open the worksheet that contains the data you want to export.

2 Click the Developer tab.

3 Click Source.

4 Choose the location where you want to save the file and click Export.

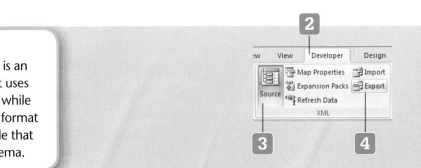

? DID YOU KNOW?

The XML Data format is an industry standard that uses its own XML schema, while the XML Spreadsheet format is a specialised XML file that uses its own XML schema.

Export data

Let's say that there is text in another file that you want to include in your worksheet. Importing allows you to open that text file in your workbook. Or if you want to copy data from one program to another, you can convert the data to a format that the other program accepts. To export an Excel file to another program format, follow these steps:

1 Open the file from which you want to export data.

2 Click the Office button, click Save As and then click Other Formats.

3 Click the Save in list arrow and click the drive or folder where you want to save the file.

4 Click the Save as type: list arrow and click the format you want. If you want to change the file name, do it now.

5 Click Save.

Import a text file

You can also import text you want to include in your worksheet. Rather than scrolling across the text and using cutting and pasting, it can be more efficient to simply import the entire text file.

1 Click the Office button and then click Open.

2 Click the Files of type list arrow and then click Text Files.

3 Click the Look in list arrow and select the folder where the text file name is located.

4 Click the text file you want to import.

5 Click Open.

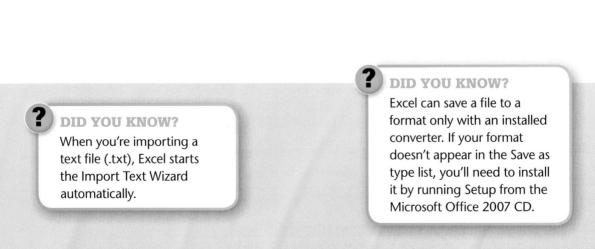

HOT TIP: If you don't need the data you're using from another source to be automatically updated if the source data changes, the best way to get the data is to cut and paste it. You start that process by clicking the Home tab and then the Copy button.

? DID YOU KNOW?

When you're importing a text file (.txt), Excel starts the Import Text Wizard automatically.

? DID YOU KNOW?

Excel can save a file to a format only with an installed converter. If your format doesn't appear in the Save as type list, you'll need to install it by running Setup from the Microsoft Office 2007 CD.

Link data

If you have a number of sets of data that are the same, resist the urge to make multiple identical entries. Instead, links are the way to go. That way you'll save time and make sure your entries are correct.

1 Select the cell or range that contains the source data.

2 Click the Home tab.

3 Click the Copy button.

4 Click the sheet tab where you want to link the data.

5 Select the destination cell or destination range.

6 Click the Paste button.

7 Click the Paste Options button and then click Link Cells.

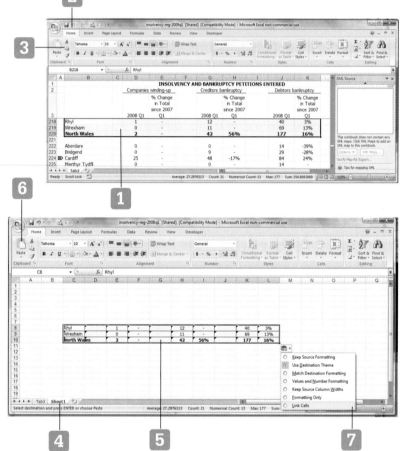

? DID YOU KNOW?

A link can be as simple as a reference to a cell on another worksheet, or it can be part of a formula. You can link cells between sheets within one workbook or between different workbooks. Cell data to be linked is called the source data. The cell or range linked to the source data is called the destination cell or destination range. If you no longer want linked data to be updated, you can easily break a link.

HOT TIP: To arrange open worksheet windows to make linking easier, click the View tab and then click the Arrange All button.

Get external data

The Data Connection Wizard connects to an external data source that has already been established. It's a good way to create a permanent exchange to a data source if you're going to be using it on an ongoing basis.

1 Click the Data tab.

2 Click the From Other Sources button.

3 Click From Data Connection Wizard.

? DID YOU KNOW?

Excel will disable your connection to external data if it detects a possible security risk. To connect to data when you open a workbook, you need to enable data connections by using the Trust Center or by putting the workbook in a trusted location.

Manage connections

It's good up to a point to be able to use your connection file for sharing connections with other users. But if you change your connection information, your connection file is not updated automatically.

1 Click the Data tab.

2 Click the Existing Connections button to open that dialogue box.

3 Click the Show: list arrow and then click All Connections or select the specific connection type you want to display.

4 Click Open.

5 Click the table you want and then click OK to open the Import Data dialogue box.

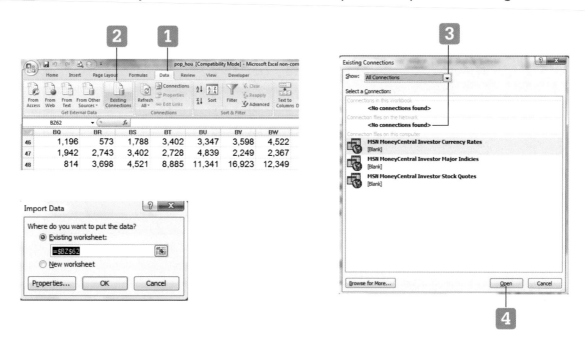

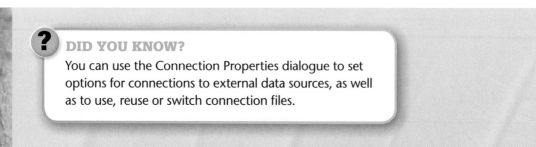

DID YOU KNOW?

You can use the Connection Properties dialogue to set options for connections to external data sources, as well as to use, reuse or switch connection files.

Top 10 Excel Problems Solved

Problem 1: Excel doesn't seem to be running properly

If you find that Excel isn't operating properly, the first line of defence is to use the Office Diagnostics application. Use it if you see an alert message or other indications that Excel can't find data, is running slowly or is experiencing mixups with data stored in the Windows registry.

1 Click the Office button.

2 Click Excel Options.

3 Click Resources.

4 Click Diagnose.

5 When a Microsoft Office Diagnostics dialogue box appears, click Continue.

6 When a second Microsoft Office Diagnostics dialogue box appears, click Continue.

The dialogue box notifies you of the progress of the check.

? DID YOU KNOW?

You can also access Office Diagnostics from Windows rather than from inside an application: click Start, point to All Programs, click Microsoft Office, click Microsoft Office Tools and then click Microsoft Office Diagnostics.

Problem 2: How do I interpret diagnostics results?

When Microsoft Office Diagnostics performs its analysis, it automatically attempts to repair any problems it encounters. Any such events are reported in the results the program sends you. If you encounter problems that can't be fixed, you should know how to handle them so you can get your Office application up and running smoothly again.

1 Scroll through the results in the Microsoft Office Diagnostics dialogue box.

2 If any problems are reported, click Detailed results to review the details.

3 If you are prompted to visit a webpage for advice with the results, follow the link provided.

4 When you've finished, click Close.

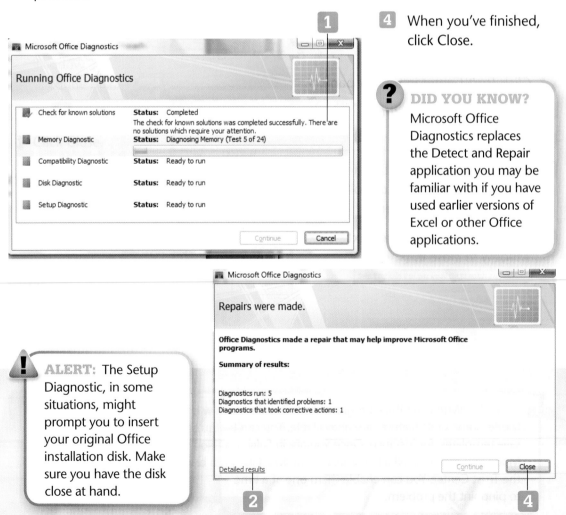

? DID YOU KNOW?
Microsoft Office Diagnostics replaces the Detect and Repair application you may be familiar with if you have used earlier versions of Excel or other Office applications.

! ALERT: The Setup Diagnostic, in some situations, might prompt you to insert your original Office installation disk. Make sure you have the disk close at hand.

Problem 8: I need to adjust a formula, how do I evaluate it first?

When you have created a nested formula, it can be difficult to determine exactly how Excel performs the calculations if you need to adjust or correct them. The Evaluate Formula dialogue box helps you evaluate parts of a formula one at a time.

1 Select the cell that contains the formula you want to evaluate.

2 Click the Formulas tab.

3 Click Evaluate Formula.

4 Click Evaluate to examine the value of the reference.

5 Continue until each part of the formula has been evaluated, then click Close.

ALERT: You can evaluate only one cell at a time.

Problem 9: An Add-in is missing

Add-ins are additional programs that are designed to run within Excel and perform specialised functions. Sometimes, functions aren't available because the add-in needed to run them cannot be found. If that's the case, you have several troubleshooting options.

1 Click the Add-Ins button in the Quick Access Toolbar.

2 Tick the box next to the add-in you need to use to activate it.

3 Click OK.

4 To check for other add-ins you have available, click Office and choose Excel Options.

5 Click Add-Ins.

6 Click the add-in to display details about it and click OK.

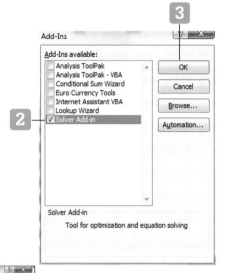

HOT TIP: If the Add-Ins button is not available on the Quick Access toolbar, click the Customize pane in Excel Options to add it.

Problem 10: How do I troubleshoot invalid data?

Data Validation enables you to ensure that data has been entered in the format you want. The rules you configure to validate data check the information and you can tell Excel to highlight data that violates the rules (invalid data) so you can make corrections.

1 Click the Data tab.

2 Click the down arrow beneath Data Validation and choose Circle Invalid Data. Red circles appear around cells that contain invalid data.

3 To clear the circles, click the Data Validation down arrow and choose Clear Validation Circles.

> ▶ **SEE ALSO:** See Create a drop-down list in Chapter 6 for an example of validation rules being added to one type of object in a worksheet.